DISCARD

FROM THE GROUND UP

FROM THE GROUND UP

Grassroots Organizations
Making Social Change

CAROL CHETKOVICH
and
FRANCES KUNREUTHER

ILR PRESS

AN IMPRINT OF

CORNELL UNIVERSITY PRESS

ITHACA AND LONDON

First published 2006 by Cornell University Press
First printing, Cornell Paperbacks, 2006
Printed in the United States of America

Library of Congress Cataloging-in-Publication Data

Chetkovich, Carol A.
  From the ground up : grassroots organizations making social change / Carol Chetkovich and Frances Kunreuther.
    p. cm.
  Includes bibliographical references and index.
  ISBN-13: 978-0-8014-4435-7 (cloth : alk. paper)
  ISBN-10: 0-8014-4435-7 (cloth : alk. paper)
  ISBN-13: 978-0-8014-7264-0 (pbk. : alk. paper)
  ISBN-10: 0-8014-7264-4 (pbk. : alk. paper)
  1. Nonprofit organizations—United States. 2. Social change—United States.
3. Social movements—United States. 4. Social action—United States. 5. Social
service—United States. I. Kunreuther, Frances. II. Title.
  HN55.C44 2006
  322.4'40973—dc22   200619349

Cornell University Press strives to use environmentally responsible suppliers and materials to the fullest extent possible in the publishing of its books. Such materials include vegetable-based, low-VOC inks and acid-free papers that are recycled, totally chlorine-free, or partly composed of nonwood fibers. For further information, visit our website at www.cornellpress.cornell.edu.

Cloth printing   10 9 8 7 6 5 4 3 2 1
Paperback printing   10 9 8 7 6 5 4 3 2 1

CONTENTS

Acknowledgments

We begin by thanking the directors and staff members of our study organizations, who were remarkably welcoming and candid in sharing their ideas and experiences. Without their thoughtful reflection and insight there would have been no book, and we deeply appreciate their willingness to participate in this project.

Our colleagues Judy Howard, Sanjeev Khagram, Kim Klein, Jenny Mansbridge, Debra Minkoff, and Francesca Polletta encouraged us in the writing of this book and gave generously of their time and expertise by reviewing chapters and providing thoughtful comments and advice. We thank them for their invaluable help. In addition, we appreciate the consistent support and excellent guidance of Fran Benson, our editor at Cornell University Press.

We also acknowledge Sarah Titus and Caroline McAndrews of the Building Movement Project staff and Linda Campbell, Helen Kim, Kim Klein, Robby Rodriguez, and Emery Wright of the Project Team, all of whom supported this effort both concretely and with their enthusiasm.

The Annie E. Casey Foundation funded the original data collection, and supplemental funding was provided through a grant for leadership research from the Center for Public Leadership at the Kennedy School of Government at Harvard University. The staff and faculty of Harvard's Hauser Center for Nonprofit Organizations, where the idea for this work was generated, also provided assistance in many forms, from feedback on the work to administrative support. In the study itself we were assisted in data-gathering and literature reviews by a wonderful group of research assistants— Kathy Hutson, Angela Johnson, Lavern McDonald, Curtis Ogden, Julia Sheketof, Elta Smith, and Mary Spooner.

Finally, we are indebted to our remarkably patient partners, Glen Tepke and Ann Holder, for providing essential sustenance in the form of both intellectual companionship and unflagging emotional support.

C.C. and F.K.

FROM THE GROUND UP

INTRODUCTION

Grassroots Organizations and Social Change

In the fall of 1999 twenty progressive social change activists from small nonprofit organizations around the United States came together to discuss their role in the larger nonprofit sector and the constraints they faced in trying to effect social change. Out of that meeting grew a project titled Building Movement In(to) the Nonprofit Sector, which aims to explore and challenge current assumptions and expectations of how progressive, U.S.-based social change nonprofits should operate and to support efforts to broaden their impact.[1] Based on the conversations at that meeting, the Building Movement project identified three high-priority issues:

- generational changes in the leadership and management of social change organizations;
- sources of funding and their effect on organizational mission, goals, and constituency involvement; and
- differences between building a movement and building organizations.

In 2001, the project brought together nonprofit activists for regional meetings in Atlanta, Boston, Chicago, Denver, Knoxville, New York, and Oakland, to explore the relationship between movement building and organization building. Representing a variety of issue areas related to social justice and activities that included organizing, advocacy, services, funding, and technical assistance, the participants explored questions about the implications of organizational mission, leadership, structure, and funding for the task of larger movement building. These conversations clarified the need for a better understanding of the challenges facing small, independent nonprofit organizations engaged in efforts to make systemic changes.

Motivated by these concerns, we began to look for relevant research. Although there is a substantial literature on social movements and an equally vast literature on nonprofit organizations, there is little that speaks directly to the kinds of questions raised by our activist informants.[2] Ultimately, with the aims of drawing attention to these organizations, informing their work, and supporting a movement-building effort, we undertook an exploratory study of social change organizations, which became the basis for this book.

Theories of Social Change Activism

Our work with practitioners across the country has convinced us that small social change organizations (SCOs) are an important feature of today's sociopolitical landscape—particularly if, as we suspect, they represent a class of organization whose numbers are sizable and growing.[3] But theoretical frameworks for understanding this phenomenon are limited, as the traditional academic approaches to social change tend to focus on movements rather than grassroots organizations operating independently. The movement literature—briefly summarized below—informs our thinking about large-scale, integrated efforts. For language and ideas about decentralized social change activity, however, we turn to the world of practice.

The Academic Frame

Among academic researchers, intentional social change is usually understood to be the product of large-scale social movements—collective efforts to change something in society—such as the early-twentieth-century labor movement, the civil rights movement, and the environmental movement.[4] Indeed, many see the rightward shift in U.S. policies since the 1970s as the result of a highly effective conservative movement constructed in the wake of Goldwater's defeat in 1964 and not countered by a unified progressive movement.[5] In this context, organizations are important in how they serve—or in perverse cases, undermine—the larger movements of which they are a part.

A number of competing theories in the literature offer different perspectives on why social movements come into being, how their activities may result in change, and what role formal organizations play in bringing about change. Early approaches—theories of "collective behavior"—focused on individual motivations, saw participation as deriving from individual deprivation or social dislocation, and, at least initially, tended to view such behavior as irrational, disorganized, and destructive.[6] Later theories, inspired in part by the social movements of the 1960s, shifted the perspective from micro to macro level analysis and enlarged the focus from a concern with the emergence of movements to include their sustenance. Some have argued, for example, that grievances are a constant in society, and what determines successful and extended mobilization is resource availability (the "resource mobilization theory" of McCarthy and Zald 1973, 1977) and/or political opportunity (the "political process" model of McAdam 1999 [1982]). More recently, theories relating to the "new social movements" — defined as less economically class-based than earlier movements—have emphasized contests over frameworks of meaning and the construction of social identities.[7]

With the shift from understanding social movements as disorganized behavior to seeing them as rational, coordinated efforts came an interest in the role of organizations.[8] McCarthy and Zald (1977, 1218) defined a "social movement organization" as "a complex, or formal, organization which identifies its goals with the preferences of a social movement or a counter-movement and attempts to implement these goals." Both resource mobilization and political process theories see such groups as providing essential movement infrastructure. Resource mobilization (RM) theory seeks to understand how social movement entrepreneurs and their organizations develop access to needed resources, particularly from elite sources outside their immediate constituencies. McAdam's political process model—based on an analysis of the civil rights movement—also highlights the role of social movement organizations but critiques RM's insistence on the centrality of elite resources. In the civil rights movement, McAdam asserts, it was indigenous black organizations, such as churches, colleges, and chapters of the National Association for the Advancement of Colored People (NAACP), that provided communication channels, practical resources, and networks of "mobilizable" participants and leaders.[9] McAdam also argues that when external elites do provide resources, their aim is more likely to be control than support.

Piven and Cloward's (1977, 1992) view of social movement organizations is far more critical. They argue that theorists using the general resource mobilization framework (in which they include McAdam) have disregarded the important ways in which mobilization and protest conditions vary according to the economic status of participants. For "poor people's movements" (Piven and Cloward 1977)—in which disruptive, violent, and/or illegal actions are necessary—formal organizations are more likely to be a drain, a distraction, or an obstacle than an essential resource. Finally, for new social movement theories, social movement organizations play a role in the construction of identities, but they are neither the only location nor (for some, at least) the most important one for this activity (Mueller 1994; Taylor and Whittier 1992).

Organizations without Movement

The central point here is that in *all* of these approaches, organizations are understood in relationship to larger movements, which are themselves the engines of change. There is virtually no attention directed at organizations doing the work of change independently of social movements. But not all organizations working for change are "social movement organizations" in the sense of locating themselves in a larger network of agents of change. In our conversations with social change activists who work with disenfranchised communities in different parts of the United States, we heard that many did not see their groups as part of a movement, even if they were interested in working for large-scale change and could see that such affiliation might be powerful. One young participant in one of these meetings told us, "I don't know what a movement looks like." Another observed, "We are not in a time of movement. We have movement strategies but not a movement."

In particular, the groups we chose to study were not for the most part movement-identified, and as such are more appropriately labeled "social change" than "social movement" organizations.[10] Small social change organizations like those studied in this book represent a different way of thinking about systemic change: they represent a bottom-up effort in which many different organizations apply varying approaches to a variety of issues in the context of their own communities. This phenomenon stands in dramatic contrast to the prominent trajectory identified by many current social movement theorists, in which movements and movement organizations are seen as increasingly Washington-oriented, professionalized, and integrated into mainstream politics.[11]

Guidance from the World of Practice

Although the term "social change organization" is not commonly used by academics, an Internet search of the phrase "social change organization" will produce hundreds of sites in which the phrase is used, usually in reference to groups engaged in "social justice" work—that is, efforts to reduce inequalities in human society.[12] For example, the website of Nonprofit Enterprise and Self-sustainability Team ("NESsT") defines a social change organization as "one that addresses systemic, root causes of social and economic inequalities and thus aims to structurally transform society to achieve greater social and economic justice" (www.nesst.org/faq.asp). For some, additional aims such as environmental protection/sustainability or peace/conflict resolution must accompany the reduction of human inequality. SCOs usually focus their efforts on a particular dimension of injustice—such as racism, sexism, homophobia, or violence against women—or on a particular disadvantaged community. A few embrace broader agendas.

The definition offered by NESsT highlights structural change as opposed to individually oriented treatment or service provision, an important distinction for those in the field.[13] An illustration of the difference can be seen in the way another nonprofit, Project PROSPER, explains how and why it is *not* a social change organization, in contrast to the program it succeeded (ESCAPE: The Prostitution Prevention Project). PROSPER's website states:

> In the Spring of 2003, PROSPER Inc. acquired the assets of ESCAPE: the Prostitution Prevention Project and launched its hybrid anti-exploitation/risk reduction program model. This differs from the political[ly] based social change organization that was known as ESCAPE: the Prostitution Prevention Project. While social change is a priority to PROSPER, we recognize that many individuals seeking services are not in a position to take on social change or political reframing. It is essential that their immediate needs be addressed. . . . We believe in a three-part process . . . : Help the individual stay as safe as possible while they're in the sex trade, provide resources to get them out, and then, if they choose, present a Social Change model to them which addresses the sex trade in theoretical terms and helps the individual to become politicized. We believe however, that not every individual requesting services is seeking to be part of social change. They may not want or be able to take part in that process. We respect their right to choose that path. (http://www.escapeprostitution.com/4.0riskreduxprosper.htm, accessed 8/8/03)

As explained below, we found the definitions and conceptual frameworks of practitioners to be a helpful starting point for the design of our research, but we also questioned, refined, and elaborated such frameworks.

Selecting Organizations for Study

Project PROSPER's statement implies a clear distinction between a service-only orientation and a social change orientation that may include service, but the dividing line isn't always obvious. Some organizations are relatively easy to categorize as SCOs because of their primary or exclusive focus on affecting policies and institutionalized practices, and some organizations are clearly not of this type, as they attend only to immediate needs. But what of organizations that serve those who have been disadvantaged in a way that is intended to encourage and build capacity for their self-advocacy? Is this "social change" work? In an Internet search, we found many programs that refer to their work in this way but that might not fit the definition put forth by NESsT or even that implied in Project PROSPER's reflective self-description.

In selecting organizations for study, we sought to exclude *purely* service-oriented groups by selecting organizations whose mission statements included the goal of systemic change. At the same time, however, we were very interested in organizations that combined service and social change work because of their special potential. Nonprofit service organizations have a broad reach: they are numerous, located in all kinds of communities, and connected to a variety of different constituencies. Indeed, some argue that such agencies have a responsibility to advocate for their client-constituents, and we have found considerable interest among service practitioners in the possibility of moving into social change work. Concluding that it would be useful to know more about groups that do combine service and social change work, we included several change-oriented service agencies in our study.[14]

Our sample (hereafter referred to as our "study organizations") included a total of sixteen organizations located in urban areas within the northeastern United States.[15] The agencies were relatively small—with staffs of at least five people but no more than fifty-four, and annual budgets between $76,000 and $3,300,000.[16] The organizations ranged in age from 5 to 111 years, with a median age of 17 years, and structures varied from relatively traditional bureaucratic forms to more organic collectives.

As noted, within our basic definition of an SCO, we included change-oriented service agencies along with organizations predominantly focused on political action. The literature usually draws a distinction between *service* and *advocacy* organizations,[17] but we distinguished *organizing* groups as a third category, and recruited roughly equal numbers of organizations in each of these three categories (see Table I-1 for a list of study organizations identified by pseudonym).[18] We use this typology to reflect an organization's primary activity, how it spends most of its resources, and its self-image. In our categorization, *service delivery* refers to the provision of services directly to individuals and families; *advocacy* means promoting change on behalf of marginalized groups through the courts, the legislature, administrative agencies, and/or the public at large (and also includes serving other groups that do this work); and *organizing* means bringing together people in a constituent community, training and mobilizing them to advocate for themselves, with the target of advocacy efforts being either political decision-makers or the public. Our categorization is not meant to suggest that these organizations are pure types with no overlaps in activities—some organizing groups provide services, and service groups advocate—rather, it reflects our understanding of their primary identity. As table I-1 indicates, five of our SCOs were primarily service agencies, five were organizing groups, four were advocacy organizations, and two were advocacy-organizing hybrids.

We also sought variation in the field of activity. The work of these organizations encompassed a tremendous range of activities, such as creating affordable housing in neglected urban neighborhoods; securing economic rights such as minimum wage claims; supporting women leaving abusive relationships; publishing multilingual newspapers that give voice and advice to low-income women and children; training young people to work against violence and advocate for change in their schools and neighborhoods; supporting self-determination in poor neighborhoods by developing indigenous leadership and decision-making skills; providing technical assistance and network linkages to residents seeking to influence environmental policy; and litigating to secure the just treatment of psychiatrically disabled prisoners, abandoned lesbian and gay youth, sex workers, and other marginalized populations.

Finally, we wanted diversity among leaders—by sex, race or ethnicity, and age. Our selection of organizations was shaped in part by the desire to understand how these different factors might affect processes of leadership. In our work with practitioners, we had heard social change activists across the country express concerns with leadership transition challenges and with generational tensions in social change organizations.[19] To investigate the ways in which leadership might vary by generation or how the process of leadership development and succession might be affected by age differences, we spoke with leaders of different generations. In addition, we conducted interviews with staff members—primarily young

Table I-1 Study organizations

Pseudonym	Basic Activities and Goals	Category
Advocates for the People (AP)	Political action, research, and networking to achieve full participation for the Latino population	Advocacy
Center for Critical Information (CCI)	Opposition research and analysis, in support of the work of progressive groups and individuals	Advocacy
Rights for All (RFA)	Legal representation and organizing of socio-economically marginalized groups	Advocacy
Urban Watch (UW)	Local-issue research and analysis to serve social justice activists and policymakers	Advocacy
Community Choices (CC)	Citizen education, training, networking, and litigation to address environmental inequalities and sustainability	Advocacy/ organizing
Community Voice (CV)	Community organizing and legal representation of economically marginalized neighborhoods	Advocacy/ organizing
Community Ownership Program (COP)	Development of cooperatively owned and managed housing for low-income people	Organizing
Faith in Change (FC)	Organizing and education of local residents for more effective political participation and advocacy	Organizing
Respect (Rt)	Self-organizing and education for the empowerment of low-income persons	Organizing
Residents Making Change (RMC)	Supporting community decision-making and control of development in diverse, low-income neighborhood	Organizing
Uniting Youth for Change (UYC)	Organizing and training inner-city youth to develop stronger schools and communities	Organizing
Dare to Dream (DTD)	Providing services and support to homeless and other low-income families in a way that promotes their movement out of poverty; advocating for policy change	Service
Growing Roots (GR)	Providing services to support the development of Black and Latino youth in poor neighborhoods	Service
Neighborhood Reach (NR)	Supporting stabilization of at-risk individuals and groups, nurturing community, bringing together economically diverse segments of the population	Service
Sheltering Our Own (SOO)	Serving particular racial/ethnic group to support women's freedom from domestic violence; advocacy and education to change attitudes	Service
Teaching Tools (TT)	Anti-violence training for youth, in service of safer, more democratic schools/ culture	Service

people—in the same organizations, who could give us the perspective of potential leaders. The final sample of organizations included eight led by older leaders, seven led by younger leaders, and one collective in which we spoke with both an older and a younger activist.[20]

Interviews were conducted by seven project staff members (all women, three of whom are women of color). Questions were open-ended, based on a topic guide that included the following areas:

- the mission and work of the organization; whether and how it contributes to social change;
- the organization's structure and decision-making processes;
- the path to the work, the personal motives, beliefs, and experiences of the respondent;
- the leadership needs of the organization and the opportunities for the development of leadership, as well as the respondent's own training in this area; and
- the effects of race and gender on leadership and decision-making.

In addition, we obtained demographic data about the respondents and their organizations. Demographic data and data from the interviews were supplemented with information from nonprofit tax returns (Form 990), organizational literature, and published media or research accounts of these groups.

The gathering and analysis of the data (described in detail in the appendix) were motivated and shaped by our interest in particular aspects of social change work and the organizations that do it. We also sought an understanding grounded in the experience and perspectives of the people engaged in these activities. In keeping with these aims, our methods were iterative: through both data collection and analysis our questions were reconfigured by the respondents' answers.

The remainder of this book is a report of what we learned, beginning with the most fundamental question of our project, the definition of social change work. Chapters are organized as follows:

Chapter 1, "Approaches to Social Change: A Framework," analyzes our respondents' comments about how their organizations approach social change, to identify the key dimensions that distinguish SCOs from other nonprofits and, in some cases, from each other. We develop a framework that specifies four alternative social change orientations (or *enacted theories of change*) associated with different organizations within our sample. In subsequent chapters we consider the relevance of social change orientation for particular features of organizations as well as relationships between them.

Chapter 2, "Doing the Work: More Than a Job," discusses the backgrounds, motivations, and capabilities of the people who staff and lead these organizations. We find common themes across our groups, as well as staff requirements that vary by social change orientation. The work offers deep satisfaction but also significant challenges to sustainability—including the problem of balancing work and other life commitments, a source of significant intergenerational tension.

Chapter 3, "Leadership: Making the Vision Real," applies a general model of organizational strategy to the work of SCOs, highlighting special leadership demands associated with a mission of systemic change, a commitment to constituent participation, and in some cases, transformative work. The chapter reviews the preparation of current leaders, ongoing staff development, and barriers to broadening leadership, and it concludes with suggestions for the preparation of future SCO directors.

Chapter 4, "Organizational Structure: Legitimacy and Accountability," examines the decision-making structures and processes of these organizations, highlighting variation along two dimensions—the concentration of internal authority and the degree of openness to clients or community. We find a relationship between the second dimension and the nature of the work (as reflected in the organization's particular social change orientation). Internal structures can be either democratic or bureaucratic, as long as the particular challenges associated with the form are acknowledged and managed.

Chapter 5, "Resources: Spinning Straw into Bricks," looks at the varying sources and levels of support available to different types of SCOs, and finds four different resource strategies corresponding to the four social change orientations. In terms of their contribution to social change effort, the strategies have complementary strengths and weaknesses; in particular, there tends to be an inverse relationship between budget size and ability to engage primarily in change-oriented activity.

Chapter 6, "Collaboration: Mission Driven Partnerships," identifies the kinds of collaborative work in which these SCOs are currently engaged. Different social change orientations are found to be associated with particular collaborative approaches, in part reflecting variation in competition and resource strategies. In all the SCOs, the desire for greater effectiveness in meeting mission drives collaboration, but organization-specific imperatives can constrain it. Leaders vary in their commitment to cooperative effort, and the deepest forms of collaboration—in which individual organizations are open to growing and changing—are rare.

Chapter 7, "Organizations, Movement, and the Future of Social Change," assesses the potential role of social change organizations in the building of a progressive social movement. We summarize the debate among progressives about centralized versus grassroots approaches to movement building and conclude that SCOs can make an important contribution. We also note the significant challenges that confront their effective participation in the building of a larger movement for change, and suggest shifts by funders, national groups, and SCOs themselves that will be necessary for more meaningful, successful aggregation of effort.

CHAPTER ONE

APPROACHES TO SOCIAL CHANGE

A Framework

Alex Montoya was one of eight children, born and raised in a poverty-stricken, predominantly Black and Latino urban neighborhood.[1] His father was an alcoholic who died young, leaving Alex's mother to care for the family on public assistance. Alex was 13, in ninth grade at "one of the worst performing schools . . . in the nation," when he "came out." "There was a lot of hostility . . . against me," he said, "because I was like basically always a little flamboyant—a little feminine, as society states—and people would pick on me, you know, like the students would call me 'faggot' and push me and things like that, and that basically traumatized me and I was scared." Two months into the school year he dropped out. But even outside school he encountered deep hostility. "I turned to drugs, basically to escape—because like even if I would go to the store, people would laugh at me. . . . I met people who I thought were my friends, but they weren't. They were also gay and they were on drugs, and I just saw them doing it and like, they would feel good and that."

Alex was addicted to heroin from the age of 14 until the age of 18, when he got help through a neighborhood church. He had once been a good student and wanted to get his life back on track. "So I went to St. Bartholomew's," he explained. "I spoke to the Father and they sent me to detoxification in a hospital. I stayed there for two weeks. When I came out, you know, that's when I started to get stronger." It was at the church that Alex met Alisha Matharu and Steven Jencks, who were beginning to work as organizers in the neighborhood. Initially they operated out of the church's basement and eventually founded their own organization, Community Voice. Inspired by the two organizers' aims of educating and empowering the community, Alex told them he wanted to help. Knowing how hard his own experience had been and seeing that some had even greater problems, he was convinced of the need to provide support. "I was a little more fortunate," he said, "because my mom was really open-minded and she accepted me. [But] I know a lot of my friends, they were basically abandoned by their mothers and by their fathers just for being gay."

When Alex explained what he wanted to do, Alisha and Steven welcomed him. "They pretty much—without even knowing me, they just said, come in . . . and I mean I never had any experience in organizing, never . . . and they just, they basically opened up their arms, and said, 'Yeah, come in with us, and we'll teach you, we'll give you training.'" For the past several years, Alex's group has been meeting with and providing support to at-risk youth, in addition to conducting outreach and education in the community. This project is only one of many initiatives undertaken by the organization, which now has a large community membership and a board elected by the community. With a small staff in conjunction with resident activists, Community Voice (CV) has worked for economic justice (taking sweatshop owners to court for unpaid wages), better access to public services for non-English-speaking residents (informing them of their rights, confronting public agencies over inadequate services), and a healthier neighborhood environment (identifying and addressing hazards such as lead poisoning or pest infestations). The organization's priorities are defined by the community, and many programs rely on resident action as well as professional staff services.

Steven Jencks describes CV's work as a blend of organizing and legal service. It brings people together for political education and advocacy, he explained, "to make some changes in the systems which can negatively affect them." It also provides assistance "so that people can deal with the way their oppression manifests itself . . . day to day," whether it be a child's wrongful suspension from school or the erroneous denial of food stamps. In addition to addressing some immediate needs and undertaking some small-scale reforms, CV also engages in a systemic change effort insofar as it challenges a social structure "predicated on enormous numbers of people being totally alienated from the political process and having very little [of] both political and economic power." Steven Jencks explained:

> We're trying to help people get collective political power and educate themselves about the kind of processes they're alienated from. And also in some instances help them gain economic power by getting wrongfully denied wel-

fare benefits or pay for their work. I guess that's kind of a challenge to the . . . wholesale disenfranchisement people feel. . . . And then . . . [our] organizing campaigns . . . would entail fundamental shifts . . . if welfare recipients were able to access the information and the benefits that they were entitled to and need. It would be obviously a big change if factory workers were paid what they should be paid or if even environmental hazards were under control.

Community Voice and the fifteen other organizations described in this book fit our definition of progressive social change organizations (SCOs)—nonprofit organizations that aim to address systemic problems in a way that will increase the power of marginalized groups, communities, or interests. They represent a grassroots response (i.e., one grounded in a local community) to systemic social problems: Faith in Change, for example, organizes local residents for more effective political participation. Teaching Tools promotes safer schools through antiviolence training. Residents Making Change provides an infrastructure for community-based decision-making and control. Dare to Dream works with low-income families to develop services needed to overcome poverty. Growing Roots builds confidence and capacity through programs for inner-city Black and Latino youth.[2]

We recruited study participants based on our understanding that their organizations met our working definition of SCOs, but once we began gathering data on these agencies, we found ourselves debating whether or not all were "real" social change organizations, usually because of our uncertainty about the extent to which they were targeting *systemic* change. Was it possible to bring about systemic change simply through individual transformation? Did systemic change require massive redistributions of power and other resources? Would systemic change occur if the rules stayed the same but different groups participated in the public decision-making process? Could the restructuring of a single neighborhood be considered systemic change?

Defining the Dimensions of Social Change Work

We asked our interview respondents directly if they saw their own agency as working toward social change and what they thought that meant. An analysis of their responses, in conjunction with our understanding of their activities, led us to identify three important dimensions of efforts for social change rather than to specify the "right" definition.[3] These dimensions—

described in detail below—include the degree of constituent engagement and participation, the role of individual transformation, and the mode of empowerment (as individual versus collective action). The first of these (constituent participation) generally distinguishes SCOs from other kinds of nonprofits, but we also find variation among SCOs themselves on this dimension. The other two (role of individual transformation and mode of empowerment) are primarily useful in distinguishing among SCOs and helping us understand the similarities and differences in their approaches.

Constituent Engagement and Participation

When we asked respondents to elaborate on their own definitions of "social change," their answers emphasized working *with* the client or constituency group (those they aimed to serve or support) rather than simply *on their behalf*—whether the agency's primary activity was service delivery, organizing, or advocacy. In this characteristic as well as in their commitment to systemic change, grassroots SCOs differ from traditional social-service agencies, which provide services or support without working to develop clients' autonomy or engaging clients in program design. Constituent participation also distinguishes SCOs from professionalized activist organizations, which engage in systemic change efforts (such as lobbying and litigation), but do so either independently of the actions of members or by mobilizing them for organizationally directed political action.[4] In either traditional social services or professional movement organizations, the key issues and plans for addressing them are identified by experts.

By contrast, the social change organizations participating in this study almost all work actively with constituent populations to promote their self-determination. (The main exceptions are the Center for Critical Information and Urban Watch, the two organizations that support other agencies and are therefore one step removed from constituent populations.[5] Even with these groups, however, there is an emphasis on empowering activist-clients by providing information and analysis for their use.) Indeed, for our respondents, social change is as much about *process* as *outcome*. As Harold deMello of Residents Making Change explained, "Well, for us the measure of social change—and we think the leverage point in social change—is the ability for people who live here, versus institutions and organizations, to make change." In his view, the residents themselves should be "at the forefront . . . driving . . . being the cause of . . . the catalyst for . . . the architects . . . [and] the engineers of the change." In a dynamic world, there would always be varying issues and needs. Thus social justice would inevitably mean not achieving a particular set of material conditions, but getting "to a place where we have more capacity here as a neighborhood to deal with issues, to deal with improvement needs and development needs in this neighborhood, and . . . effecting the type of change that we think is important." Pete Veratek offered a similar view in describing the mission of Faith in Change. "It's meant to be a power organization. . . . not a housing group . . . not an anti–crime group . . . not an education group . . . not a good government group. It's meant to create a locus of power among institutions and people who don't normally have their own." Members would learn about power, use it, and then "assess the amount of change that they're able to create with the power that they built."

In the most extensive form of participation, the constituents *are* the organization—as in the low-income women's collective, Respect. Even as the members advocate and speak out for the needs of poor families, they also develop their own skills, practice leadership, and work to overcome the social divisions within their own membership, while struggling with their own poverty. An older member, Linda Jefferson, explained that a primary focus of the group is "to publish a newspaper that is by, for, and about low- and no-income people. And [to] present views that people won't find in the . . . mainstream media." Through their newspaper and other activities, members educate the public and politicians about issues, increase poor people's awareness of benefits and services available, and give voice to their own powerful feelings. Given the difficult conditions of the members' own lives, their work is challenging but also supportive. "Sometimes you feel like, oh God, I'm so tired, I can't do it anymore. And then you meet the next person. . . . And the next thing you know you're pulling their energy in, you're giving them energy and they're giving you energy. And you begin to see that, yes, we can do this."

Respect is the only membership collective among our sample of organizations, but there are three other organizations in which staff members report to constituent boards. Community Voice has a large resident membership from which its board is elected, and the board works with the staff to set priorities in the agency's work for social and economic justice. Residents Making Change and Faith in Change not only follow an agenda set by constituents, but they also focus almost entirely on membership action: community empowerment is the primary goal.

Respect, Community Voice, Residents Making Change, and Faith in Change all have formal decision-making structures that empower constituents—a feature that will be examined in greater detail in chapter 4. The other groups in our study give less formal authority to constituents, with paid staff members and non-constituent boards ultimately determining the agenda and the shape of programs. Nevertheless, these groups emphasize the goal of self-determination and create space for constituent empowerment within their activities. Uniting Youth for Change, for example, takes its own approach to youth training and organizing into schools, but within each project, it is the young participants who identify the key issues they will address through collective effort. At Growing Roots, youth development programs include projects proposed by young participants as well as services designed by the staff. Dare to Dream engages its clientele in its strategic planning, takes program suggestions from the community, and includes formerly homeless people on both its staff and board.

Even in cases where the constituent influence over the organization itself is limited, SCOs are concerned with connecting to the constituency and building its capacity for action. At Advocates for the People, director Antonio Mena determines the agenda, but he is concerned with promoting community capacity. AP wants to connect its research to organizing and advocacy but often finds that the community's institutional infrastructure is very uneven.

> So we find a lot of times we're also creating . . . these makeshift infrastructures around different issues. So, for example, around redistricting and voting rights, election reform, there really are very few . . . organizations that deal with that. I mean most of them are very, very local, so we've had to actually go out there and try to structure like a regional infrastructure of committees. . . . [But] we don't do the plans for them. We just provide them with mapping and legal support, and then these community groups, or coalitions usually, are the ones that do the work.

Finally, several agencies promote constituent self-determination through the provision of particular kinds of services or resources. Community Ownership Program, for example, helps low-income residents become home-owners in cooperatively owned and managed buildings, but the work goes far beyond the provision of housing. When constituents become engaged in their housing, they develop a variety of skills, such as bookkeeping, maintenance, and the politics of co-op management; they also gain confidence. As director Roger Cochran explained,

> They have a success in controlling a piece of their lives . . . [that] translate[s] into other parts of their lives. . . . And then . . . particularly the leaders in these buildings, but even the regular [co-op] members . . . tend to be active in their neighborhoods, not just in their buildings. Once they finish their build-

ings, you see the same people in the community gardens. You'll see them on the housing committees of their churches. You see them on the local school boards and community boards and precinct councils. . . . [A]ctivism . . . in one part of their lives spills over into others, and they take those skills and experiences and use them.

Like several other study organizations, COP engages in some policy advocacy independently of its work with constituents—but when speaking of *social change*, COP leaders discussed not organizational policy advocacy but their direct work with constituents. And the result of that work was not a static outcome, but an ongoing process of development and self-determination.

The Role of Individual Transformation

When the executive director of Community Ownership Program spoke of how program participants became activists, he was articulating a practical theory of change that includes not only an increase in the engagement and self-determination of a community but also a transformation of individuals that is integral to larger change efforts. Indeed, the importance of individual transformation is even clearer in the comments of Henry Mathis, a project director at COP. "What we try to do," he said, "is not hold your hand through the process, but . . . give you the tools that you need to fight for yourself, to deal with the government agencies, to go and deal with [the housing department], to go to the department of finance and dispute a tax bill." The meaning of this capacity-building process was most evident to Henry when he saw how clients reacted to the certificate they received on completing COP's training. Henry had initially thought of the certificate— something suggested by funders—as nothing more than a "marketing ploy."

But when I realized how people felt about getting that piece of paper in their hand, it really taught me something. . . . You know, that's social change if we can raise your level of confidence . . . and if we can give you some skills that you can take outside of the building and have enough confidence to go and apply for a certain job, give you some leadership skills. Maybe make you a better role model for your children or for other people in the building. That's social change. It's giving someone something that they never thought they would have.

Whereas constituent participation is common to most SCOs and distinguishes them from many other nonprofits, individual transformation is central to the work of some SCOs and not others. In particular, we find that individual transformation is prominent in the theories of change articulated by those in organizing and service groups but not in advocacy organizations. For both organizers and change-oriented service providers, constituent transformation encompasses increased awareness of how social systems affect personal circumstances, development of personal capacity for effective self-advocacy, and increased confidence that success is possible. For those in service SCOs, the transformative work actually constitutes one form of social change; for organizers, individual transformation is an essential element in motivating and sustaining the collective action through which change occurs.

Service provision is often distinguished from social change work because of its focus on individuals, but several of our service-agency respondents cited individual work—in addition to direct efforts to influence public policy—as an important aspect of their efforts to cause social change because of its transformative quality.[6] In this regard, their work is similar to the liberation pedagogy developed and practiced by Brazilian educator Paulo Freire and others.[7] Freire argued against a "banking" model of education, in which teachers deposit knowledge in student minds—analogous in some ways to a traditional service-delivery model—and for a process of learning that would draw on the student's life experience and lead to greater consciousness and action.

Such a vision of change was reflected in the comments of Maureen Lynch, Dare to Dream's administrator, who explained, "Social change is happening on different levels." At the macro level, she said, their director was working in the policy arena to influence legislation affecting low-income families. "But then [we operate] at the micro level as well, working with the families to help them realize that they are a victim of the system. Lots of times they come in thinking they are the cause. . . . So [we're] helping them recognize that [larger system] and . . . become advocates for social change."

At Sheltering Our Own, these two different levels of change were highlighted by different respondents. Not surprisingly, executive director Madeleine Lee answered our question about SOO's social change work by describing their efforts to change social attitudes toward domestic violence in the local immigrant community through public education. But staff member Kamla Chowdhury emphasized the element of change in their work at the individual level. The communities, she said, "have their traditional notions of domestic violence and . . . male superiority, and we're trying to move away from that. In educating our clients, our women . . .

into . . . life here, how they're in a different position now and they kind of have to be independent, that in itself is change. With one woman you're creating social change. Seeing one woman move from where she was to where she is, is social change. It's minuscule, but still it adds up."

Respondents at other service agencies echoed these sentiments, asserting that transformative work produces social change. Growing Roots co-founder Monroe Harris observed that through their primary work of youth development, "Social change is inevitable. . . . [I]f you're helping to create a generation of young people who care about each other and care about their community and are fighting against problems—then that's social change." Similarly, Teaching Tools program director Frank Haynes saw the potential for profound change in youth non-violence training. If young people "see that cooperation is more interesting than competition and that fairness and kindness and taking a stand matter as much or more than winning and getting over . . . that's really radical social change."

In our service agencies, respondents described two distinct venues for their social change efforts—their own political advocacy and transformative work with clients that was expected to result in client self-advocacy over the long term. In organizing groups, individual transformation is a necessary but not sufficient condition for activism and advocacy; as constituents become more knowledgeable, confident, and skilled, the organizing group provides a platform for their political action. Marsha Madison, a young member of the organizing collective Respect, recounted how her own transformation—reminiscent of what Maureen Lynch sought for DTD's clients—connected to the advocacy and activism she undertook through the collective:

> I also think social change can happen on an individual basis. . . . [A]ll I can speak of is my own experience with this, and that is that . . . when I first came to Respect . . . I was a low-income woman in a domestic violence situation. I was on welfare and deeply ashamed about that, because I left my abuser and found that I couldn't afford to support my kid on the wages I was making. . . . And then my son was diagnosed with [a serious illness]. . . . And I really believed that it was just my own personal bad decisions until I met these other women and started to see a *system*. . . . It affected me so much that I completely changed the course of my life and in turn became an activist, and in turn became an educator, and in turn spread this reality to other people.

Marsha saw other women who came into Respect undergo the same shift of perspective wherein a personal story becomes political. That transformation, she said, is "one of the things we provide" and it enables mem-

bers to effect change in their own lives and beyond. "The stronger I became," Marsha explained, "the less shame I had, the more I was able to
do." She edited the collective's newspaper, created a writing curriculum,
and spoke to large public audiences where her words had a galvanizing effect. "I've had people come up to me at events . . . [like] young women in
college, and they'll say, 'Marsha, I heard you speak at such and such a
place, and you changed my whole perception of homelessness. And now
I'm an activist because of you, or now I'm a feminist.' " Marsha defined
this kind of impact as a form of social change. It might not be the same as
changing laws or policy, but in the long term it could lead to that. "I think
that if you don't [get] individuals in your society changing their minds, or
transforming, or becoming aware of root causes, then you can't change society, because who's making up the societies but individuals?"

Uniting Youth for Change, another organizing group, also relies on a
framework in which individual learning and development foster collective
action to effect institutional change. UYC's model of youth organizing be-
gins by helping young people see their own behavior in the context of
larger societal dynamics, and then identify targets for change in local practices and policies. As site director, Mark Lightner elaborated: "Our goal
is . . . to change behavior patterns among young people and adults, within
institutions or communities, and thus . . . [to] change the structure of . . .
[those] institutions . . . to take in the views and roles of young people . . .
so that they become full participants."

In contrast to the organizing and service agencies, those emphasizing
advocacy activities—such as class-action litigation, political research and
analysis, and networking or coalition building for political action—tended
not to articulate theories of change in which individual transformation
played a central role. For these groups, the removal of structural obstacles
facing marginalized groups was the goal; personal growth or transformation might result but was not an explicit element of the change process. A
lawyer with Rights for All explained his motivation for RFA's work by reflecting on the difference that legal assistance can make for poor people. In
his experience, legal assistance could keep people from "falling through
the cracks." This was particularly true in dealing with the problem of
homelessness.

I thought there was a key role for lawyers to play in helping people to prevent
eviction, and moving beyond that, I thought that there was a fundamental inequality in the one landlord versus one tenant equation. . . . [I found myself]
wanting to balance it out. To balance out that equation and put tenants on a

more equal footing with the landlord. . . . [On] the notion of . . . individual client self-determination that I've talked a little bit about . . . my role as a lawyer has been to empower individuals and not to make them just reliant on another person.

As mentioned, two other advocacy organizations—Urban Watch and the Center for Critical Information—provide information and analysis to activist groups and individuals, and do not therefore have the kind of constituencies typical of organizing and service agencies. The leaders in these organizations both offered qualified responses when asked if their agencies did social change work. At CCI, the director said, "Well, absolutely we do, but I really see us as a backup organization for the activists who are working on the front lines for social change. We supply them with the information and analysis that they need to do their work. But we don't do the actual organizing and activism ourselves. It's in the service of social change." Similarly, at Urban Watch, the director said she knew "the folks who do social change. And they would probably say that we're not that." But in contrast to the mainstream media, they played a critical social change role, "essentially serving the people who do social change."

Individual Empowerment or Collective Action

The final dimension on which our SCOs' approaches varied was the mode of empowerment. For some, change was expected to occur through individual self-determination, as previously marginalized people obtained the rights and resources needed to take control over their own lives, thereby exercising more power on behalf of themselves and their communities. For others, individual empowerment might be desirable, but systemic change would come through collective action.

The focus on individual versus collective action interacts with but is not identical to the relative emphasis on individual transformation in social change. Organizations may work with a theory of change that includes a central role for individual transformation and yet be oriented toward collective action. Conversely, the theory of change may be focused on empowering individuals (often as members of a marginalized social group) without attention to individual transformation. In figure 1–1 we locate our SCOs' theories of change with respect to these two dimensions; the result highlights a relationship between social change orientation and primary type of activity.

On the left side of figure 1–1 are the organizations for whom individual

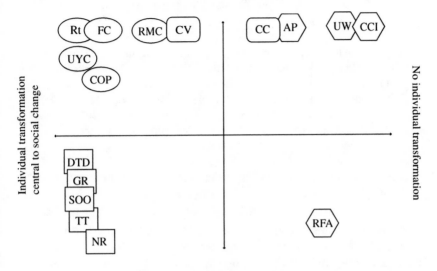

\P=Advocates for the People; CCI=Center for Critical Information; CC=Community Choices; COP=Community Ownership Program; CV= Community Voice;
)TD=Dare to Dream; FC=Faith in Change; GR=Growing Roots; NR=Neighborhood Reach; Rt=Respect; RMC=Residents Making Change; RFA=Rights for All;
;OO=Sheltering Our Own; TT=Teaching Tools; UYC=Uniting Youth for Change; UW=Urban Watch;

Key: □ = service; ○ = organizing; ○ = advocacy; ○ = advocacy + organizing

Figure 1-1 Enacted theories of change

transformation is central to their theories of change. In the upper left quadrant are SCOs that link individual transformation to *collective action*—
these are the organizing groups. In this social change model, constituents
are educated, motivated, and inspired; then they are brought together for
collective action, which when successful results in even greater transformation.[8] Faith in Change, for instance, encourages local residents to identify and attack common problems, whether it be cleaning a vacant lot or
demanding services from the city. FC's director Pete Veratek explained
that when the organization began, the neighborhood was economically and
politically "off the map"—nonexistent as far as the rest of the city was concerned. The first task for FC was to activate constituents by helping them
acknowledge both their disadvantage and their potential. The second task
was to demand attention and resources through collective action—to re-
build the neighborhood, to repair parks and pools and transit stations, to
demolish abandoned buildings and construct homes on vacant lots. Over

two decades, Pete said, the community effected "an extraordinary amount of physical improvement and change." But at least as important as the physical changes was the psychological impact of their efforts:

> People know they can do things. They don't need some third–rate City Council person to talk to about something that the City Council doesn't have the least interest in or power to solve. They know they can just go, organize, prepare, research, act and get it done. Large numbers of people, not just three leaders or ten pastors or—hundreds of people, thousands of people. Because they've all done it. They've been in successful action that's led to successful results and they know that they can win.

SCOs that link individual transformation to *individual empowerment*— the lower left quadrant—are primarily our change-oriented service agencies. These groups provide various forms of training and support that enable individual constituents and families to achieve greater control over the conditions of their own lives and to reshape communities and institutions through their actions. When Teaching Tools trains young people in conflict resolution and peace-making techniques, it promotes both individual development and a shift in the culture of the school. When Neighborhood Reach provides services that allow low-income, elderly residents to remain in their homes, they serve individual needs but also support a diverse community. NR's Jean Patterson argues that the outcomes of their efforts not only promote individual success, but are "really fundamental to the healthy growth and development and sustenance of the community that we're serving here."

On the right side of figure 1–1 are the organizations whose change-theories do not emphasize transformative work with constituents. In the upper right quadrant are SCOs oriented toward collective or community-level action, which are primarily political advocacy groups. Some of these SCOs simply do not work directly with individual constituents (unless they happen to be community leaders). For those that do work with individuals, the change-model starts with changing community conditions, rather than individual transformation (though the former may produce the latter). As an example of this approach, Advocates for the People supports political action by the Latino community and engages in capacity building at a community level (as described by Antonio Mena above), but AP's vision does not highlight individual transformation as central to the political mobilization process. Urban Watch and the Center for Critical Information both provide information and analysis in support of organized political action but not through individual constituents. Finally, one of the advocacy-organizing hybrid organizations (Community Choices) is placed in this quadrant; originally an advocacy organization, CC seems to emphasize a non-transformative model of organizing. In contrast, the other hybrid (Community Voice) was founded to do both organizing and advocacy and tends toward more transformative work.

The fourth approach to social change emphasizes *individual empowerment* without transformative work (the lower right quadrant) and is reflected in the work of Rights for All, an advocacy organization whose primary activity has been litigation on behalf of marginalized groups. As with any organization operating primarily on a legal advocacy model, RFA seeks to secure legal rights and services for people who belong to systemically disadvantaged groups. Social identities are relevant to this approach—rights are sought on behalf of individuals because of group membership—but collective action is not the aim.[9] If our sample included more legal advocacy groups, this quadrant of the figure would contain more organizations.

The relationship between different theories of change and SCO types should not be taken as absolute. As illustrated in figure 1–1, there are differences between agencies of the same type: some service groups work toward more collective or community action than others; some organizing groups place a stronger emphasis on individual transformation than others. Additionally, agencies that shift their activities over time are likely to represent less pure prototypes; for example, Community Choices is turning toward organizing from advocacy, but with less emphasis on the transformative theory of change common to traditional organizing groups. Nevertheless, the framework does capture important distinctions in approaches to social change articulated in the reflections of our respondents and evident in the work of their organizations.

Parts of the Whole

In figure 1–2 we summarize the primary work of each of the four orientations, showing that these quadrants represent complementary rather than alternative approaches: interdependent pieces of a larger effort. The work of agencies in the lower right quadrant is to dismantle formal barriers that prevent individuals from accessing needed support; for example, ensuring that those struggling with drug addiction are not illegally harassed for par-

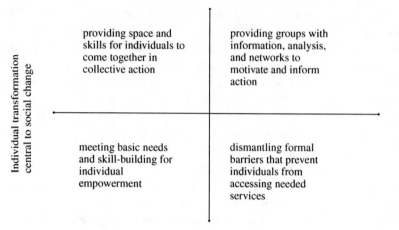

Figure 1-2 The work of social change

ticipating in needle-exchange or methadone treatment programs, or that homeless people are able to secure the public benefits to which they are entitled. Such work both facilitates and is facilitated by the activities of groups in the next (lower left) quadrant, including the building of awareness and capacity for self-advocacy along with service-provision at the individual level through training, shelter, psychological support, and family services. When these skills are developed and needs met, individuals can come together for collective effort, the domain of the third (upper left) quadrant. These collective actions—along with the legal advocacy of the first quadrant—make use of the information, analysis, and networking efforts of groups in the final, upper right quadrant.

All of these approaches are necessary but individually insufficient to meet the larger aim of systemic change. It may be possible for single organizations to do the work of more than one quadrant (usually through different programs housed in the same agency), but it is not realistic for a single organization to encompass effectively all four aspects of social change work. Understanding an agency's particular competence and the role it plays in the larger picture is a critical task of leadership in SCOs, for both targeted success and collaboration with others.

Understanding Organizations in the
Context of Purpose

Much of the literature on nonprofits—particularly that which focuses on management or performance—treats these organizations in generic terms, offering analyses and sometimes prescriptions intended to apply across agencies with varying missions and activities.[10] We argue that a full understanding must take into account what organizations are trying to accomplish and how they go about doing this—in the case of SCOs, full understanding requires taking into account their theory of change. We expect the emphasis on constituent engagement and participation among our SCOs to have a bearing on such organizational concerns as staffing, decision-making structure, leadership, and resources. In terms of structure, for example, these organizations are likely to be more permeable than other nonprofits, but also to show variation among themselves in line with different emphases on constituent control. Similarly, the ways in which these agencies differ with respect to the role of individual transformation and the mode of empowerment should have implications for their operations: staffing, structure, access to resources, and external relationships are likely to vary with the four different social change orientations.

Furthermore, these dimensions are relevant to the challenge of broadening impact through movement building. The location of organizations in figure 1–1, for example, highlights similarities and differences that might be strategically important in networking efforts, as SCOs with different orientations may well face different constraints and opportunities for collaborative effort. Additionally, to the extent that different change orientations are associated with different organizational characteristics and capacities, the strategies for engaging different groups and making the best use of them in a larger effort will vary. Finally, for deeper collaboration to occur, it will be essential for those using different approaches to understand and respect their differences.

In subsequent chapters we look closely at how SCOs function—their staffing, leadership, structures, resource strategies, and partnerships. In each area we will find commonalities that distinguish SCOs from other types of nonprofits, and we will also find important differences. In many cases, these differences are related to the organizations' differing social change orientations, suggesting that one-size-fits-all organizational prescriptions are inappropriate.

CHAPTER TWO

DOING THE WORK

More Than a Job

I always knew . . . growing up that different people were treated differently,
because of the color of their skin or who they were, whether they were female or male, whatever it was. I would be aware of this but not as much in
a social context—that obviously I had to develop, had to figure out how
systems work and institutions work. That was something I really came to
be passionate about. . . . I don't feel that I did come out of a social justice
background. Most of the people that we interview now . . . [have] been
doing a lot [in this area]. . . . I wouldn't even get this position now if I
wasn't hired before. I was much more like a basic person.

MARK LIGHTNER,
Uniting Youth for Change

SCOs are not unique among nonprofits in looking for a good fit between
the values of individual employees and the organizational mission.[1] But to
align closely with an SCO's mission, an employee's belief system must go
beyond the "basic person" viewpoint described by Mark Lightner—which
acknowledges and laments unequal treatment but does not link inequality
to social and economic systems.[2] Specifically, SCO staff members must
see that the difficulties constituents face are shaped as much by larger systems as by individual circumstances or choices, have a sense of how those
systems operate to disadvantage certain groups and hold a commitment to
changing structures of inequality.

Getting the Analysis

How do SCO staff members come by their critical perspective? Our respondents reported a variety of paths to their awareness. For some—often people of color—it was less a distinct learning process than a matter of early socialization: a commitment to social justice was woven into the fabric of their family and community life. As Growing Roots' co-leader Denise Stewart put it, "We have parents who are activists and educators. And those values were instilled in us at a very young age." It could be hard to sort out the effects of nature versus nurture, she said, "because you just grew up in it."

For others, the development of critical consciousness resembled what adult educator Jack Mezirow (2000, 8–9) calls "transformative learning:" the "process by which we transform our taken-for-granted frames of reference . . . to make them more inclusive." In Mezirow's view, transformative learning occurs when people reflect on long held beliefs that have become problematic. Through a process of critical analysis, the learner—often with the help of others—examines his beliefs and the assumptions behind them to arrive at a new point of view. The transformation itself can be sudden or incremental.

The process is evident in the experience of Pete Veratek, long-time director of Faith in Change. Growing up in the 1960s, Pete found his exposure to the civil rights movement raised questions for him. A turning point occurred when he took a summer job with a local housing group at the same time as he was seeing the all-white neighborhood of his youth turn all black.

> It was like seeing archeology. It was like seeing a mountain cut open, and you see all the layers of rock. I was seeing, again mostly by accident, all the layers of what happens to white families, when they're scared out of their homes by white realtors, who are ripping them off. What happens to the black families, who move in, who are sold the same, basically lousy houses for three times their value, when they're trying to escape the ghetto. What happens back in the ghetto they just left, because that's where they bought their homes on contract and were being evicted or under threat of eviction all this time. So I just got this very early, deep cut into political reality and social reality that told me that something was going on. And it had very little to do with anything I was hearing in the normal political arena, or even the normal religious arena.

Soon after this experience, Pete set aside his ambition to be a writer and became a community organizer.

Pete's growing awareness was shaped in part by his experience of the civil rights movement, and he was not alone among our SCO leaders in reporting that the process of transformative learning had been prompted or supported by the progressive movements and thinkers of the 1960s and 1970s. For younger SCO staffers who have less exposure to such movements, or those who are not from communities with strong social justice traditions, the opportunity to develop a systemic analysis in the workplace is essential.

For Mark Lightner (who is a generation younger than Pete Veratek), the social analytic framework provided by UYC enabled him to transform a vague discomfort over witnessed inequities into a larger understanding of social systems. At Uniting Youth for Change, social justice training is explicit: the organization introduces new hires to a social analysis that underpins the work they do with youth. The model does not discount the importance of individual behavior, but places it within a larger context, calling attention to social and economic forces that constrain individual action. Such an understanding allows UYC staff members to support client development in which young people assume responsibility but also avoid self-blame, and furthermore begin to develop a political awareness that will help them advocate for themselves. Reflecting on his own increased understanding, Mark noted, "I feel a lot of me has grown up here."

In the case of constituent staff-members whose awareness is undeveloped when they join their organizations, the transformative learning process can affect both their work and the way they view the circumstances of their own lives. In Marsha Madison's case, it was hearing and seeing others in similar situations that led to her reinterpretation of her own experience. When she arrived at Respect, she was overwhelmed with a sense of personal failure for her inability to support herself and her child after leaving an abusive relationship. "As I got involved in the group . . . I saw other women are having this same circumstance. I began to realize, oh my god, there is a system that's really making it impossible for some women to be full citizens on purpose. And then I began to think about history. And then I began to learn history, a different version of this history." Her own increasing awareness of the larger context became a central aspect of her ability to support other women and to work for change generally.

I feel like everyone who's in our group should understand how Corporate America works. I feel like they should know that CEOs are making, I think it's 525 times the average worker right now, and they should know that because that's what we're up against. There should be things that we understand, and how did that get to be, and the history of wealth in this country. . . . I also think we need to understand about internalized shame. . . . And I don't think you get that just from organizing in the streets.

Marsha's thoughts were echoed in comments by older Respect member Linda Jefferson, who noted that keeping up with the training of new members was a critical challenge. "As we bring in new members, we want to get them up to speed before they think, write or say something that really expresses internalized oppression." It was important "to really have them express what's happening to them in a way that gives a deep yet connected analysis. And in order to do that, sometimes you have to go back into history and train them of how to think and why this happened and did you know that this used to be done this way and not the way it is now." Those who founded the organization "came with a certain analysis from the civil rights struggle and the women's struggle and all that." This is a perspective that honored the work and lives of the poor. "We are somebody. We contribute to this country. . . . [E]verybody is worthy and we all need to have a piece of the pie." For young people who missed the social critique of the 1960s, "if they never had that feeling that this country doesn't do everything right, that everybody's deserving, that we all contribute to the society, we have to give them that. And we have to get it instilled in them before they say or write something that says, well, I deserve it but not everybody does."

Linda's comments illustrate the importance of a systemic understanding of inequality for the work of social change organizations. Although some staff members come to the work with this perspective, it is critical that the organization support a learning process for those who do not.

The Fit between Staff Qualities and Social Change Work

SCOs' common commitment to social justice requires staff members to have or develop a systemic analysis of social problems. But as explained in chapter 1, SCOs differ in their approaches to social change in ways likely to affect staffing requirements and working conditions. All groups engage in multiple kinds of activities, but the critical tasks vary by social change orientation. Table 2–1 summarizes the nature of these tasks and the quali-

Table 2-1 Critical tasks and staff requirements by social change orientation

| | Social Change Orientation | | | |
| | Collective Action | | Individual Empowerment | |
	Individual transformation	*No individual transformation*	*Individual transformation*	*No individual transformation*
The work	Providing space and skills for individuals to come together in collective action	Providing groups with information, analysis, and networks to motivate/inform action	Meeting basic needs and skill-building for individual empowerment	Dismantling formal barriers that prevent individuals from accessing needed services
The central task	Motivate	Reveal	Recognize	Entitle
Staff qualities: skills, knowledge, abilities and values	• Listening • Connecting experience with analysis • Building unity • Belief in the power of collectivity	• Curiosity about social structures • Embracing outsider status • Serving others' activism • Belief in the power of analysis	• Acknowledging immediate needs • Providing support, nurturing, love • Belief in the power of caring	• Knowledge of law • Respecting constituents • Belief in the power of legal rights
Sources of satisfaction	• Seeing people stand up for themselves	• Producing practical knowledge	• Promoting human development	• Winning a legal battle

ties required of staff members who engage in this work. In brief, for those that link individual transformation to collective action, the central task is to *motivate*—that is, to engage constituents in the work. For groups supporting collective action without individual transformation (those providing analysis to other activists) the task is to *reveal*—to uncover and disseminate knowledge needed by change agents. In SCOs promoting individual transformation for individual empowerment, the task is to *recognize*—to see the worthiness and potential in constituents who are struggling to overcome disadvantage. And finally where the aim is individual empowerment through dismantling legal barriers rather than individual transformation, the task is to *entitle*—to ensure that the protections and guarantees of the law are extended to all. In the following discussion we explore the particular kinds of work activities associated with each of these domains, and the staff qualities that reflect both capacity and comfort with the work.

Motivating: Turning Anger to Action

Prominent community organizer Saul Alinsky (1989, 116–117) said that an organizer "must first rub raw the resentments of the people" in order to mobilize them for action. "The job then is getting the people to move, to act, to participate; in short, to develop and harness the necessary power to effectively conflict with the prevailing patterns and change them." Although not all SCOs that mobilize individuals for collective action do so by using Alinsky's methods, they must somehow succeed at identifying, recruiting, and engaging constituents.[3]

There are several important elements to this process—listening, connecting experience with analysis, building unity, targeting winnable issues, and developing strategies for action, and all can be seen in the work of Uniting Youth for Change. Working in local schools, UYC site director Mark Lightner identifies candidates each year for the position of youth organizer. Once organizers are hired, they are trained in the social justice model used by the UYC staff. As director Jonathan Stein explains, "It starts with society's values, around race and class and gender and sexual preference and so forth, race and class being the primary values that society orbits around. . . . [We look at] how those values get translated into policies, practices, and institutional capacity and resources. So if you look at your school and you say, my school's a mess . . . it's like, well, why is it?" Organizers are encouraged to locate local problems in the context of larger social issues, and then to think about what kind of interventions can be taken in the local setting.

Listening skills are critical in this work, for Mark, as site director, and for the youth organizers themselves, as they connect with other students to identify meaningful issues. Once an issue has been highlighted, Mark will coach the organizers in researching and analyzing the nature and causes of the problem. By way of illustrating the process, Mark told us of a case in which students were concerned that rules were not enforced fairly and consistently in their school. To find out more and determine what should be done the youth organizers conducted a survey, gathering data from six hundred students and approximately one hundred teachers as well as administrators and other personnel. "And after [compiling] the results of the survey we had a series of meetings that were made up of students, teachers, administrators. . . . We had them come up with a series of solutions, actually, look[ing] at a proposal that was developed by the students . . . [and] working with the administration to develop a more consistent discipline policy and ways to enforce it, school-wide."

Mark takes UYC's youth organizers through a process of transformation in which they analyze their own experience and then he shows them how to engage in collective action, including issue identification and strategy development. The young organizers develop a common language and understanding of the system as a result of applying UYC's model to their own life experiences. As Mark helps them build unity among themselves, he also teaches them to extend this process to others at the school.

What type of people work in SCOs with this approach? Staff members in these groups are highly skilled at taking constituents from understanding to action. They believe in "people power"—that those who have been disadvantaged can make significant change by working together. And they derive enormous pleasure in seeing constituents stand up successfully for themselves in political struggles. Talking about a city planning meeting he'd attended with residents, Residents Making Change staffer Alvin Jackson said, "I really love the passion of most of these residents. I mean last night . . . we had the City here with their draft RFP and just how the residents really just kept on, you know, taking a shot with the City and saying, no, I don't like this, I don't like that, scratch this, scratch that." Stephen Jencks noted that there were many things he enjoyed about his work, but he found especially satisfying the many kinds of impact Community Voice could have through organizing:

> It's very beautiful actually to see a space where people can come together and feel comfortable and find companionship, and also win concrete things,

changes in their community life. It really just transforms people's relationship
to the world to not just go to a hospital and be humiliated and confused, but to
go the hospital or go to the welfare center and see that after you have a meeting with the director that suddenly signs are hung up on the walls in Spanish
and people get their caseworker switched and really I think that that's enormously satisfying. . . . [A]nd seeing members' children start to see their parents as powerful activists, as opposed to confused non–English speaking
people who can't navigate this variety of hostile bureaucracies, I think is really, really powerful and fantastic.

Recognition as Seeing the Dignity and Potential in Others

In "The Politics of Recognition," Charles Taylor explains the importance of giving groups who have been disadvantaged recognition or standing in society. Arguing that our identity is shaped in part by the recognition
we receive, Taylor (1994, 25–26) observes that "a person or group of
people can suffer real damage, real distortion, if the people or society
around them mirror back to them a confining or demeaning or con-
temptible picture of themselves. . . . Due recognition is not just a courtesy
we owe people. It is a vital human need."

When SCOs focus on transformation for individual empowerment, staff
members recognize constituents both by acknowledging and meeting their
immediate needs and by supporting their efforts to change the conditions
affecting them. These groups attract staffers who understand how "mis-
recognition" (in Taylor's terminology) can harm people, and who are able
to honor those they serve. As they provide training, care, safety, and other
forms of support, these workers also convey a sense of the constituents' potential, strength, and worthiness. As Tanisha Howard, a young Growing
Roots staffer explained, "All of the programs really are to give the youth a
view of how they can make themselves better, how they can make their
communities better and how they can affect change in this world in a positive way. . . . [W]e do want every child that comes out of this program . . .
to leave knowing that they have the strength within themselves to make the
world the way they want to make it."

This approach differs from that taken by more traditional nonprofit service agencies, which Salamon (1999, 110) defines as providing "forms of
assistance, other than outright case aid, that help individuals and families
to function in the face of social, economic, or physical problems or needs."
Change-oriented service groups take their work beyond the stage of meet-

ing immediate needs to helping clients understand how their lives have been affected by a larger system of inequality and what they can do to make change. As noted by Dare to Dream's Marueen Lynch, clients often blame themselves for their plight, and DTD sees part of its role as correcting that impression and encouraging self-advocacy. Indeed, transformation and empowerment are embedded in the service work of these groups. Susan Ho explained that at Sheltering Our Own, advocates work with clients to challenge the constraints of their traditional roles and claim their autonomy:

> Women particularly . . . [they've] been dependent on someone or the other. Their families, their dads, their brothers, their husbands after they're married — the sons even, once they're grown up. So if they come to you for help they're obviously bringing with them years of dependence. It's hard, because you don't want them to put all their hopes in you. You don't want them to depend on you for every little thing. You want them to come out on their own. . . . You have to encourage them to speak up on their own, you can't do the work for them.

Many of these SCOs conduct their work in groups, a method in which client needs are met not only by staff members but by other clients. In groups, constituents learn they are not alone in their experiences; they offer each other support, observe how others are able to make change in their lives, and develop a sense of competence as others witness their progress. Dare to Dream's adult education program, instituted at the insistence of constituents, was modeled on Freire's popular education approach. In this context, the women support each other in a variety of ways: they share their growing understanding of how personal struggles are connected to social structures, challenge systems of dominance by small acts that challenge the classroom teacher's authority, build networks of support inside and outside of the program, mentor others, and speak up for each other. "It's been extraordinary to see their development," according to director Dorothy Morrison.

At Growing Roots, programs ranged from group after-school activities to a class that taught the history of how people of color won their freedom in different parts of the world. Describing the philosophy behind this work, GR co-director Monroe Harris said, "We do create a different social atmosphere, where we create a different way of living, where we demonstrate kind of community responsibility and community working together in a different way. . . . It is about loving other people, loving ourselves, loving our community."

The commitment of staff members to their work in these SCOs often was strengthened by a connection to the staffers' own experiences and/or identification with the constituent group. For example, Susan Ho at Sheltering Our Own revealed that her mother was a victim of domestic violence, an important motivator for her entering this type of work. Teaching Tools' director Jay Stanley was also motivated by having experienced "a significant amount of violence growing up as a kid." One way to avoid turning that experience against himself or others was to organize. Of people who chose this path, he said: "They take their anger and they understand that it's not an internal thing, it's not an external thing, but it's kind of a systems thing. And I got lucky in that, as a fairly young kid, when I was nine or ten, I took this anger and directed it into organizing." In some cases, staff members valued the work because it was with their own community, even if they had not personally experienced disadvantage. In part, this identification reflected the SCOs' intent to match staff with the constituency group. Growing Roots, for example, is designed to help young men of women of color, and its staff is comprised entirely of people of color. Sheltering Our Own works across several immigrant communities that are also represented in the staff demographics. This kind of identification is meaningful for many staff members; as Jean Patterson of Neighborhood Reach said, "Working in the context of a community of people where I see myself reflected is satisfying to me."

Those who work in these SCOs believe in the power of caring—that through an empowering style of service they can not only meet constituents' immediate needs but also provide them with the knowledge, skills, and awareness that can enable them to change conditions for themselves and their communities. This sense of their work came through in staff members' comments on sources of satisfaction. As Dorothy Morrison of Dare to Dream said, "I enjoy women and families who were once struggling and who had such a poor image . . . move up and out of poverty and come back to make a difference for other families. . . . To see them from being in Dare to Dream as a shelter to being colleagues and spokespersons . . . that to me is the most meaningful thing." For Susan Ho at Sheltering Our Own, "The satisfaction is greater than anything when you see a woman standing on her own, being very independent, gaining the skills that she could have, and taking care of the children or family, and being away from the violent situation." Growing Roots' Tanisha Howard takes heart in the expectation of what GR's clients are being prepared to do. When things are going badly in the world, she said, "I can always say well, when the kids that I'm working with are ready, they're going to go out there and just really show themselves and do something great."

Revealing: Providing Information for Action

In SCOs that support collective action through information and analysis, staff members are committed to changing systems through knowledge production. At Advocates for the People, director Antonio Mena said, "Our idea is not to do academic research, but to . . . develop research as a tool for advocacy and organizing." Through relentless and careful investigation, these SCOs make visible how systems of dominance operate and provide other change agents with the information needed to be more effective in their work. Staffers in these SCOs listen to the needs of activists on the ground and simultaneously monitor social, political, and economic developments. "It's sort of early warning work," said Ellen Mayhew of the Center for Critical Information. "That's one of the roles we play, to let people know what is coming and give people an analysis of it before it actually hits. . . . [W]e need people who can keep up, who can manage to monitor a lot of different activity on a day to day basis." In CCI's case, that effort includes keeping track of antidemocratic activities including efforts to undermine public education, immigrant rights, reproductive freedom, and economic justice.

Antonio Mena referred to his work as "gorilla research—you know, pick up whatever crap you can from the street and turn it into weapons." AP's projects have included Census analyses of the Latino population to inform voting rights projects, reports on bilingual education that are helpful to education reformers, and an inventory of Latino nonprofits useful for networking and infrastructure development in the community. Urban Watch looks at "anything that affects the quality of life" in low-income or moderate-income communities, trying to ensure that neighborhood activists and community developers have the information they need to organize, secure funding, and fight political battles. In its advocacy work, Community Choices provides technical assistance to groups working for environmental justice, including scientific analyses as well as information about relevant policy and law.

In contrast to the political or personal skills needed for the work of motivation or recognition, the qualifications for the work of revealing systems of inequality include more technical capacity in research, analysis, or writing, plus a drive to ferret out useful information. This type of SCO attracts people who are driven to understand how things work and who are dedicated to seeing such knowledge inform action. As Marianne Foley at Urban Watch explained, "I'm just personally fascinated by the way the world works. . . . I like to understand what's really going on. . . . [I like] recognizing where things don't work but rather than giving up on it or saying, 'Oh, we can't do anything,'—to realize that you can both have knowledge and act on that knowledge . . . is, I think, very exciting." However, staff members seeking more direct political involvement can feel unsatisfied by the distance between this work and the struggle it is intended to affect. At CCI, staffer Maral Azimi expressed her ambivalence, saying that although she thought the work was important, she didn't know if she was "the kind of person who's going to love reading books, reading Web sites all day long for the rest of my life." She wondered if she should look for "something else that would really rev me up and feel more vital and more immediate than what we do here."

A belief in the power of knowledge motivates those who do this work. Skilled at finding the Achilles heels of powerful institutions, they often revel in their outsider role. One of Antonio Mena's favorite moments was an occasion when his "rinky dink" little group was able to embarrass a large corporation by critiquing its labor practices. "The most fun," he said, "is being able to do things that you're not supposed to do, or have unexpected results." Director Rachel Beck of Urban Watch also had a strong sense of leverage in her work. "I've seen the power of really useful analysis, or a useful article in terms of shifting thinking on things. And . . . since I've been at the front lines watching municipal government for almost twelve years now, I've seen that change is possible and doable and actually relatively easy if you know what you're doing."

Entitlement: Removing the Barriers

One of our SCOs—Rights for All—takes a legal advocacy approach to social change, aiming at individual empowerment by dismantling legal barriers rather than through transformative work with constituents. In contrast to traditional legal aid services, RFA's work includes aggressive outreach to potential constituent groups in an effort to understand the structural problems they confront and a respect for constituents that honors their own view of their needs. RFA staffers take pride in working with constituents often ignored by other legal groups, and they spend considerable time developing relationships on the constituent's turf—whether it be in soup kitchens or group homes. RFA's director Daniel Cohen notes that "almost all of our projects do some sort of outreach to groups that don't [usually] get representation. . . . And we're very much doing both individual advocacy as well as systemic advocacy."

Tony Capra, an RFA attorney and project director, exemplifies the type of staff member attracted to this work. Explaining how the work moves beyond simple legal representation, Tony expresses his enthusiasm for the job:

> And I think the thing I love the most about [the work] is the fact that we do things differently, that we really do our best to recognize and uphold the dignity of our clients, and provide services . . . the client determines that he or she needs, and are in the client's best interests rather than providing services that the lawyer finds are the things that the client needs. . . . [O]ur approach— which combines lawyering and social work, direct services, community organizing, individual representation, systemic advocacy—that sort of multitiered interdisciplinary approach is very exciting, and we're one of the few places in the country that does it in such an integrated fashion.

RFA is also unusual in the degree of entrepreneurialism it seeks in staff members, particularly project directors. Projects are independently funded and operate with considerable autonomy. To join RFA, project directors must convince Daniel Cohen—and to a lesser degree the other project directors—that they have a viable and important program. This means identifying an important unmet area of need as well as a source of funding.

Staff members in an SCO like this one believe deeply in the power of legal rights. They use the law to ensure access to welfare benefits by the homeless, safe housing for those with mental illness, protection for people in needle-exchange programs, and fair wages for service workers. Winning class-action or precedent-setting cases is a tremendous source of satisfaction, because of the expectation that these will lead to systemic changes as well as individual remedies. Daniel says of his own motivation, "I care about justice, and I care that things are not just . . . and people get screwed. . . . [I]t gives me great satisfaction to be part of creating more justice." While the work empowers individuals, it also has an impact on a community of constituents. As Tony explains:

> I don't see myself as being some superman who can walk into a community and change it. I see myself as playing a role in helping community residents get control over their own lives and their own neighborhoods and their own communities. So multiplying that empowerment times the number of people that you're trying to serve. Self-determination for a community group.

"Creating more justice" was an important source of satisfaction for those working through legal advocacy. Like those in other types of SCOs, Tony and Daniel spoke enthusiastically about the rewards of their work. At the same time, however, all SCO leaders and staffers acknowledged that the demands of the work could be significant.

Sustaining Social Change Work

The participants in the study were for the most part extremely positive about their work and that of their organizations. They talked about the pleasure the work gave them—their contact with constituents, their ability to see the impact of their efforts, the sense that they were really making a difference. Indeed, we were surprised at the number who volunteered how much they loved their jobs. Yet some of these same people were conflicted about whether they would be able to continue over the long term, because although the work was enormously gratifying, it also posed challenges for both directors and staffs. Concerns about job satisfaction and long-term sustainability arose in the context of three areas: the blessing and burden of strong commitment to the work, the difficulty of balancing work and personal life, and the importance of a suitably supportive workplace environment.

The Benefits and Cost of Commitment

Few people could be more enthusiastic about their work than Dorothy Morrison at Dare to Dream. As a religious woman, her work was truly her calling, so it was no surprise when she enthusiastically claimed, "The mission of Dare to Dream is the mission of my life. So it's totally consuming for me." Despite being over sixty years old, Dorothy reported working fourteen-hour days and had no intention of slowing down. Like other directors and staff members who found their work completely absorbing, she was fueled by the demands of the job and the possibilities of greater change.

However, the culture and mission of the work that were so gratifying to Dorothy were more problematic for her deputy Maureen Lynch. Although deeply committed to the organization's mission, Maureen was more hesitant in her comments about the organization's work culture. Asked what she found challenging, she replied, "It's all absorbing, meaning it isn't work you leave behind at the end of the day; I think about it when I get up;

it's emotional." She went on to explain, "Work takes most of my life because when I am not here I am thinking about it. . . . Even when I am talking to my friends long distance, I find myself talking about the work I do
here." When asked if she would consider becoming the organization's next
director, Maureen reflected that although she was philosophically in tune
with the organization, she worried that it would be "too absorbing to do
this and live a life." Thinking she would like to have a family some day, she
didn't think this job would be the best thing for her at that point.

Commitment to social change work was a mixed blessing. On the one
hand, it could nourish the staff member's sense of connection and authenticity in her job. On the other, it could lead to burnout through trying to do
too much with too few resources. As a result, some staff members would either find themselves having to leave their positions, or worse, staying without the energy and engagement needed for the work, doubting their own or
the organization's effectiveness. No one would question Maureen's commitment to DTD's mission, but the emotional toll taken by the work, even in
a primarily administrative position, made it difficult for her to think about
her future at the job. For Dorothy, being "consumed" by the work was a
good thing, a source of motivation; for Maureen, it could be draining.

Managing Identity, Boundaries, and Constituent Expectations   Issues
of commitment were sometimes intensified by the staffer's relationship
with the community served. Almost half of those we talked with identified
either as current members of the constituent community or as people who
had once been constituents. Another quarter spoke of a strong personal link
to the constituent group through shared characteristics of race, class, gender, and community residence, or a common life experience. An older staff
member at Sheltering Our Own revealed that her own experience of witnessing (and perhaps experiencing) violence in her community made this
work especially important to her. The organization's director felt a connection to their clients based on hardships she had also faced as a new immigrant. At Residents Making Change, the director and young staff member
both grew up in the community and had long histories with the organization, resulting in a strong sense of connection that could be problematic
when it seemed unbounded. Director Harold deMello explained:

I've been feeling some of that [pressure] recently. . . . [O]n my walk home
I'm talking RMC. I've got a neighbor, we've been friends forever, but the
other day he apologized to me because now all he talks about are . . . RMC-

related issues. So he's talking about the yard that needs to get cleaned up behind his house and how we're going to do that, when we're going to do it. . . .
He's talking about houses that are being sold up the street. And then . . . he
paused, and he said, "Harold, I'm sorry. When I talk to you, I'm always talking business."

Harold enjoyed his engagement with the community but was also aware
of its demands. "There are no breaks or relaxation," he said, in part because
of his own reluctance to take time away from work that always seemed so
urgent.

Among the social identity factors that influenced staff and director work
experience, race was particularly prominent.[4] Staff members of color, especially in predominantly white organizations, often had to negotiate between the community and the organization. As front line workers, they
were in a position where they had more permeable boundaries when it
came to the needs (and demands) of constituents, which only increased
when they were current or former constituents themselves.

Directors of color explained it was difficult to escape issues of race and
cultural identity, even when they did not want these to dominate percep-
tions of their leadership or the work of their organizations. Several reported
having been challenged by constituent groups about their ability to represent different ethnic interests outside of their own racial group. Dolores
Santiago recalled having to assure a predominantly African-American
community that as executive director she would not turn Neighborhood
Reach into a "Puerto Rican agency." Similarly, Harold deMello noted, "In
terms of the race piece . . . my being black is important. In a neighborhood
like this, representation or race in leadership is huge." He went on to explain, "I am not West Indian, I'm not African American . . . and there's this
huge question mark . . . do you really consider yourself black . . . like us?"

This type of direct challenge to an SCO leader's commitment to the
whole community was not mentioned by white leaders, but some of them
did feel that their legitimacy might be questioned, particularly if their staffs
were not sufficiently diverse. To these directors it sometimes seemed that
an emphasis on racial or ethnic identity could displace appropriate concerns about other staff qualifications. Community Voice director, Steven
Jencks mused,

Does a person, in order to be an effective organizer, need to have shared lived
experience with the people they're organizing? . . . I think in our experience
it's clear that there are some significant benefits. And I think that not with-

standing those benefits it's important to understand that an organizer is an organizer and not a representative of the constituency. . . . So we could have a
Latina organizer who was on welfare and she might share a lot of experiences
[with constituents] but actually that doesn't mean that our members have any
more power relative to her. They might have more in common but it's important organizationally to not let that symbolic representation act as a substitute
for actual accountability and democracy within the organization.

The difficulty within organizations of talking about these issues was expressed by Marsha Madison, a white staff member of Respect. She described a situation in which the collective was divided by race over who to
hire as a coordinator. Speaking of that experience, she openly discussed
the struggle of addressing the different "isms" in the organization and the
importance of doing so.

I think we have to be really willing to unflinchingly look at our racism, our
own sexism, our own homophobia, our own ageism, and classism because we
are conditioned from the time we are born and socialized in this country to
have all of these "isms". . . . I don't think you can escape it. . . . I think we
have to be able to point out those things with love . . . [and] really realize that
the other women who are in this group are doing this because they really care,
and we're in this together. So I get nervous about that. I feel like there could
be rifts, divisions that could really split us. They never do, but it doesn't mean
that [they] . . . won't.

For Marsha, and many other staffers that had been constituents, the work
was central to their lives. It was deeply satisfying but its demands could be
overwhelming.

Balancing Work and Personal Life

Another major concern expressed—especially by staffers—was the conflict they felt in fulfilling their work responsibilities and still finding time to
have a personal life. As noted above, Maureen Lynch at Dare to Dream
wondered if it would be possible to stay with this work and have a family.
Her concern was not only the long hours of the job but the emotional commitment entailed in the work.

The problem of balancing work and personal life has become a major
concern for many workers. Literature on Generation X asserts that those
born between 1964 and 1979 are more concerned than their predecessors
about spending time with their families, and the data are particularly striking among men. Studies conducted by both Catalyst (2001) and the Rad-

cliffe Policy Institute (2002) report that younger men are far more likely than older men to rate the ability to have time to spend with family as an important consideration in choosing a job. Bennis and Thomas (2002, 74) found in their interviews with older (pre-Baby Boom) and younger (Generation X) leaders, "No issue or attitude divided geeks from geezers more dramatically than the importance of balance in their lives."

Our respondents expressed conflicting feelings about the demands of their work. On the one hand, most felt compelled to put in long hours, motivated by a desire to do more for constituents. As one person said, "I can't do enough of it, there's not enough time, not enough people who want to do it, and there's not enough resources out there to do it right." Another person commented, "There's not enough time in the day to do everything that you want to do." And a third lamented, "Saying no to probably more people than we say yes to is difficult. Heartbreaking! And yet we have to do it every day." Staffers in one organization spoke with pride about how they only hired people that were available "24/7." For very young staff members there was great enthusiasm for the time they devoted to their job. Their colleagues were like family and the workplace a substitute home, reinforced by the long hours where relationships among staffers were strengthened.

On the other hand, there were already cracks showing in staff members' ability to keep up such taxing schedules. Respondents in their late twenties and early thirties were particularly concerned about how to balance work demands with the needs of personal lives. Several young men expressed uncertainty about their futures as they anticipated conflicts between family needs and heavy work requirements. Mark Lightner talked at length about this dilemma, reflecting on his situation at UYC:

> I want to be able to maintain a healthy family relationship when I have kids, and I don't want to have work be too much that I can't spend time with my family as much as I want to do. . . . I just happened to be single when I started here and [only] 23, so it didn't matter to me. . . . A couple of people that were great for this organization . . . just knew that they couldn't keep up with what had to be done [when they had children]. . . . There's a lot of choices that I'm going to have to make about what's manageable and what can be done, to be able to sustain it.

Time commitment was usually the first challenge that younger people noted when they thought about their future. Money, though mentioned less often, was also a concern. Attorney Tony Capra of Rights for All noted that at the moment both he and his wife were in nonprofit jobs, and though they loved their work, he wasn't sure this arrangement would be sustainable. "If I'm able to create a position for myself where I can work decent hours, have a family, balance economic needs with the needs of a family, that would be great. I would love to have this job for the rest of my life. I don't know if that's going to be possible." One fairly new director in her mid-thirties who had two young children acknowledged that she was able to manage only because her husband was in a well-paying job, and even in these circumstances she wondered how long she could stay. "Sometimes I don't see my kids in two days," she said. She noted that the private sector was better able to support workers with families and wondered how non-profit organizations like hers could meet this challenge.

Some of the demands for more personal time reflect a life cycle issue—the very young and those with either no children or grown-up children are less focused on this dilemma. But in addition to life cycle issues, times have changed. More families need two wage earners to make ends meet, younger people are carrying a higher debt load from college educations, and the assumption that staff members can devote unlimited time to work is facing a serious challenge.[5]

Several of our young SCO founders were trying to address the need for personal time through new organizational structures that spread decision-making responsibility among co-directors or leadership teams. For the most part, however, individuals were struggling to bridge the gap on their own.

The Workplace Environment

Oster claims that people are attracted to the work of nonprofits for two main reasons, the values or mission of the organization, and the expectation of greater autonomy in the work.[6] We found that a third critical element, the atmosphere in the workplace—often shaped by the leader(s)—could enhance the job or make it much less desirable. In part this was a matter of fit between the staffers' needs and the organizational style: in some SCO work environments there was a strong emotional bond among coworkers that staff members found appealing, but in others a sense of respectful collegiality and independence was valued. In most cases, the prevailing climate seemed to suit most if not all workers, but in one organization the lack of warmth was a serious problem for many.

In several of the organizations, at least one respondent made reference to the idea of the organization being like a "family" or "home"—sometimes for clients or community members, sometimes for the staff, sometimes for both. Among those organizations with a familial quality, the connection between the organization and the community seemed to be an important element of this environment; only one agency, Community Choices, was described as a "family" for staff only. Residents Making Change, Growing Roots, Dare to Dream, and Community Voice were all depicted as places in which community members as well as staffers (groups that sometimes overlapped) considered the organization to be something like a second home. Two of the respondents at RMC had first come to the organization as children—sometimes accompanying adults who worked in or with the agency—and had in a sense, grown up there. "My aunt worked here," explained one of the men. "And when I was younger, I couldn't go many places without my family. And because my aunt worked here, it was OK, my mother would allow me to come. Or I would actually feel OK coming in here."

Tanisha Howard at Growing Roots said she'd met the agency's co-founders while she was in high school: "And I just always stayed in contact with them. Some people, as soon as you meet them, you can tell right away, you're never going to lose contact with them. You know? And they just became part of my family." As a member of the staff, she continues to feel this strong connection. "I don't know if you think it's corny, but I just really love that fact that I . . . come to work with such a great group of people. . . . And the fact that I know that I'm doing something that's helping somebody is icing on the cake." Her story echoes the terms in which one of GR's founders describes their work. "It is a labor of love . . . I mean we didn't create the organization because we needed a job. It's that we really had a deep feeling of the need to heal our community, to purvey this space where . . . we do create a different social atmosphere. . . . Providing an alternative to what's out there. And also providing what any family should provide, a space where people feel safe and cared for and aware."

Dare to Dream literally provided a home for some community members when its founders, members of a religious order, realized that they had more space than they needed and that this was something they could offer those in need. The sense of connection to the community is so strong, according to the new administrator, that "Everybody talks about the Dare to Dream family, and how it feels like a family here, and when they come back it's like coming home again." According to the director, the feeling is shared by many staff members, in part because of how they support each other through difficult times. Stephen Jencks, co-founder of Community Voice, saw his organization as "an incredibly warm, vital, exciting work place where there are thirty, fifty, eighty people here who are always saying that this is like a second home to me, and there's tons of young children, and it's very beautiful actually to see a space where people can come together and feel comfortable and find companionship, and also win concrete things, changes in their community life."

Not everyone seeks a strong emotional connection to coworkers, and the environment at Rights for All provided a different kind of satisfaction to staff members. Director Daniel Cohen had spent many years developing an organizational structure that allowed projects to work independently within a collegial and supportive office. Project directors could obtain intellectual guidance and practical advice from colleagues and the executive director, and project staff members could draw on each other for stimulation and support. "And there's no bureaucratic infighting or turf fighting because I'm not passing out any goodies," Daniel explained. Project directors and their staffs were in command of their own work. At the same time, because of the staff members' commitment to social justice and to RFA's projects, it wasn't "just a matter of labor" but a shared endeavor, and people appreciated each other.

In Daniel's case, and for other long-time directors, the tone of the organization reflected their interests and style, and sometimes the result didn't work for everyone. In RFA's case, operations director Susan Crane felt the culture was a deterrent to establishing systems needed to keep things running smoothly and fairly, but her view did not seem to be widely shared. A more significant divide existed in another of our SCOs in which the reserved style of the long-term director was a source of discomfort to many staff members. For his part, the emotional needs of the staff were somewhat baffling and a diversion from the work, but others were critical of his manner. One program director explained:

> The vision is there. But that needs to translate into tangible things. "Hi, how are you? How was your weekend?" Things like that . . . [but] he is just not that type of person. . . . [A] staff person would pass him in the hallway, and he wouldn't speak. . . . They would be like, "Well, you know what? You don't even speak to people." . . . [I]t's so much on a subconscious level he would say, "Of course, I speak when I pass you." But he really didn't. He wouldn't speak. So that all kinds of things are running through peoples' minds, that this guy's a racist, that he's not comfortable around minorities. And you've got to alleviate those fears and those thoughts.

The exclusive focus on work was satisfying for the director and a few long-term staff members, but not for many newer employees. And the di-

rector's inattention to people's needs for a more supportive work environment was a source of significant tension.

Supporting the Work

In many ways the human resource needs of SCOs are similar to those of
other nonprofits and organizations more generally. But we find two areas
of concern that, if not particular to social change organizations, are especially prominent in this work. We suggest that attention to these areas
would help SCOs attract appropriate people and support them as productive members of these organizations. The first issue has to do the transformational learning that is a common element of SCO staff preparation, and
the second with the challenge of making these jobs manageable for a new
generation of workers.

Given how central transformational learning is to those working in social change, it is remarkable how little discussion or thought seems to have
been given to how to support this process among potential employees.
Those who came of age during the social movement era of the 1960s and
1970s found social support for their interest in social change and places
where they could reflect with others on the experience of injustice and its
systemic causes. Today organizations must take on this work more consciously—both for the personal transformation of constituents and for the
training of new staff members. As part of this effort, issues relating to race,
gender, and class—that often divide people but go unattended—must be
addressed.

Only one or two of our organizations had developed a framework for
this type of teaching, but a number of other groups have developed useful
programs based on the theories of popular education and transformational
learning.[7] Common elements of these programs include starting with constituent experience (which is informative for staff members and motivating
for constituents), looking at this lived experience in the larger context of
social and economic patterns, examining locally relevant policies and practices and investigating who benefits and who loses, acquainting staffers
and constituents with historical and international examples of political mobilization, and engaging in action followed by reflection. Raising awareness of such methods and applying them more widely within SCOs could
help to attract and maintain new workers in these groups. Other educational settings open to critical pedagogy, including adult education pro-

grams and even some colleges and universities, could also include this kind of training for students interested in social change work. An opportunity to reflect on lived experience in the context of a structural analysis could bring more social change workers into the field, and expose others to the importance of this work.

SCOs face major challenges in accommodating new generations of workers who enter with very different needs and expectations from their predecessors. The social and economic context of the U.S. has changed over the past thirty years in a number of ways relevant to social change work—including the professionalization of nonprofit work, the increase in two-income families, and changing expectations about family life. Although many SCOs continue to survive because their staffs put in long hours and receive relatively low salaries, this arrangement may not be sustainable. As difficult as it will be, SCOs and funders must acknowledge the need to relieve the pressure on workers, rather than expecting that a system that has somehow worked in the past will continue to be viable.[8]

Among our SCOs we found that some younger directors are experimenting with different organizational structures that allow them greater flexibility to enter and leave their organizations and to share leadership responsibilities. Other types of restructuring and resource-pooling may be possible. For example, recognizing that local organizers often work in settings without retirement benefits, the National Organizers Alliance has begun to pool resources to develop a pension fund for these workers. Combining other benefit programs such as health care coverage could help SCOs meet employee needs and possibly free up support for higher salaries or other benefits. Another form of mutual support on the rise among nonprofits is co-location in multi-tenant centers, where groups share common space and services to reduce overall costs.[9] Co-location has the added advantage for small groups of building a community for staff members and directors, as they work together toward social justice. Foundation- or government-sponsored educational loan forgiveness programs for staffers of social change and other community-based nonprofits is another way to make this work more sustainable. Although constraints on salary and time are not easily solved, ignoring these issues may have the unintended consequence of creating dissonance between the external values the organizations espouse and their internal operations.[10]

Given current employment patterns in which the median job tenure for American workers at age twenty-five and over is less than five years, it is unreasonable to expect that staffers will stay for life.[11] SCOs want to offer some kind of stability to their employees and want also to reap the benefits that come with staff longevity, but it is unrealistic for them to try to meet the needs of all workers. One way of addressing this tension is for SCOs to think of themselves as offering employment opportunities and training as a field rather than solely as individual employers. For example, United Way-funded nonprofits in New York have developed a support and professional development program across different organizations that enables staff members at all levels to move more easily between different organizations. The result strengthens the field and helps to ensure that talent is available to take on executive-level positions when directors leave, as many reported they were planning to do within the next five years, according to a United Way study.

Finally, older directors thinking about leaving their current positions often have a hard time finding ways to do so that are financially viable, emotionally satisfying, and structurally sound for the organization. How these older leaders can be honored and supported in their departures is an important problem for SCOs, and a crucial piece in thinking about current and future leaders in social change work. To address this issue, there have already been a number of succession planning services offered to departing executives and their boards by nonprofit management support organizations.[12] This work focuses not only on succession issues but also on the departing leader who often feels responsible for the long-term viability of the organization even beyond his or her tenure. These and other challenges of SCO leadership are explored in the next chapter.

CHAPTER THREE

LEADERSHIP

Making the Vision Real

I think first of all, [you need someone with] a vision . . . a dream initially of what they want, what they see the organization as. Then you need someone who's willing to take actions, who's willing to take initiative, who's willing to do what it takes to get it there. But also [to] consider everyone's opinions. . . . So you don't want someone who's just obsessed with their own thoughts and ideas. You want someone who's accepting of other beliefs as well. . . . I guess you just need a dreamer, a thinker, and a doer.

KAMLA CHOWDHURY,
Sheltering Our Own

Nonprofit leadership encompasses a wide variety of responsibilities from mission-definition and staff management to board relations and fundraising.[1] These diverse tasks can usefully be aggregated into the elements of Mark Moore's "strategic triangle" framework,[2] which argues that leaders must attend to the alignment of an organization's value/mission, operating capacity, and authorizing environment. In other words, the nonprofit leader's work broadly consists of providing direction for the organization, overseeing the operations that produce mission-relevant services, and interacting with the environment to secure support and ensure relevance.

All of the basic tasks of nonprofit management are relevant to SCO leaders, but—as suggested by the quotation above—these tasks are complicated by the characteristics of social change work. Concern for systemic change, commitment to a high level of constituent participation, and (for some, at least) the goal of motivating change though individual transformation—all shape the tasks of leadership in SCOs. These additional leadership demands produce three particular challenges that relate to the elements of Moore's triangle. First, mission or direction must be defined in a participatory way, not by the leader alone. Second, within internal operations an environment must be created that supports participation, growth, and transformation. And third, interacting with the external environment entails not only ensuring organizational support and relevance but an understanding of the organization's role in larger change efforts and the balancing of conflicting demands of organizational maintenance and movement building.[3] We describe each of these challenges in turn and then ask how our SCOs' current leaders have developed their capacities, what their own practices are for developing leadership in others, and where there seem to be shortfalls in terms of producing the kind of leadership required by SCOs. We conclude the chapter with possible avenues for strengthening SCO leadership development.

Providing Direction with Participation

In SCOs as in most organizations, it is expected that formal leaders will hold and articulate a vision of the organization's aims that will guide and motivate others in their work. Organizations allocate this responsibility to leaders not only because of who they are, but because the formal position they occupy is often the only one with a perspective that is holistic, outward-looking, and future-oriented. As Henry deMello, the young director of RMC put it, part of the leader's job is "to remember what you're trying to do and keep the bigger vision in front of you, the values clear. Because it's so dynamic, so changing, so crisis-oriented, so now, now, now, now, but yet you're looking at the future, future, future."

When asked what it took to lead organizations like theirs, our respondents in both director and staff positions highlighted the need for *a vision fueled by a conviction* that would help to propel the organization. As Mark Lightner at Uniting Youth for Change explained, "It's hard to lead any of us without being able to see the world being a better place, whether the outcomes happen or not. . . . I think you have to have a certain level of intensity . . . to be able to drive forward when things get difficult." Not only vision, but persistence and determination are often necessary to sustain organizations with difficult work and limited resources. As Growing Roots co-founder Monroe Harris explained, "You have to have a lot of faith . . . that you're going to be able to accomplish your goals, because you take risks." An SCO leader must be bold, he said, "because you are challenging . . . conventional thinking." And Linda Jefferson, an older member of the collective Respect said simply, "The first word that comes to me is guts. . . . It takes guts to provide an alternative view from the popular view—especially in a day when they're trying to malign everybody [who needs help]—and certainly conviction, absolute conviction."

Because the challenges are so great and the resources so limited, SCO leaders must be exceptionally motivated. Among the qualities needed, according to Stephen Jencks of Community Voice, "probably the number one thing would be that they are interested in being effective leaders. In some way they're motivated to try and push stuff forward." He described his own strengths by saying, "I have a lot of energy for work, it's very important to me," adding that the enjoyment he took in the job "helps me come to it with a little bit of energy." Energy, ambition, and drive are not simply personal attributes, but are fueled by the leader's personal connection to the mission of the organization—particularly in organizations led by founders, as many of these are. Some leaders go so far as to say that "the mission of the organization is the mission of my life."

The rub is that it is not up to the leader alone to determine mission. Indeed, in many organizations today, leaders are urged to undertake the task of direction-setting with some degree of consultation and collaboration on the assumption that such an approach provides for more innovative problem-solving, more effective implementation, and more motivated and effective employees.[4] In SCOs, the argument for inclusive practices is even stronger and more fundamental, given their commitment to constituent empowerment and participation. SCO leaders must strike a balance between the need to motivate and guide and the need to listen, reflect, incorporate, and sometimes defer to the views of others—including constituents, board, and staff members.

When our respondents spoke of leadership with regard to mission, they conveyed a notion not of an independent, forceful visionary, but of a collaborator who clearly understood her interdependence with others. "It's not just about you," said young staffer Maria Reyes of Advocates for the People. "[O]ther people share your vision, because you brought people into that vision. That vision wasn't just created by you, but developed by you and other people." The idea of shared agenda-setting was particularly prominent in the comments of those working in SCOs with constituent boards or resident activists. At Residents Making Change, an organization controlled by the community, a young staff member noted that "being an effective leader means that you have to take your belief and put it aside and incorporate everybody else's beliefs." His director explained that the process of vision-setting entailed considerable interaction: "And when I say articulate vision, articulate the vision of the people that they're leading. . . . It's figuring out what their visions are and then bringing them in, being able to articulate it, sell it, move it forward, share it."

For many, the effective leader was also grounded in a strong connection to the community the group was trying to serve. These respondents linked leadership vision and commitment explicitly to the work of social change, noting the importance of "knowing who you're trying to help" as one staffer said, or "having a deep and consistent commitment to social change," as a director put it. Alex Montoya, the young CV staff member whose story opens chapter 1, went so far as to insist that a primary quality of good SCO leadership would be

> Life experience. Definitely. That's a hundred percent of the quality, life experience. I mean, it is nice that we have white people here, who are lawyers and who . . . come from privileged families. And they could be making $200,000 a year. They don't have to be here working, making $30,000, $35,000 a year. . . . [But] like personally to me and to my other co–workers, it's life experience. We've been there. We know how it is. We were raised in poor families. We were raised in the projects. . . . We were raised with rats. We were raised with food stamps. We were raised with peanut butter and water or Quik with water.

Like other leaders, directors of SCOs must provide guidance, inspire with commitment, and demonstrate unflagging determination. At the same time, the missions they serve cannot be theirs alone, but must be open to multiple voices, and grounded in the experience and needs of constituents.

Supporting Growth Internally and Externally

A second major area of nonprofit leadership has to do with operational oversight, including the functions of managing financial and human resources along with benchmarking and monitoring program performance. Among these functions—all of which are affected by SCO work and values[5]—human resource management is arguably the most challenging in these organizations. SCOs' commitment to participation and, in many cases, to personal growth and transformation sets a high standard for the quality of internal relationships at the same time as limited resources and demanding work can make meeting that standard exceptionally difficult. Not surprisingly, the internal aspect of leadership most often highlighted as essential by our respondents was the management of interpersonal relationships or what Fletcher (1999) aptly calls "relational practice."[6] Two leadership requirements were identified in these comments: a highly attentive, inclusive approach to management and an active concern for supporting the growth and development of staff members.

In line with the democratic missions of SCOs, both directors and staff members insisted that decision-making must be transparent, clear, fair, and participatory. They spoke often of the leader's need to *listen*—to heed others, to be open to their ideas, to be willing to learn from them. "You have to be open also to learning new things and to recognizing that everybody's got something to teach," said a co-director of Growing Roots. A personal attribute cited by several directors as characteristic of effective leadership was enough confidence or security not to need to be in control or to have power. CCI founder Ellen Mayhew noted, "I don't have to exercise power in order to establish myself." For some respondents, the work of leadership was so much about collaboration and connection that they downplayed the notion of single leaders. When Jay Stanley of Teaching Tools was asked about leadership requirements, he said, "I don't know what Teaching Tools will need, but it won't be a leader. It'll be a mixture of people. Teaching Tools doesn't need me. They need a team."

In addition to their democratic orientation, some SCOs—particularly organizing and service groups—work toward transformative growth in constituents as part of their approach to social change, another feature of their work that shapes relational practices. Many practitioners feel that those working toward such a goal with clients must themselves be actively supported in their growth and development.[7] The need for such support is particularly acute in situations where the work is emotionally demanding—such as at Sheltering Our Own where workers support women at risk of losing their lives from domestic violence—and/or where the staff includes people from the community being served—as at Dare to Dream or Community Voice. SCO leaders in these groups must be especially attuned to staff needs and ensure that the organization provides appropriate support.

Growing Roots works with its young clients in a context of emotionally supportive, healthy relationships—relationships of love. "For some kids . . . [our care] is going to be the most affection that they get," explained Denise Stewart. In this context, it's not surprising that her co-leader insisted that a critical feature of leadership was being good with people: "You really have to find a way to help people be inspired and help them to learn and to grow." Similarly, SOO's director recognized the need to support staff members dealing with victims of domestic violence. The staff should see that this is "teamwork." "They won't be alone out there to do that battle." Among other things, there must be a "communication channel" that allows staff members "to share, to grieve, to process." Everything they do "is always going back to the service of the battered woman," but there's a chain reaction in the quality of that service. "Because if the staff, they're not happy, they're very stressed out, they cannot be supportive to the battered women."

Many SCOs are staffed in part by constituents—people who are themselves experiencing or have experienced the kind of disadvantages the organization aims to address. In these cases, understanding and supporting staff members is required not only by the terms of organizational mission but by the special vulnerability of staff members in these situations. When Dare to Dream's young COO detailed the qualities of leadership, she concluded by saying, "Also you have to have a lot of compassion and understanding that is not [just] compassion for families [we serve] but also employees. Some staff are not far from being homeless and are still struggling, and understanding their personal needs [is important] . . ." For her, a definitive organizational achievement would be to bring the skill level of a constituent to the point where such a person could become the organization's executive director.

Even in organizations not routinely facing crisis situations, or employing constituents, the work of social change can be daunting and the people who do it need support. "[D]oing this work sometimes takes a lot of really baby steps," said Jean Patterson at Neighborhood Reach. "It's very important to continue to remind people of the progress that they've made and to keep them challenged in the miles that they have yet to go." When a leader fails to provide this kind of support, the organization and its work can suffer. One staff member expressed concern about a director who was insufficiently attentive to relational work: "People don't like to feel that they're working in a vacuum. . . . They don't like to feel disenfranchised. They don't like to feel like they're cut off from their source of support. . . . Now, when we're [physically] separated, a lot of the staff feel like we have an executive director that doesn't really care about us. . . . There's no problem with his vision. There's no problem with his intellectual capacity. . . . [But] he needs to increase his people skills." As another leader himself put it, "I think that initially my biggest weakness was . . . having a very intense and personal relationship with work and expecting other people to have it." He wasn't quick to anger, but when it happened he could hurt people's feelings. When people asked for help he couldn't always tell if it was because they were scared or lazy, and in those situations he didn't know how much support he should offer, or how.

For leaders facing multiple demands and limited resources, it can seem that attention devoted to staff support detracts from attention to the work, that staff needs and internal processes draw energy away from mission accomplishment. There can be a temptation, another director noted, to focus on winning battles at the expense of the people who are doing the work. But, he recognized, in the long term that's a mistake. Such an approach not only conflicts with basic organizational values about how people should be treated, but directly undermines the accomplishment of mission, especially (but not exclusively) when workers are themselves constituents.

Balancing the Demands of Organizational Maintenance and Movement Building

The third element of strategic nonprofit leadership entails attention to the organization's external environment. Like any other nonprofit, an SCO must achieve a fit with its environment, targeting a niche in which it can provide something of value to constituents that will be supported by funders, and that does not duplicate what others are already doing well. Although organizations encounter their environments in a number of ways, the strategic interactions—generating support, ensuring relevance, and scanning for threats and opportunities—are usually a formal leader's responsibility. For those leading SCOs, the depth and breadth of mission make environmental relations particularly critical and challenging.

Our respondents did not speak often or at length about the external tasks of leadership, but when they did, they referred to the need for relationship building, networking, collaborating, partnering, maintaining legitimacy with funders, and establishing access to political resources. These efforts are relevant to nonprofits generally, but relationship building may be particularly critical for social change organizations, given that the mission of achieving social justice is so large, and the capacity of any one SCO relatively limited. Although several respondents noted the importance of collaboration and network building, one staff member's observation was particularly telling. She said one of the skills a leader needed was "an awareness of what your organization is capable of handling, what your organization is capable of growing into . . . and an awareness of what all else is out there and how we might tap into that. . . . [S]o that we can partner or refer . . . [and] we're not trying to do everything." The objective is to get the work done, not necessarily to build large organizations.

In relating to their environments, SCO leaders face a set of difficulties beyond the challenges typically faced by other nonprofit leaders. In many nonprofits, leaders confront difficult trade-offs between margin and mission (i.e., doing what is good for organizational survival versus doing what is consistent with mission accomplishment).[8] For SCOs, the underlying commitment to systemic change creates an additional tension—that between dedication to a single organization's mission and fidelity to the larger cause of social justice. SCO leaders must struggle with the question of how organizational leadership may differ from and perhaps be at odds with movement leadership—by which we mean not an individualistic, charismatic approach but a collaborative effort to build something with others.

We heard a variety of different perspectives relating to this question. Some directors maintained that a leader should be cognizant of the greater aims to which organizational mission is connected, and be guided by those rather than organizational success. Ellen Mayhew of the Center for Critical Information was one who insisted on a kind of generosity as a central quality of social change leadership, even as she understood why it was difficult to act in this way:

> It takes a very collaborative, open person who is not easily threatened, who has a generosity toward not just your own staff but toward other organizations. And it's the lack of those qualities that I find the most frustrating part of my job from outside the organization, that we don't have enough leaders in the progressive movement who have internalized an instinct for collaboration and [for] . . . giving support to other like-minded people.

She didn't blame individuals because she recognized they were all competing for the same pot of money. But the result was that "we're steadily losing, if we ever had, the really strong absolutely basic instinct that collaboration comes first and mutual support comes first. And to the extent that we lose that, it *really, really* weakens the movement." The competition for resources and attention promoted by the funding system was "a very destructive pattern of behavior."

Others didn't necessarily see a need to worry so much about collaboration and emphasized that the need to be combative on constituents' behalf went hand-in-hand with a more general external aggressiveness on behalf of one's own organization. A project director at Rights for All said that while it was important to be team-oriented *inside* the organization, "At the same time, you have to be aggressive externally. You need to be aggressive to get money. You need to be aggressive to serve your clients. . . . [Y]ou have to stand up for your staff or you're not going to have any credibility with them." For some, the aggressiveness that fuels legal and political battles may mean that organizations are less inclined to collaborate, even when it makes sense to do so.

In addition to tension between organizational survival and external cooperation, there is the question of whether an SCO should ensure impact by "going to scale" as a single organization or by engaging in cross-organizational movement building. Some argue that SCOs or other non-profits will have a significant impact only if they come to operate their own programs on a large scale; others feel that the aim should not be replication of an individual model but a reciprocal effort involving numerous agencies and approaches. For instance, the organization, Teaching Tools, was wrestling with this question. Having spent his first several years figuring out how to run a program and build an organization, director Jay Stanley explained that the next four years would need to address the question, "How does Teaching Tools help lead a movement or be part of a movement?"

Recent school shootings had created a "window of opportunity" for dealing with youth violence. Standard policy proposals overemphasized psychological causes of violence to the exclusion of structural factors and also ignored the potential for engaging young people in problem solving. Jay saw the potential for TT and others to build a movement "to change the dialogue in those two areas" and was asking his staff and board to consider how they could contribute to the broader mission. A long-time TT program director expressed his ambivalence about achieving impact through organizational growth. "I always said to Jay, I don't want to be a part of McTeaching Tools. That's not what I came to do. If that's what you want to do, great I guess. But that ain't me. And I think we're perilously close to McTeaching Tools. . . . But at the same time, if you want to do movement building, you can't do it in three schools. Well, maybe you can. I mean, Dorothy Day did."[9]

The organization undertook an extensive, systematic survey of the field to explore needs, opportunities, and challenges, and developed a set of alternative approaches to growth. "I'm not a natural proponent of growth and replication," Jay noted, but at the same time he felt it was important to expand to address unmet needs. TT would do this in two ways. First, it would establish a "national training institute" that would offer training and technical assistance to other nonprofits. Second, the organization would try replicating its own program in other locations, beginning with the opening of an office across the country. Jay saw the expansion as an opportunity to refine the program by implementing it with varying partners in different communities. In the end, though, he maintained that the goal had to be the achievement of mission and not simply organizational growth. "Our mission isn't to build Teaching Tools into a powerful, multinational organization. Our mission is to prepare kids to be peacemakers. And inherently, that's better done by systems than by folks outside the system. It's better done by schools, universities, businesses. And if we can help be a catalyst to get those groups together to build in some infrastructure, that's great. And then we're done."

For most SCOs, mission accomplishment can be thought of on at least two levels. Jay Stanley's comment reflects concern with mission accomplishment at the level of a particular issue and/or population targeted by the organization (e.g., violence affecting youth; lack of political power among low-income Latinos; economic need in a poor neighborhood). At this level, success is achieved if an issue is effectively addressed and/or the constituent population's condition is improved. But mission accomplishment can also be thought of at a second level on which the issue or population is situated in a structural web of inequality that must be addressed for long-lasting, systemic change. In the case of Teaching Tools, thinking about the second level might mean recognizing the ways in which youth violence is shaped by race and class structures. A strategy emphasizing organizational growth over movement building may serve the first level better than the second, but neither level can be achieved entirely without collaborative effort. In dealing with their environments, SCO leaders must understand the location of their organization in the larger social change network, and be prepared to work across various types of boundaries with other groups.

Preparation of Current Leaders

These are major challenges for organizational leaders. What prepares people for this kind of work? The directors in our study were not *trained* to lead social change organizations. Rather, their work as leaders was informed by a blend of personal experiences, formal education, and informal tutelage by mentors and role models. They developed skills, knowledge and an attitude of comfort with the position—a sense of efficacy, optimism, and self-confidence—in whatever ways were available to them, driven by individual resourcefulness and dedication. In general, their preparation was strongest for the content of the organization's work—understanding what they were trying to do for constituents, how to go about it, and why it was important.[10] They were less prepared for tasks of organization building and maintenance, but managed to develop these skills to some degree through trial-and-error. Their most limited preparation was in the three challenges identified above: participatory direction-setting, relational practices supporting growth/transformation, and balancing organization and movement.

Training for the Organization's Work

Not surprisingly, our SCO leaders were well grounded in the content of the work done by their organizations, whether it was legal advocacy, youth development, sheltering and supporting battered women, organizing low-income neighborhoods, rehabilitating housing, or providing research and analysis to social activists. Multiple sources of professional development contributed to their ability to define and engage in mission-relevant work. These included personal experience, formal education, prior engagement in social movements, practice, and learning from or with others.

Personal background—especially when it included sharing some aspects of the constituents' experience—was cited by many leaders as important in their ability to do their work. In some cases, leaders who were not personally subject to hardship were schooled in the problems of injustice and inequality through their engagement in social movements. Being sensitized to racism, sexism, poverty, violence, the vagaries of the immigration process, or the impact of political power on neighborhood resources not only motivated leaders but gave them an understanding of the systemic problems facing their constituents and the kinds of actions that would help. According to Pete Veratek of Faith in Change, an intuitive sense of political reality and power is critical for doing his work, and unlike many other relevant skills, may not be easily taught. In his case, it was the result of processing early experiences growing up in an urban environment "where power was a common, public visible thing" and seeing the impact of the exercise of power. An organizer wouldn't need to have *his* particular experience, but "you've got to have some sense of power and the way the world really works and what's real and what's not real."

Pete wasn't sure this kind of understanding could be taught, but two leaders—members of the women's collective Respect—did mention developing their political awareness partly through formal education. Linda Jefferson and Marsha Madison had themselves experienced poverty but had come to their systems-awareness through interaction with peers and exposure to social theory in higher education. Unlike most students, however, these women had sought out college programs known for their attention to social problems—and even in these contexts, they experienced oppression along with enlightenment (Marsha referred to her field of study as "political silence").

More commonly, leaders cited their formal education as a source of other knowledge and skills relevant to their work. In some cases, education provided professional or technical knowledge (training in law, architecture, social work, education/youth development, and environmental engineering were relevant to some practitioners); in other cases, it produced more generic skills that were essential to the work (such as research and writing). Other sources of content-relevant preparation were short-term formal training (for example, in organizing) and practice over time—usually with some assistance from others.

Organization Building and Maintenance

None of our leaders had studied management, though a few had taken short courses over the years, and two younger directors had worked in the private sector. Establishing, building, and maintaining an organization were tasks they learned how to do primarily as a matter of trial and error. "You don't get a set of instructions with a nonprofit," said Roger Cochran, the longtime leader of Community Ownership Program. "You just start one. No one tells you how to run it or . . . how to do the budget . . . you just sort of make it up as you go along." The 54-year-old founding director of the Center for Critical Information, Ellen Mayhew, had used her network to develop the tiny amount of funding needed to start the organization, and "then it was just a matter of putting one foot in front of the other." She went on, "I'm part of a generation who did not have any training whatsoever, and so I bet that that profile I painted of a poor administrator who had the original vision for the organization, that was so true of so many organizations that started around the late '70s and early '80s. We didn't have any training at all. But we had a very exciting and volatile political atmosphere. . . . I think we were all born of the political climate at the time, when there was so much possibility and so much excitement."

Two factors did give some structure to the process of learning-by-doing for these leaders. First, almost all were able to draw on some coaching or mentoring (sometimes from peers or even subordinates). Second, most also had some experience with *program* management before having to take on responsibility for an entire organization. The background of the director of SOO illustrates the latter point. Madeleine Lee began her work in domestic violence through an internship in the local district attorney's office, then "realized this was really what I wanted to do for my life." Her next job as a legal advocate for a domestic violence program gave her the chance to establish a program to put advocates in two local district courts. As the volume of work grew, she became a coordinator and then program director, positions providing exposure to a variety of institutions and people, in which she could develop her skills "step by step." She gained additional business experience in the private sector, and eventually, when the former director of SOO was leaving and encouraged her to apply for the position, she was ready to do it.

Younger leaders in our study were particularly likely to report learning *with* others, through co-leadership arrangements or by relying on feedback from subordinates. For example, Jay Stanley of Teaching Tools had limited experience being supervised, so he said, "I haven't learned how to manage from being managed. I've learned how to manage from the people that I've managed—if that all makes sense—which makes me an incredibly responsive manager because that's how I've learned what success looks like, is feedback from people." When Rachel Beck moved up from her previous position at Urban Watch to become director, she found that she needed to change some of the attitudes and perspectives that had served her well in a narrower role, and the way she did it was by listening to co-worker subordinates. Sometimes her behavior would so irritate one of them that he would "scream at me coming out of meetings." She figured out that she needed "to be open and to listen to people . . . because I needed a ton of advice at that point and that meant getting advice from all of my staff."

By contrast, although older directors had mentors or role models, when they spoke of learning by doing, they often described a more independent activity—as illustrated in the comments from the directors of CCI and COP above. Ellen Mayhew mentioned having had "role models" but not in the context of program or organization development. Roger Cochran alluded to administrative lessons he'd had early on from a bookkeeper in the organization, but he didn't describe having developed as a manager with anyone's assistance. Part of the reason for the difference in stories related by younger versus older leaders may be that younger directors are still engaged in the learning process and may be more conscious of how much they rely on others. Another explanation may have to do with generational differences in approaches to work (younger people are said to be more team-oriented).[11]

The Missing Pieces

If preparation for organizational maintenance was uneven, it was far better than preparation for any of the special challenges of SCO leadership identified earlier—facilitating constituent/staff participation in direction-setting, managing staff members in a way that supports their own transformative work with constituents, and balancing organization with movement. A handful of leaders had some kind of training (usually, but not always, informal[12]) in constituent participation and empowerment, and some had received instruction in a service model that entailed supporting growth and transformation in *clients*—which might or might not be applied to staff relational practice. Virtually none had any real preparation for working on systemic change through collaboration or movement building.

Learning Participatory Practices   Many SCO leaders are inclined to lead in a highly participatory way, as this type of leadership is consistent with the substantive goals of their agencies. But valuing this approach is not the same as being able to practice it effectively, and very few leaders reported any real preparation for this challenge. Difficulties were apparent in a number of ways: some staff members reported confusion about when and how deeply they could influence decisions, some groups struggled with tensions between collective authority and individual responsibility or power based in expertise, and some organizations that began with highly democratic structures ran into serious conflicts.

The few leaders who described background preparation for this aspect of leadership mentioned two sources of guidance: social movement influences and coaching from older mentors. On the first point, two women spoke of the guidance they received from the women's movement. For Ellen Mayhew, the effect was primarily to incline her toward consensus-based decision-making, but for Dorothy Morrison there was a systematic developmental process. In the aftermath of the Second Vatican Council, Dorothy and others in her religious congregation had engaged in an explicit effort to develop participatory structures and leadership skills:

> And what happened in religious congregations all across the country is that we became conscious much more of the women's movement and . . . much more aware of leadership and . . . owning it, and then we engaged in a collaborative process across the country to change the structures of our own life. And most of those structures were parallel to the Catholic Church. They were hierarchical structures about authority and obedience. And . . . we transformed them and . . . created participative structures in our own religious con-

gregations all across the country, and . . . supported one another in that process. And then we worked together to find ways of dealing with the Bishops
and others in the various states that we worked with to get them to be more
participative.

Dorothy now leads an organization in which clients and staff members
(some of whom are former clients) actively participate in program design
and implementation.

The one SCO leader who, when asked about his own skill development,
recounted a story explicitly about learning participatory practices from
mentors was Harold deMello of Residents Making Change. Harold grew
up in the local neighborhood, and his leadership training began when he
used to drop in at the RMC offices and watch his aunt at work.

> And I started asking questions. And one of the first questions that you ask as
> a kid is *why*. Why do you guys do what you do? . . . And she says, "because
> the community wants us to do that, because you guys say we should do it."
> "What do you mean 'you guys'? *I* didn't say you should do that." "Well, you
> know, we have community meetings where people come in and they tell us
> what they want to do. . . . If you want to come in, you should tell us what you
> want to do and then we'll do it." "You mean I could tell you what to do?"
> "Yeah, you could tell me what to do." "Well, then I want you to do this." "No.
> You can't tell me to do that. You have to do it collectively. You have to do it
> with everybody else. If everybody else agrees that that's what they want me to
> do, then that's what we do."

Harold laughed as he told this story. He went on to describe getting
more involved, working with RMC's Youth Committee, and organizing activities. All along, his elders provided advice, pulling him aside and giving
him tips and feedback. When he expressed interest in developing a "youth
agenda," they advised him to call a meeting to discuss it. He recalled with
amusement how when he arrived at that meeting: "I already had an agenda
for myself. I sat some youth around a table and I said, 'Well, here's a youth
agenda.' Which really wasn't a youth agenda. It was a Harold agenda,
right?" When Harold resisted their alternative suggestion, his aunt and another organizer pulled him aside and said, " 'Harold, if you're going to organize youth, then you're going to have to be willing to hear what they
want to say.' "

Harold—who was about 15 years old at the time and wanted to learn
about his African roots—was interested in setting up an after–school program. But the other teens were younger, and wanted a party. "They wanted
to get to know some youth from the other parts of the neighborhood,"

Harold explained. His own response to this was negative, but his aunt cautioned him, "'You've got to listen if you're going to do the collective. Sometimes the people who are at the lead try to not lead but drag.'" She went on to say that "if you're going to facilitate a conversation that's going to come out with a youth agenda, you're going to have to hear the youth voice." He took this early lesson to heart, and they had a party, which was quite successful. "I learned a lot out of it," he said. "A lot of good came out of it [the party]. There was a lot of community building that happened because of it." As a result of experiences like this, Harold came to understand the importance of constituent participation, how to facilitate it, and how effective it could be. These were critical lessons for someone who would eventually direct an organization that exists for and reports to the community.

No other SCO leaders in the study explicitly referenced preparation for participatory work, though some had trained as organizers and presumably encountered relevant lessons in that process. The two respondents who came to Respect from their own experience as welfare recipients were committed to learning democratic processes through reflective practice—and they worked hard at this—but it wasn't something for which they had any training. Several other leaders were struggling to develop skills in this area. For example, the co-founders of Community Voice also lacked preparation but were working with the rest of the staff and the community board to figure out how to run a non-hierarchical organization. For advice and support they often looked to colleagues in other collectivist SCOs, who were facing the same kinds of challenges.

Supporting Staff Members Doing Transformative Work Most of our SCO leaders reported essentially no preparation for relational work within the organization, and some found it challenging and frustrating. One director observed that it was common among nonprofits of their size and type to promote people who were well-grounded in "content" (the substantive work of the organization) but unprepared for "running an organization," including doing the work of "personnel management"—and he put himself in this category. Although he maintained that he did "a good job in supervision" he also noted that "on the day-to-day personnel management things . . . I guess I get tired of . . . the personnel problems and issues." It sounded as if he knew how to work with people who for whatever reason didn't require much interpersonal support, but he wasn't so effective in meeting stronger staff needs—an impression that was confirmed by the comments of a staff member. The problem of a manager with substantive expertise but weak relational skills is by no means unique to SCOs, but for reasons already discussed, it is especially critical in organizations doing social change work.

Of course, in at least some SCOs, the "content" involves transformative developmental work with constituents, and a number of directors come to this work with some kind of training in human development. Within the ten SCOs oriented toward a model of change emphasizing individual transformation, at least four directors had academic backgrounds in social work or education, and another had pursued formal but non-academic training for his work with youth groups. But it isn't necessarily the case that this preparation translates from constituent services to effective relational practice with staff members. From the reports of staff members in some organizations, it seems that as skilled as some leaders may be in working with clients, they either fail to recognize the importance of relational work with the staff, or are unable to accomplish it. The result can be ineffective performance or burn-out and turnover.

Balancing Organization Needs with Collaboration and Movement Building Our SCO leaders mentioned almost nothing in the way of preparation for collaborative work. To the extent that they had learned how to do it, the learning was through trial-and-error, and the work itself was generally limited to the accomplishment of the organization's activities rather than joining forces to build a larger effort. Those who engaged in the broadest or most frequent collaborations tended to be organizations directed by leaders who drew inspiration and/or lessons from social movements—such as Center for Critical Information (whose leader is quoted above, on the subject of collaboration), Dare to Dream, or the low-income women's collective, Respect.[13]

Ongoing Leadership Development in Social Change Organizations

Civil rights leader Ella Baker once said, "I have always thought what is needed is the development of people who are interested not in being leaders as much as in developing leadership among other people."[14] Leadership development is a concern for SCOs not only for sustaining their own work but for meeting the larger mission of systemic change and self-determination for those who have been disempowered. How do SCO directors—with their own somewhat uneven preparation—go about training the next generation of leadership for social change? What opportunities and support for staff or constituent development have they structured into their organizations? What types of leadership roles are different groups (staff versus constituents) being prepared for? And what are the areas of skill, knowledge, or attitude in which development occurs?

How Learning Occurs, Who Benefits, and What They Learn

We begin by distinguishing between activities aimed at developing grassroots leadership for community activism (usually targeting constituents) and efforts to develop leadership for social change organizations (usually involving staff members). Grassroots leadership development is integral to the mission of many organizing groups, and many of them provide formal instruction toward this end. Faith in Change, for example, sends core constituents to national training sessions, and Residents Making Change has recently established a Resident Development Institute to formalize leadership development in recognition of the increasing complexity of neighborhood issues and the challenges of community self-determination. Additionally, some service organizations whose missions include client capacity building are adding explicit leadership skills to their educational programs. Dare to Dream has begun a special project in which participants, who are selected for both leadership potential and commitment to give back to their community, are trained to make their voices heard in institutions that affect them. The skills developed in formal constituent training tend to be those of political activism and self-advocacy, useful but not sufficient for organizational leadership.

The process for developing organizational leaders tends to be more ad hoc, essentially relying on situated practice—that is, engagement in relevant activities accompanied by feedback and support.[15] In our SCOs, we found that staff members and sometimes constituents could practice leadership in three ways: by participating in general organizational decision-making, by helping to implement projects, and by taking responsibility for specific projects or programs (the least available, but arguably the most powerful).[16] Regardless of the form their practice took, learning was greatly facilitated—in some cases only possible—when accompanied by mentoring or coaching to provide both instruction and support. The process was illustrated in the comments of Rachel Beck at Urban Watch, as she described the development of her program directors. They had their own staffs, she said, and "they're expected to grow their programs as they wish. . . . with[in] this sort of this larger strategic sense of what we could be." She relied on them to "manage their own people and to . . . think about where they want to be going." But she also kept an eye on them and worked with them when it seemed necessary, as she did with her program director Marianne Foley.

> She was managing a relatively large team of people, and she wasn't doing a great job at it, because those are interpersonal skills that you gotta learn. There's a faith in yourself that you gotta develop, and I went through the exact thing when I took over as executive director, and I basically talked her through that whole period, and I'm like, "All right, here's what's going to happen. Here's what you're going to feel like. Here's some tips. Here's some ways to psych yourself up. It's all mental."

Something similar was described by Advocates for the People's program coordinator Maria Reyes, whose boss Antonio Mena gave her responsibility accompanied by "on-the-job mentoring." In the week of our interview, she explained that she had spent the first three days in out of town meetings, and had scheduled things "so that I didn't have a moment to breathe, except for Tuesday night, where I had dinner and I just relaxed and was talking to Antonio on the phone for like two hours about everything that had just taken place." Interestingly, it was when she was asked what made for effective leadership that she brought up her boss's support of her own development.

> I can tell when Antonio trusts me on certain things, because he'll give up his—like if somebody calls and says, "We have a conference we want you to speak [at]" . . . he goes, "Well . . . you know, Maria's really the one who's been doing this and you should talk to her." And . . . I'm going, you know, man, he didn't have to do that. He could've just juiced me for the information and he could have run with it. . . . But he's about developing leadership, so I think a good leader is not scared of putting anybody else in an equal position . . . or teaching them everything or showing all their cards, you know, because you confide in that person and [then] . . . you're developing other people.

Maria contrasted her current experience to an earlier position (in development), in which she'd had no coaching. "I mean, I was dying in development," she said. "I had no one leading me there. I was doing things on my own and I was going, all right, this can't be possibly right." But without guidance she didn't know how to proceed. Coming to work with Antonio, she said, "salvaged me."

Although some degree of leadership practice is available to staff members in virtually all of these organizations, the opportunities for their leadership development are limited by two factors: first, not *all* staff members are given significant responsibility, and second, insufficient attention is paid to coaching in several organizations. Active coaching plus opportunities for practice seem to be present in under half of our organizations, and the extension of these leadership-development elements to most staff members is even less common, probably characteristic of only a handful of the organizations. Access to practice-with-coaching for a limited number of staff members (e.g., program directors) can be found in organizations with all types of structures, but the extension of opportunities to broader segments of the staff is primarily found in those organizations with more democratic structures and responsiveness to the community. In part, this may be because such agencies see their missions as specifically including empowerment and they apply this aim internally as well as externally.

Just under half of our SCOs give constituents some opportunity to develop leadership skills through organizational practice. The most extensive participation occurs in the collective Respect, in which the constituents essentially staff the organization and take full responsibility for making projects happen. The limitation of this model is that there may be inadequate coaching resources when almost all members are at a relatively early stage of professional development. Alternatively, at Dare to Dream the constituent participation is more limited (giving input for program design, serving as spokespeople in public arenas, sometimes chairing local initiatives) but is accompanied by somewhat more structure and support. In organizing groups like Uniting Youth for Change, constituents are trained in the organization's model of group interaction and then assisted as they organize for action in their own school or community environments. UYC and community organizing groups like Faith in Change or Community Voice aim to develop skills in constituents so that they can conduct their own political actions—but the organization continues to provide infrastructure, staff support, and on-going training.

Perhaps not surprisingly, the content of lessons about leadership is strong in many of the same areas as the current leaders' own development, and tends to be weakest in areas where they have the least preparation. Within the organization, staff members who take or share responsibility for the running of programs learn a great deal about both the content of the work and basic organizational functions. In terms of the key challenges relevant to SCO leadership, however, their training is uneven. In some organizations, they learn something about democratic decision-making and constituent participation through experience, though it's not clear how well structured the learning process is. Training in appropriate relational practice occurs only where the current leader models and encourages effective behaviors (which seems to happen infrequently). Even more limited is training for collaborative work that goes beyond meeting the organization's programmatic needs.

For constituents who don't become staff members or run projects, development is more related to the content of their own activities, including basic skill development such as written and oral communication and working with others to accomplish collective action. In other words, they are learning about social change work in the community but not necessarily about what it takes to establish or sustain an organization that can support this work.

Leadership Succession

One clear sign of leadership development opportunities within an organization would be the accession to a director's position by people inside the organization. Among our SCOs, this was relatively unusual: only two had directors promoted from within. Fully half (eight) of the study organizations were led by people who came to their positions through founding, co-founding, or transforming the organization (this number includes both older and younger leaders).[17] Three groups (19 percent) had hired directors from outside their organizations (in two cases, the incoming director was known to the founder), and another had hired someone from outside who had previously worked extensively within the organization. The remaining two organizations were led by, in one case, an individual who was placed in the position by a national parent organization and in the other by a collective of individuals coming to the work through personal connections. In other words, very few of the directors were the product of internal leadership development efforts within the organizations themselves.

There are many reasons why these organizations would be unlikely to have developed leaders internally. A number of them are relatively young organizations headed by young founders, and it seems premature for them to be addressing this question (though some are thinking about it). For older organizations headed by founders, there are many difficulties and tensions associated with leadership transition. In addition, many staff members—even those inclined toward leadership—are not particularly anxious to lead the organization in which they're currently working. And, of course, limited resources also pose a challenge.

Transitioning from a Founding Leader

Founding leaders tend to be so strongly identified with their organizations that leadership development and transition can be very difficult. Older founder-leaders often spoke of the degree to which their position, even the organization as a whole, had formed around their vision or become heavily identified with their particular ideas and expertise. When Antonio Mena of Advocates for the People said, "You just can't hire somebody for this kind of job," he was in part alluding to the way in which he had figured out how to do it as he went along, but also to the fact that "a lot of [the work] is driven by my vision." "Basically, my biggest challenge the whole time is this, since I started the center, I've always had kind of the founder's syndrome . . . trying to figure out a way to institutionalize it so it goes beyond my personality." He went on to talk about resource constraints, but periodic references to his own specialized role seemed to reflect concerns about how well someone else would do the particular work that he had envisioned.

In many cases, it was the leader's ideas, energy and commitment that brought the organization into existence and maintained it over time. In addition, for many founders, the organization's work is also their life's work. In this context, to open leadership to new ideas is to threaten the organization's integrity; to turn the organization over to someone else is to give up one's own mission. Furthermore, for the agency's external partners—funders, collaborators, constituents—often the leader *is* the organization, and his departure can result in a major loss of credibility and support.

A few of the older founders in our SCOs had given some thought to leadership transition issues, and some were struggling to come up with workable plans. One clear dilemma concerned the role of the departing director: should all ties be severed or should she remain active in some capacity? In the former case, the organization might lose its focus, but in the latter case, the founder's influence could prohibit the new director from exercising effective leadership. Ellen Mayhew, founder of the Center for Critical Information, expressed these concerns. Asked about her role in the future of the organization, she discussed her expectation that the organization would be transitioning to new leadership within the next five years. Within this process, she said, "I see my role as making sure that during that transition the organization doesn't lose its footing. . . . [that] it stays a stable, strong organization, with clear, articulated principles. I'm not wedded to preserving any particular aspects of the program, as much as I am . . . [to] passing on the general political principles on which we have operated for twenty years." The problem would be negotiating the balance of stepping back while at the same time ensuring that principles remained intact. She worried both about "making sure that the organization is open enough to accept new leadership" with the changes it might bring and about "losing our political principles."

Ellen's comments reflect a clear tension between organizational openness to new ideas and faithfulness to guiding principles, a tension for which the resolution isn't obvious. How much could a new director change, and still be true to the organization's founding principles? The question is a difficult one under any circumstances but particularly hard for people who have established organizations and worked tirelessly to sustain them for decades. In addition to establishing the vision or guiding principles, founders or long-term leaders also become repositories of important knowledge relating to the organization's work. Because some of these organizations are *so* identified with their leaders, in some sense any change of leadership would probably by definition mean a significant change in the organization's work, and it is understandable that a founder would be nervous about this. At the same time, change is inevitable if the larger effort is to continue.

One possible way to work toward a smoother transition would be to try more consciously to bring others—particularly younger staff members—along as the organization develops, but this requires time and other resources, and there is no guarantee that those people the leader brings along will stay with the organization. Some organizations are simply so small that it would be hard to develop an internal leadership track, but even where there is the structural space to do this, other obstacles—including the leader's own demands—can interfere with the process. One founding director spoke of challenges in a way that highlighted these problems, explicitly and implicitly:

What tends to happen is people come into the organization and they want to [be] and are successful here, do in fact take on leadership positions . . . but they leave. . . . So then . . . how do you develop that ongoing continuity? . . . If we were doing something that wasn't innovative, if we were doing day care or an after school program or whatever and you started the program and now you're going to get into DSS funding streams . . . [then] basically, you need generic leadership to carry on the mission. But here . . . the program is constantly developing and growing and changing and it's very specific in nature. So the leadership has to come out of the people who've come in here and developed their leadership here and then know this organization . . . this set of philosophies and . . . methodologies, are committed to and have the talents and abilities to carry it on.

It is understandable how founding leaders can have high expectations for subsequent leadership in their organizations, but overly high demands or excessive rigidity can inhibit effective staff development and ultimately organizational survival.

The organizations in which we saw the emergence of these issues were older ones, led by older leader-founders. But some of the comments of the younger founders suggest that they have an attachment to their organizations that may put them in a position similar to that of the older founders as they age. For example, Stephen Jencks said he and his Community Voice co-founder hadn't thought much about succession, just about the minimum time commitment each of them would make to the organization. He observed that their ten year commitment seemed a long one, but when asked about how the organization's work fit into his larger life goals, he said, "I think it fits very centrally there. I would just as soon stay here if I felt . . . like it remained a challenging environment, and . . . [one] that I felt was positive and also catalyzing the type of social change that I am interested in dedicating my life to seeing happen. So I could stay here I think, for my entire life."

The leaders of Growing Roots had come up with a structural model—a "director's circle" to facilitate the movement of individuals into and out of leadership. When one of the three directors left to attend graduate school (with a plan of coming back), they brought another staff member into the circle. They emphasized developing leadership in the organization and the flexibility of the structure as ways to prevent the rigidity that often happens when "the old guard" of an organization holds on too tightly. At the same time, though, they had intensely strong attachments to the organization. "I think we'll always feel that this is our center, this is our home," said Denise Stewart, "but that there will be times when we want to go off and do different things." When asked how long they saw themselves continuing to do "this kind of work," Monroe Harris said, "I think forever. It's not going to stop. . . . I don't think any of us will ever pursue other passions so that we are not involved at some level with what's going on here."

Leadership Interests of Younger Staff Members

Many factors inhibit leadership succession in founder-led organizations, including the leader's own difficulty in letting go, the wish to find someone else with similar qualifications and passion, and funders' identification of the organization with the older leader. But some leaders also note that even if they were willing and able to leave, it's not obvious there would be people available to take over. As Antonio Mena said, "You get criticized for it because people say, make room for somebody else. But there's nobody to make room [for]. Nobody wants this job. Doesn't pay enough and it's not prestigious enough so nobody actually wants it."

In fact, only one of the sixteen younger staff members we interviewed expressed a clear desire to be the executive director of the agency at some point, and one other said she had thought about it, but with some doubts about the fit. Two of the younger staffers said they would *not* be interested in this position; one because she wanted to work in a more directly activist organization at this point in her life, and another because he felt there was too much "baggage" in the organization's existing staff structure. Two more spoke of developing leadership skills in their current organizations, but they also had dreams of starting their own organizations in program areas closer to their own interests.

SOO's Kamla Chowdhury saw opportunity for her own growth in the agency, even expected she could develop a program, but in all likelihood would eventually want to do her own thing. She was happy for the time being doing outreach work but ultimately hoped to exercise her skills in other capacities. "I think as the organization grows . . . there'll be a stage where there's more positions opening up, where I can kind of expand my own growth in the agency." Asked where she'd like to be in two or three years, she said she had always wanted to have her own organization, dedicated to serving the women of her own community. For now, "the whole experience of working in an . . . [ethnic] women's organization" was definitely something she needed to do, to prepare herself. "I mean just to observe what Madeleine's doing at her position, what everyone else is doing at their position, how this organization's being run. I'm definitely taking this job as a learning process for myself." When asked what sort of training she thought she would need to run her own agency, she said that simply observing others and learning from their actions and mistakes, followed by with her own trial-and-error process once in a director's position would be adequate. In essence, doing her current job for a few more years would be "training enough."

If this young woman's comments are representative of other young staff members, SCOs may do more for leadership development in young people by providing consistent participation opportunities, coaching and support than by offering internal tracks to their own executive positions.

Structural Barriers to Broadening Organizational Leadership

Many people working in or with SCOs have expressed concerns both about whether there are enough young leaders to take up the work of the retiring baby-boom generation and about how to ensure that social change leadership includes diversity by race, ethnicity, sex, and other dimensions of social identity.[18] Though the situation may not be as dire as some have feared, our interviewees did highlight some important structural barriers to broadening leadership in these organizations, even when there is a desire to do so.

Antonio Mena of Advocates for the People complained that he was "kind of stuck," partly because "you just can't hire somebody for this kind of job." He saw the need for new leadership, but he felt himself spread too thin to do both the necessary training of younger people and the work itself. There were limited opportunities for staff mobility ("the organization's not large enough to have any upward mobility unless I drop dead"), leading to somewhat high turnover among the staff, which in turn increased his own training burden. At the same time, he didn't have access to the resources needed to hire more senior people who could share the responsibility. It could be particularly difficult to recruit qualified Latinos for skilled work at low pay: there was a "pool of whites who can take pay cuts, who can take low salaries" but "in terms of Latinos, what we find is that there's such an economic polarization in the community that you have people that are very, very poor who . . . aren't even eligible for these jobs . . . and then you have people who are credentialed, who have expectations . . . that they're going to make a certain amount of money." In addition, there were generational trends away from social change work and toward the private sector, he said, but "I'm beginning to see a shift a little bit in that thinking."

The net result was that he didn't have staff members with as much experience as he would like, though he did see the potential in his young subordinates. "They're all kind of leaders in different ways," he said. "Basically these are people who are running their own areas but have a ways to go yet." With more resources he could hire additional senior people for a better "mix"; with more institutional opportunities, the young people could go farther.

Mena's leadership development was focused on young people from the Latino community who had good skills but needed more experience and guidance. For organizations that might try to develop leadership among the most disadvantaged, the barriers were even greater. Myung Kim of Community Choices had a vision of future leadership coming up from the community, but he thought that it would take five to ten years, not one, to develop such leadership. CV's Stephen Jencks said that with "experience and . . . some sort of nurturing or apprenticeship . . . people could do a lot of what I do." But he didn't agree with some in the field who would argue that in community organizing, the aim is to "work yourself out of a job."

> I don't think that it's realistic. . . . I think that I can work myself out of a lot of aspects of my job and that is really important, to be focused on having people developing the skills and leadership, to be pushing things forward. I do think the fact that I went to school for about 25 years in this country means that I'm going to be more comfortable writing in English than people who didn't. And given the way foundations decide who to give money to, I think it makes sense for me to write grant proposals. . . . I think that the amount of training we can offer to people isn't going to fundamentally make it so that people are suddenly able to magically do everything that an organization needs to do.

Residents Making Change was unusually successful at developing community leadership, and indeed its current director came from the community and developed some of his own skills growing up under the tutelage of older members of the organization. But Henry deMello had left the neighborhood to attend an elite college, and then gained additional skills through internships and work in the private sector. It remained to be seen whether a young staff member from the community without such education and experience would be able to attain his own dream of some day becoming the executive director.

In sum, SCOs face a set of challenges in trying to broaden their own leadership. People whose educational backgrounds or professional training might make them good candidates are not necessarily eager to work for low pay in small organizations with limited opportunities for upward movement. But people without those advantages require much more training by already busy current leaders, and in some cases no amount of development the organization can realistically offer will be enough to make up for lack of formal education or professional experience.

Leadership Development for the Work of
Social Change

The tasks of leadership in social change organizations are complex, and the ability of SCOs to grow their own leaders is constrained. Even where current leaders are inclined to develop others, their own uneven training makes them ill-equipped for this responsibility. In addition, they may feel a tension between fidelity to organizational mission—that is, getting the work done—and the need to prepare new leadership.

To be sure, if the mission of an organization is explicitly about empowerment and the development of capacity in others, then the conflict between doing the work and developing new talent is lessened, though there may still be too many demands on limited resources to meet all aspects of the mission. And for some social change activists, the definition of leadership entails nurturing growth in others. When Marsha Madison of Respect responded to a question about leadership, she insisted that a good leader wasn't necessarily "somebody who had charisma, stood out from the rest" or "knew how to take charge."

> A good leader is somebody who can really get the other people going, help the other people. I don't like the word "empower" because I don't think you can give other people their power, but I know that I've had people in my life who helped me realize my power and helped me access my power in a way and learn how to do that. And a good leader will let people make mistakes. A good leader will know that mistakes will happen and they need for the person to progress.

Indeed, constituent leadership development is central to the model of organizing groups like Faith in Change, and the result of their efforts is broad capacity for leading political action. As Pete Veratek put it, "A lot of organizations get a leader day one and that leader is identified forever. And they're good organizations and they're good leaders. It's not to criticize them. . . . [But] we can go, on any given day and any given meeting . . . with 50 different leaders and it won't matter in terms of our quality."

But it takes considerable time and effort to build other people's capacity—especially to let them make mistakes—and although many of the leaders we interviewed would probably agree that this is an important feature of leadership, they wouldn't necessarily say it took priority over getting other work done. In addition, the kind of constituent capacity building done by organizing groups like Faith in Change does not produce organizational leaders (nor is it intended to). In this model, community members learn how to take responsibility for political action, but the organizing group continues to provide support and ongoing development and must sustain its own staff in other ways.

Complicating the challenge for leadership development in social change organizations is the high probability that staff members (or other participants) tutored in any given organization will not go on to lead that organization. Because these agencies have such limited resources, unless they can develop staff members through the course of the work itself (without investing significant amounts of additional time in this process), it will seem unwise on an agency level to commit heavily to internal leadership development. At the same time, without such effort, valuable expertise may be lost and new leadership development may be less effective than it could have been. In some cases, organizations will disappear.

Looking Beyond the Organization for Leadership Development

How promising is the possibility of training a new crop of SCO and other nonprofit leaders through formal professional education, as in the nonprofit management programs that are now offered by a number of postsecondary institutions? We asked directors and staff members about the value of such programs, but their responses were not generally enthusiastic. Although both groups would appreciate additional managerial skills, they were skeptical about the ability of generic programs to deliver on these, given how much even their administrative work is shaped by context. In addition, directors were particularly critical of the mainstream perspective likely to be inculcated in such programs. As Antonio Mena commented, "I find that when you deal with people who have trained in public affairs schools and stuff like that, they've been trained basically to work with people who have power. They don't know sometimes how to work with communities that don't have power, and it's a lot different. And so the question is, can you get some people like that and untrain 'em, retrain 'em, you know."

When Ellen Mayhew was asked if she would have found such training useful, she was doubtful, for the reason that with formal training, "you can't just take what you need, you tend to be marched through a program that may or may not be relevant to what you're doing. . . . And it can, I think . . . encourage you to think inside boxes, when a lot of the work of the program director or the founder or the visionary . . . is to think outside the box and to see possibilities where they weren't obvious."

Ellen Mayhew wouldn't have wanted training in a "certain way to do this work," if that way reflected political principles different from those she held. In such a case, she "would have learned a lot of methods without the political principles that really should be guiding the methods." In addition, it seems particularly unlikely that current formal training programs would provide adequate preparation in areas we have identified as critical to social change work, including participatory direction-setting, relational practices supporting growth/transformation, and balancing organization and movement.

A more promising approach, according to some of our respondents, would be for formal educational programs to work directly with social change organizations to design training that integrates service learning (some programs already do a little of this). For such an approach to be most effective, the educational institutions would have to work closely with the organizations to identify appropriate skills to be developed and a formal curriculum that would support the service-learning components. To open up the work to a diverse group of students, there would be a need for support to underwrite internships, not only for student time, but also for organizational resources to be devoted to the leadership development process. Programs could be made available to people within the organization as well as students from outside.

This training process should include the critical analysis relevant to social change, and should support development in the central functions of SCO leadership such as participatory direction-setting, relational practice, and movement building. Although these functions draw on personal attributes as well as learned skills, they can be strengthened in training, particularly in settings that entail actual work in organizations. Participatory visioning must be informed by an analysis of social conditions and interaction with constituents, and these can be motivated and grounded through work in social change organizations. On this point, members of Respect indicate that an indispensable element of new-member training is political education that counters internalized oppression and enables the new member to connect her experience to a larger social context. And relational skills can be developed only in the context of practice, ideally within an environment committed to constituent growth and transformation. Finally, skills of collaboration and movement building will require reaching beyond the boundaries of single organizations, and learning by doing, accompanied by critical analysis and reflection.

Formal education can foster important analytical skills and technical knowledge, while service-based learning provides exposure to the challenges of practice. The right mix of these could better prepare the next generation of SCO leaders to meet the particular demands of their work.

CHAPTER FOUR

ORGANIZATIONAL STRUCTURE

Legitimacy and Accountability

Community Choices was from its beginning a staff-driven organization. The co-founders were the co-directors. . . . [As] an assistance organization, you know, we basically made decisions about what to take on based on what people came to us with and what we felt we had the resources to actually serve. But as we evolved, we began . . . [doing] a lot of coalition building and eventually spawning direct organizing projects out of what we did, which meant that we were building up our own direct constituency base. . . . So . . . the bottom line for us [now] is establishing a membership structure for the organization. So we are kind of evolving . . . into our next phase . . . having a much more direct decision-making process whereby our constituency, but through membership, can shape our agenda. . . . [W]e're doing a lot of our work now with the eye towards how do we build long-term constituency and a power base. And really the thrust of our strategic plan is how do we achieve systemic change? . . . [S]o building power was one piece of our move to a membership structure. The other piece was accountability. We wanted to make sure that, if we really are about empowerment and constituency leadership, that that doesn't stop at the project level. . . . So governance also became something that membership was involved in—governance of the organization. Not just governance over the campaign.

MYUNG KIM,
Community Choices

Organizational "structure" refers to the ways in which work roles are divided and grouped, the formal allocation of decision-making authority, formal channels of communication, and written rules or regulations (Mintzberg 1981, 1983). Our examination of structure in social change organizations focuses primarily on decision-making for two reasons: it is the dimension of greatest variation in relatively small organizations and decision-making procedures are substantively relevant to the work of organizations aimed at redistributing power.

The second point is clearly illustrated in Myung Kim's description of strategic decisions at Community Choices. Having recognized that their deepest impact resulted less from professional advocacy than from community-based collective action, CC staff members committed the organization to the latter approach. They believed that this new orientation would require a change in organizational structure, and they undertook a multi-phase transition from a staff-driven decision-making model to one that would explicitly empower constituents. The CC case exemplifies a particular linkage between an organization's structure and the theory of change on which it acts. Does a relationship between structure and social change theory hold for other SCOs with different approaches? To answer this question we begin by depicting the array of structures we found and examining some of their complexities, including the interaction of formal and informal factors. After this review, we identify important influences on SCO structure, including social change approaches, environmental demands, and values. We conclude that structure should be responsive to the requirements of mission and offer some suggestions for managing the particular challenges associated with different structural choices.

Decision-Making Structures

The literature on structure in activist nonprofits tends to focus on the contrast between bureaucratic and collectivist-democratic forms, and views most real organizations as blending features of the two forms.[1] Our study highlights two related but distinct dimensions of decision-making in social change organizations: the way authority is distributed internally (among directors and staff members) and the openness of the organization to client or constituent influence. We find that our SCOs vary in terms of both the concentration of internal decision-making authority and the type of influence they grant to constituents and that these dimensions are not always correlated in predictable ways.

Concentration of Internal Authority

In terms of the concentration of internal decision-making authority, our organizations reflect a variety of configurations that range from traditional

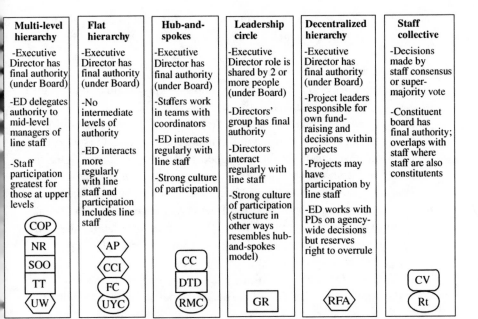

Multi-level hierarchy	Flat hierarchy	Hub-and-spokes	Leadership circle	Decentralized hierarchy	Staff collective
-Executive Director has final authority (under Board) -ED delegates authority to mid-level managers of line staff -Staff participation greatest for those at upper levels	-Executive Director has final authority (under Board) -No intermediate levels of authority -ED interacts more regularly with line staff and participation includes line staff	-Executive Director has final authority (under Board) -Staffers work in teams with coordinators -ED interacts regularly with line staff -Strong culture of participation	-Executive Director role is shared by 2 or more people (under Board) -Directors' group has final authority -Directors interact regularly with line staff -Strong culture of participation (structure in other ways resembles hub-and-spokes model)	-Executive Director has final authority (under Board) -Project leaders responsible for own fund-raising and decisions within projects -Projects may have participation by line staff -ED works with PDs on agency-wide decisions but reserves right to overrule	-Decisions made by staff consensus or super-majority vote -Constituent board has final authority; overlaps with staff where staff are also constitutents

AP=Advocates for the People; CCI=Center for Critical Information; CC=Community Choices; COP=Community Ownership Program; CV= Community Voice; DTD=Dare to Dream; FC=Faith in Change; GR=Growing Roots; NR=Neighborhood Reach; Rt=Respect; RMC=Residents Making Change; RFA=Rights for All; SOO=Sheltering Our Own; TT=Teaching Tools; UYC=Uniting Youth for Change; UW=Urban Watch

Key: □ = service;   ○ = organizing;   ◇ = advocacy;   ▢ = advocacy + organizing

Figure 4-1 Internal decision-making configurations

multi-level hierarchies to democratic membership collectives, but also include models in which executive directors share authority to varying degrees with middle-managers, leadership teams, or quasi-autonomous project directors (see figure 4–1). By necessity, the typology here is a simplification, with variation among structures in each category and no pure prototypes in reality. In addition, formal structures may not reflect the informal influence of individuals that derive from special expertise, moral authority, or long-time association with the organization. Nevertheless, we do find significant variation in the concentration of decision-making authority and some interesting configurations arising out of the SCOs' efforts to meet multiple and sometimes competing demands as elaborated below.

Multi-level hierarchy. In this category and the next, we include agencies in which authority is clearly concentrated in the executive director, as reflected by accounts of decision-making in these organizations. In multi-level hierarchies, the director delegates authority to middle managers or program directors who oversee front-line staff members. The structure of

Neighborhood Reach depicted in figure 4–2 is typical of such agencies: a board of directors sets policies and appoints the president/executive director, who works with a "senior director team" responsible for program service areas as well as such functions as marketing and development. Reporting to the directors are managers and site coordinators who in turn supervise groups of front-line staff members.

Final authority clearly resides with the executive directors in multi-level hierarchies, but executives often delegate program oversight responsibility to their mid-level managers, as explained by Madeleine Lee at SOO, another organization with a multi-level hierarchy. "Of course," she said, "ultimately, all decisions have to go through me to review, but I do like to have participation from the staff, and [for] the responsible supervisors to take the lead to brainstorm about . . . what is the best thing to do for their programs, for their services." Major decisions relating to funding or the agency's financial status would have to involve her, she said, because she was ultimately responsible. "But [in] day to day operation I would like to have the supervisors to be part of the decision-making. Because I think this is how you encourage people to take the initiative, to be more involved with their job."

Similarly, at Teaching Tools the formal multi-level hierarchy is modified by the director's practice of working closely with a formal leadership group that shares in the making of at least some agency-wide decisions. By way of example, Jay Stanley explained that when they were reviewing possible new program sites proposed by different members of the group, anyone on the team could have blocked a particular site. At the same time, though, the director noted that "far too much stuff still comes through me." In part this was due to his own "issues of control," but another factor was the relatively short time most of his senior staff had been with the organization.

Flat hierarchy. The organizations we have characterized as flat hierarchies differ from multi-level hierarchies in that there are no intermediate levels of authority between directors and front-line staff. In some cases, there are "team leaders," but they don't have the degree of delegated authority given to program directors in multi-level hierarchies. At the same time, the small size of most of these organizations and the regular direct contact between directors and all staff members means that decision-making processes are often highly participatory. In Uniting Youth for Change, for example, staff members are "required" to engage in regular and highly interactive meetings, in which program decisions are fleshed out. "I have authority and I use my authority to manage people, mostly to supervise technical assistants and so forth," explained UYC's director

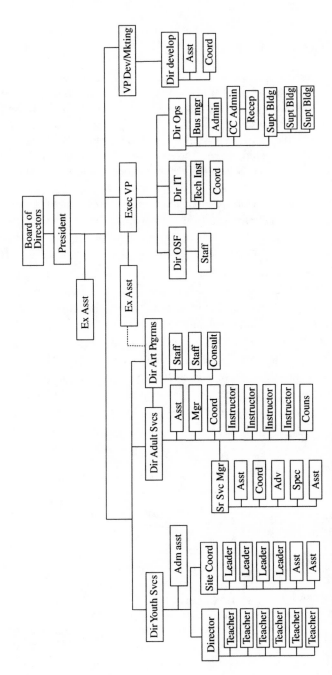

Figure 4-2 Neighborhood Reach organization chart

Jonathan Stein. But program content is determined more interactively, he noted, as in the case of a project recently undertaken.

> [T]he shape of the program . . . was done as a group with a lot of back and forth and different ideas and different questions. . . . And certainly . . . the leadership has power within that context . . . [to] set the agenda, and there's all kinds of subtle ways in which I have a lot of power. But there's a lot of input and the actual decision is one that's reached through a process of building consensus. . . . And in fact, people who wouldn't participate in that process, who wouldn't want to be heard, *that* would be a management issue.

Hub-and-spokes. In what we label a hub-and-spokes structure, the executive director plays a central role and retains final authority but staff members at all levels routinely participate in program and staffing decisions, often as part of teams. DTD's deputy administrator Maureen Lynch illustrated their procedures by explaining how the organization had dealt with the departure of their shelter-program coordinator (one of four program-area team coordinators—see figure 4–3 for an organization chart). Team members, the director, and her deputy interviewed several candidates for a replacement. When none of them seemed an appropriate choice, they discussed the idea of the team operating without a coordinator. "And we went through the responsibilities that each team member would have . . . and how to coordinate," said Maureen. "So we did that for a while . . . and I couldn't tell you how many times we went off and came back and met . . .

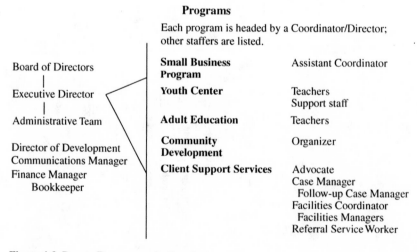

Programs

Each program is headed by a Coordinator/Director; other staffers are listed.

Board of Directors	**Small Business Program** — Assistant Coordinator
Executive Director	**Youth Center** — Teachers / Support staff
Administrative Team	**Adult Education** — Teachers
Director of Development	**Community Development** — Organizer
Communications Manager Finance Manager Bookkeeper	**Client Support Services** — Advocate / Case Manager / Follow-up Case Manager / Facilities Coordinator / Facilities Managers / Referral Service Worker

Figure 4-3 Dare to Dream organization chart

[but] it was a team decision that we needed a coordinator. It just—things slipped through the cracks. If there isn't somebody who sort of has ultimate authority—I hate using that because that sounds so—but, you know, to get that accountability." It was a participatory process involving all team members, but "in some ways, Dorothy weighs in on that decision in a different way because there are certain things that she . . . needs to be able to make sure happen."

Staff members in hub-and-spokes structures tend to have a strong expectation that decisions will be made collaboratively; at the same time, they can find the process difficult. Tonya Allen, a young staffer at Community Choices reported that interactions could be quite stressful when there were heartfelt disagreements, and director Myung Kim noted that his role included providing a sense of stability without being overly directive. He believed that the organization could achieve a balance of stability and full participation by holding itself accountable to principles and values flowing from the mission, rather than relying on a leader-driven command-and-control approach.[2]

Leadership circle. One organization, Growing Roots, has something similar to a hub-and-spokes structure but is headed by a small leadership circle that makes its decisions collectively (see figure 4–4). The existence of the "Directors' Circle" means that decision-making is not concentrated

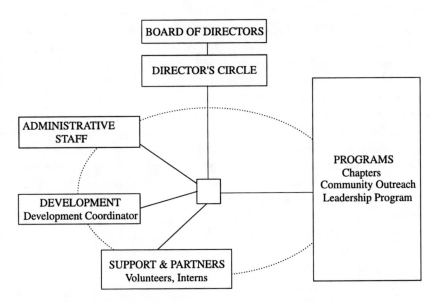

Figure 4-4 Growing Roots organization chart

in a single leader, and that leadership has some fluidity: individuals in this group can leave (and return) without the organization going through major upheaval. Speaking of the Circle, Monroe Harris explained,

> And it's a collective, so we're all equal within the circle, we all supervise, or oversee the entire operation of the organization collectively. We divide up responsibilities so that each of us has certain things that we're primarily responsible for and generally we try to align those responsibilities among lines of our strengths, our interests, but sometimes it's just about delegating things to different folks.

They choose to work in this way, he said, in part "to demonstrate this balance and equality, gender equality especially, but also because we recognize that the idea of the traditional hierarchy within a nonprofit organization, with any kind of organization, has its limitations. And [it] also doesn't model the kind of society that we want to see created." Sharing leadership responsibility allows them to draw on each other's strengths and "to accomplish a lot more by working collectively." It also enables them to continue their program activities—maintaining contact with those they serve—at the same time as they do the less satisfying but essential work of sustaining the organization. Finally, the flexibility of the leadership circle could keep the organization responsive to change and open to new leadership. One new member had been a chapter leader and community liaison before joining the Directors' Circle. "And that's a cycle we want to see happening," said Monroe. "The youth becoming part of the staff, becoming part of the Director's Circle and us eventually onto other things." This design could address "one of the problems we see in a lot of organizations, the old guard holding on very tightly to their power and to their roles and not really creating spaces . . . for new people to come in and develop leadership and take on responsibility."

A young program coordinator confirmed that the leadership group at Growing Roots strongly supports participation from all other staff members. She said that "everybody has a say," and explained that new program ideas could come from anyone, including young constituents as well as staffers. Not all decisions would be made in a participatory manner, but even when something came from the leadership collective, "they would bring it to the staff members and say we've been talking about this, that and the other and just wanted to let you all know or we've been talking about this, that and the other and we're going to take a vote on it."

Decentralized hierarchy. An alternative structural model, decentralized hierarchy, is exemplified in Rights for All, an umbrella organization composed of a set of independently funded, fully autonomous projects.[3] Here the project-specific decisions are made by project leaders (in conjunction with their staffs as they see fit) and overall organizational decisions are made by the executive director and project leaders. As in Teaching Tools, there is a formal leadership team comprised of project directors that works to arrive at consensus decisions, but final authority rests with the executive director and not all decisions are put to the group. Some give-and-take is required in particularly difficult decisions, such as a recent one concerning the criteria for bringing on new projects. Daniel Cohen wanted the organization to be "available to young, energetic people, if they can get money and we like them, they're a good person who will fit into our culture here." But some of the project directors thought RFA should only accept larger projects with more experienced directors. After talking over the problem at some length, they resolved it by deciding that new projects that did not fit the specified criteria could be brought in, but their leaders would occupy a lesser position as "project coordinators" rather than "directors." For Daniel, including smaller projects "was something I wanted, I wasn't going to let go, and so everybody compromised a bit. . . . And so that worked out . . . it's generally decisions by a very loose, informal consensus. . . . That was a decision that took a little more work."

Collective. The most democratic internal structures, collectives, are found in Community Voice, which has a full-staff collective that reports to a community-elected board (see figure 4-5), and Respect, which is a membership collective in which "staff" members (mostly unpaid or minimally paid) are also for the most part constituents, and decisions are made by the group.[4] CV began with a more traditional structure directed by two cofounders, but was restructured both in response to staff concerns and in recognition of the need to be more directly accountable to its constituents. According to Stephen Jencks, the staff is now "structured as a collective so everyone on staff has an equal say . . . and we decide things through some sort of modified super-majority voting system that tries to capture some of the benefits of consensus decision-making, but not capture some of the disadvantages." Working out the operational details of a democratic structure hasn't been easy, but it has been "interesting and challenging and important." Stephen described the process of trying to figure out an appropriate salary structure:

> When we set out we believed in equity, so it was a totally flat salary structure. And then, that doesn't make sense . . . if someone has a child or someone has been working ten years and someone just got out of college. And so we're try-

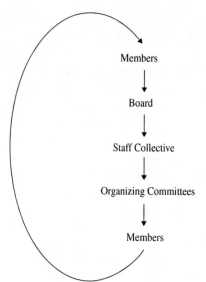

Figure 4-5 Community Voice organization chart

ing to figure out the structure that addresses all these different concerns, [and it] is enormously challenging, time consuming, but also really interesting and exciting. . . . And it happens in every facet of the work, whether it's the salary structure, the benefits plan, or the grievance procedure.

In Respect, members *are* the organization—there is no full-time paid staff—and they make all decisions by consensus. Marsha Madison reported that the effort was both difficult and essential. Their struggles to overcome internal divisions along with severe disadvantages "are the things that sort of worry me about the future," she said, but "they're also the things that inspire me, because when I look around . . . I don't see that many organizations that are really surviving by actually organizing the people themselves to be leaders in the group. I see a lot of people who aren't in the situation creating the organization and then involving the people who they want to affect . . . but then not really letting them have leadership roles."

Constituent Influence

A second important dimension of SCO decision-making is the degree to which organizations are open to influence by members of the community they serve. Although all of these agencies listen to their constituencies, and clients are active participants rather than passive recipients, the groups vary in the extent to which they regularize or formalize client influence. We identified five different approaches to constituent participation among our SCOs, ranging from a basic responsiveness to client needs (the most limited form of constituent participation) to having a constituent board set organizational direction (the most powerful form of constituent participation). The approaches are described below, and the characterization of specific organizations by both internal structure and form of constituent participation is shown in figure 4-6.

Awareness of client circumstances and needs through the work itself. In the most basic form of client involvement, SCOs learn about client needs and attitudes by paying careful attention to client experience and attitudes in the course of their work. Informed by their interaction with clients or constituents, SCOs change their products or services and sometimes design new ones. Teaching Tools modifies the delivery of its curriculum according to the needs of particular school sites; Sheltering Our Own creates new programs when public policy changes create new problems for the women in its shelters; the Center for Critical Information develops new re-

	Multi-level hierarchy	Flat hierarchy	Hub-and-spokes	Leadership circle	Decentralized hierarchy	Staff collective
Level 5: Agency agenda set by constituents		(FC)	(RMC)			(CV) (Rt)
Level 4: Constituents participate in program design			CC / DTD	GR		
Level 3: Constituents identify own priorities		(UYC)				
Level 2: Agency actively seeks constituent input	NR					
Level 1: Agency learns of constituent needs through the work itself	(COP) SOO* TT (UW)	(AP) (CCI)			(RFA)	

AP=Advocates for the People; CCI=Center for Critical Information; CC=Community Choices; COP=Community Ownership Program; CV= Community Voice; DTD=Dare to Dream; FC=Faith in Change; GR=Growing Roots; NR=Neighborhood Reach; Rt=Respect; RMC=Residents Making Change; RFA=Rights for All; SOO=Sheltering Our Own; TT=Teaching Tools; UYC=Uniting Youth for Change; UW=Urban Watch

Key: ▢ = service; ◯ = organizing; ◇ = advocacy; ▢ = advocacy + organizing
*SOO clients do participate in some site-specific agency decisions

Figure 4-6 Internal decision-making structures and forms of constituent participation

sources for its activist clients in response to a shift in the kind of assistance they request; Rights for All identifies legal strategies based on what it learns through outreach to marginalized groups.

Active solicitation of constituent input. Some SCOs go beyond the first level, and actively seek out constituent ideas and feedback—not only from direct clients but from other community members. Josh Klinger described Neighborhood Reach as "a participant–driven organization," in which "at the core of our mission is trying to keep our minds and hearts and mission wrapped around the pulse . . . of the community." They try to respond not only by modifying existing services but by offering new ones. They assess community needs (and assets) in three ways: by looking at published data on social and economic trends in the neighborhood, by obtaining anecdotal evidence in the course of their work, and by conducting formal and informal community forums and focus groups. "So we might hold a town forum in which we spend an afternoon or an evening prioritizing the community's interests, and then coming back and picking the ones that float to the top and maybe doing a little bit more investigation as to, what do people mean when they say affordable housing? What do they mean when they say programs for youth?"

Constituent identification of priorities for their own activity. In some SCOs, the basic program model is set by the organization but in implementation the clients work on their own agenda. For example, Uniting Youth for Change employs a particular approach to youth training and organizing that relies on the young people themselves to specify the priorities on which they will work. The clients don't shape UYC *per se*, but they do have significant influence over what they do in the program. Jonathan Stein explained that there are "multiple layers of decision-making and issue identification. . . . On the level of young people, there's a whole process in place by which they identify issues that they face, prioritize those issues, and then begin to plan to address those issues." Through an extended, interactive interview process, UYC screens young applicants for its organizing positions and in the process has them brainstorm issues and priorities. Once organizers are selected, "their job is to identify the issues in their community or school where they work, determine which are the most powerful issues that will have the biggest impact on . . . social change . . . and then develop a strategy to impact those identified issues." Because the process exposes young organizers to the ideas of many of their peers, their priority-setting and strategizing reflect not only their own ideas, but broader concerns in their communities.

Constituent participation in program design. In some organizations, clients not only engage in the design of services, but can substantially influence what services are offered. Dare To Dream, Growing Roots, and Community Choices have all shaped and/or offered programs on the basis of constituent participation. The idea for DTD's adult education program, for example, came from constituents who sought a program that would provide the kind of services (such as day care) and learning support that they needed. "So they asked us if we would develop an adult learning center," explained Dorothy Morrison. "And I wasn't really in favor of it because there were other adult learning centers in the area and I said I don't want to duplicate this. Well, you know, those women convinced the whole Board and the whole group that we should do that. And they were right and I was wrong. And so, we began an adult learning center . . . [and] we have 35 women who are in it now. And most of those women dropped out of school and had no hope. It's been extraordinary to see their development."

Agency agenda set by constituents. In the most powerful form of participation, constituents have a formal agenda-setting role in the organization. Four of our SCOs—Faith in Change, Community Voice, Residents Making Change, and Respect—operate on this basis, and a fifth, Community Choices, is moving toward this kind of structure. In many nonprofits, client interests are represented by one or two board positions, but in these organizations, the board or other superordinate decision-making body consists largely or entirely of constituents—and this process is seen as integral to the mission of the organization.

The details of decision-making systems vary among the agencies in this category. RMC has an elaborate board structure with several designated categories of membership, including representatives from small local businesses, social service and religious groups, different racial and ethnic groups in the resident community, and young people. Members are chosen through community-wide elections, and the board is involved not only in giving explicit direction to the staff but in implementing program activities.

The board of Community Voice consists of neighborhood members who are elected by the organization's full membership of about five hundred local residents. In addition to the core membership, the organization interacts with a larger number of people who are not members but come to weekly meetings or participate in various activities. Stephen Jencks explained that "we're trying to create staff accountability to the membership and the community" and that the board not only sets policy direction but has final authority for personnel decisions. Hiring is done by a committee of board, staff, and membership; firing is done by the staff collective but can be reversed by the board.

As noted, Community Choices is moving in the direction of constituent-based decision-making, with plans for a board consisting primarily of people elected by the membership that will set priorities and strategies for the organization's social change efforts. The staff will continue to be headed by a director but operations will be closely guided by constituent-driven decision-making.

Faith in Change's small staff is financially supported by local religious institutions and sees itself as answerable to the community in which those institutions are embedded. The staff relies on a concentric set of community leadership groups to make certain administrative decisions as well as to set direction for the agency and community's efforts. A "strategy team" of some thirty top leaders meets monthly, approves the budget, and has hiring and firing authority. It is in this group where the most "mature" discussion and deliberation about action priorities goes on. Beyond this level is an "action team" of about 150 to 200 people that meets less often, primarily when an issue merits much broader deliberation. And finally, there's an "assembly" of about 1,000 residents that meets relatively infrequently. In contrast to organizations like Residents Making Change and Community Voice, the community leadership teams behind Faith in Change are not elected but come from networks of activists in the religious organizations that support the organization.

Finally, Respect may be the least formally representative organization but the most embedded in its community. Decisions are made by a board comprised of active members, most of whom are low-income women (the organization's constituents). Although there has been talk of a more formal membership structure with board representation, to this point the participants have preferred to allocate their resources to direct action rather than to organization building.

Challenges and Complexities

The preceding discussion has outlined the basic features of two critical dimensions of decision-making structure. Before exploring the relationship between these dimensions and approaches to social change, we look at the extent to which the two dimensions correlate in our SCOs, and at some of the challenges and complexities of SCO structure, including the role of boards.

In figure 4-6 (page 93) we locate the organizations in terms of both internal structure and constituent participation. Although there is some relationship between hierarchical internal structures and diminished responsiveness to constituent influence, it is by no means perfectly linear. Among the organizations with the strongest form of constituent participation, we find internal structures ranging from flat hierarchies to collectives (though no multi-level hierarchies), suggesting that SCOs may be highly responsive to constituent communities without necessarily having democratic internal structures.

Furthermore, as noted, there are virtually no "pure" structural types here. The most traditional and hierarchical organizations include some, even regular, opportunities for wider staff and possibly client participation, and the most democratic organizations confront problems of informal influences in tension with their formal democratic procedures. In addition, organizational form can change over time in various directions. We have seen that Community Choices is moving toward a more constituent-driven structure, but it is also common for democratically structured organizations to evolve into more hierarchical forms as a result of growth, funding, and staff changes. One of the agencies in our multi-level hierarchy group in fact began with a highly participatory, committee-based structure—designed in part to fit with the organization's social justice mission—that was eventually replaced by a more hierarchical one, after staff divisions and discontent led to legal problems for the organization.

Formal and Informal Influences   In organizations with concentrated formal authority, the degree of inclusiveness is highly dependent on the style of the director and expectations of the staff. As a result, staff satisfaction may derive as much from informal norms as formal structure. In Advocates for the People, for example, director Antonio Mena characterized himself as a "benevolent despot" and said decision-making "very much revolves around me" though he made ongoing efforts to consult his staff, the board, and community members. "There's a lot of consultation that goes on," he said, "we try to make it as collective as possible. But it's imperfect. It's not something that—this is not a collective; this is not a democratic organization. . . . That's not the way it works." Coming from the director, this kind of characterization could mean anything from nearly solitary decision-making to genuine inclusiveness. In this case, Mena's staffer Maria Reyes confirmed what he said about extensive staff consultation, reporting a considerable sense of involvement and an appreciation for Mena's strong efforts at leadership development in others.

By contrast, at another formally hierarchical but informally participatory organization, a staff member had a somewhat different view of organizational decision-making than did the director. The director explained that although a hierarchical model had been required by the organization's exposure to political and legal attack, "It has never really run that way. Internally we operate with as much power sharing and sharing of decision making as we can manage. It's always been, in my opinion, a great strength of the organization that we do operate that way." The younger staff member agreed that the "generally collaborative" style of the organization worked "pretty well" but raised a concern that it was not always clear when staff members would be full participants and when they would not, which could lead to staff frustration. She also said there were times when it seemed "a little bit too collaborative in that sometimes everyone is forced to sit in on a meeting where it's really clear that a few people there, because of their jobs or whatever . . . really don't have any stake in what the decision is."

In the organizations we have characterized as "hub-and-spokes" models, there is a formal authority vested in the executive director and board, but such a strong culture of participation that not only would the director be unlikely to make most decisions alone, the same would be said of program or project directors. Myung Kim described Community Choices as a collaborative team in which most decisions are made by group consensus rather than individuals; staffer Tonya Allen agreed, saying that Myung was the final authority but that he wouldn't make a decision without consulting others.

In a "decentralized hierarchy" such as Rights for All, with its autonomous projects, one prominent issue concerns the degree to which the executive director will defer to project leaders in agency-wide decisions. But there are also special issues that arise out of RFA's decentralized form. As project director Tony Capra explained, "At the same time [as] I think that the project structure is a good one . . . I [also] think it's showing its weaknesses." One of these was the growth of projects beyond a "manageable group," coupled with the problem that the director of a relatively large project would have "the same vote as somebody with one staff member." He also felt strongly about having a say in how RFA was run and resisted a proposal that the projects be less involved in overall management. He believed that the larger projects should have a significant say in the functioning of the agency, both because of their overhead contribution and the need to represent the interests of project staff members.

Highly democratic organizations struggle with the practical challenges of collective decision-making—including balancing process against the need to get work done and the difficulty of sustaining equality when individuals come with widely varying capacities and endowments. Respondents at both Community Voice and Respect spoke powerfully about these issues. At Community Voice, though the staff had been structured as a collective that reported to a community-elected board, there were still ways in which people with special talents, training, or organizational history might have disproportionate influence. As Stephen Jencks explained, special credentials and skills would endow professionals with particular responsibilities even in an organization formally structured as a collective. Furthermore, in his own case, "just having been here the longest, having people know that . . . definitely this gives people some level of deference. . . . It's easier for me to feel comfortable bringing something up . . . than it might be for someone else. . . . Ideally it wouldn't be too much the case." His observation about his own informal authority was echoed in the way staffer Alex Montoya answered a question about how decisions were made. "Decisions? Well, we have a Board of Directors, number one. The Board of Directors is up here, then the co-directors, then the collective, the staff collective." In other words, the co-directors were in some sense *above* the staff collective.[5]

Both of the collective/board members interviewed at Respect also spoke of the challenge of power-sharing when individuals brought different attitudes, expectations, and resources. Marsha Madison said of a middle-class member, "[she] has never been poor. . . . She has the luxury of time. And so she's able to go to more meetings. She's retired. She doesn't have to work. She has a pension. She has a husband. Her children are raised and gone. A lot of the people in our group, their children are not raised and gone. So they don't have the same amount of time to commit." The result was that by default this member could exercise more influence. "And that's not necessarily in the best interest of a collective. And on the other hand, if she weren't to do it, who would do it?" Her older colleague Linda Jefferson said they "used to do it better" and "we're going to move back toward more collaboration, because we can see that we haven't been doing it as collaboratively as we would like." But she acknowledged the reality that "there's so many stresses in people's lives that somebody else will take something on and then they begin to feel ownership of that particular piece." The resulting tension was something that simply had to be confronted and worked out.

The Role of Boards　　In theory, boards of directors play a critical role in nonprofit organizations, and they are legally vested with final decision-making authority. In reality, the nature and extent of board involvement varies dramatically by organization and can vary over time within a single organization depending on whether the kinds of issues that almost inevitably involve boards (major policy decisions, director replacement) arise.

We heard about active boards in two very different types of agencies: those that were structured to be highly accountable to their communities, and those more traditional service organizations that relied on boards for extensive fund-raising as well as programmatic advice. In the first category are organizations such as Residents Making Change, Community Voice, Faith in Change, and Respect (where board and staff overlapped)—all of these groups are dedicated to constituent participation. Contrasting cases of high board engagement are Neighborhood Reach and Teaching Tools. The former is a long-established agency that has come to rely on its board for significant fund-raising activity in addition to setting program priorities and joining in agency-wide strategic planning. The latter is a newer agency in which board members support the director and other staff members by lending their expertise in fund-raising and other skills relevant to nonprofit management and agency work in general.

At the opposite end of the spectrum of board involvement were agencies in which a director had founded and/or been with the organization for a very long time and board activity was pro forma. As a staff member in one of these organizations said of the director, "He doesn't have to listen to the Board. He can do whatever he wants. . . . [H]e has created this agency." In another agency, the founding leader hand-selected the board for advisory purposes only. When a project director was asked about the board's role, he answered simply, "The board isn't involved." Decisions were made by the director in consultation with project directors.

In between these organizational models were organizations in which boards were engaged in major policy questions, the approval of budgets, the review of financial statements, and in taking responsibility for replacing directors when needed (sometimes with significant staff involvement). In a few cases, directors reported using boards to test ideas or seek guidance. One director clearly thought of board involvement as entailing significant trade-offs. As currently constituted, her board was "laid back." "As a result," she said, "I don't get much out of my board. . . . [T]hey really see my track record has been good, and there's no way any of them can question it." She did not think they saw the organization's potential in the way she did, and she appreciated not having them get in her way. "I don't want them to have any power over the organization," she said frankly. But at the same time, she recognized that "to create a big, large, powerful organization, I'll probably have to recruit a much more aggressive board of directors and keep them under control."

Influences and Implications

We turn now to possible factors shaping SCO structure, including variation in approaches to social change. The literature on organizations suggests a variety of influences on structure, including size, age, funding sources, type of work performed, environmental complexity and stability, and values or ideology.[6] In terms of the first three factors in this list—size, age, and funding—we find some support for expectations derived from the literature suggesting correlations between size, age, and government funding, on the one hand, and greater formalization and hierarchy, on the other. For example, our multi-level hierarchies are on average older and larger than our collectives, and they tend to rely more on government funding. In addition, those organizations with the strongest forms of constituent participation have on average smaller staffs and budgets, are somewhat younger, and tend to have staffs that are more racially and ethnically diverse. But there are also deviations from expectations. Within the most hierarchical organizations are some that are relatively young and small, and some that have no government funding. In addition, among the many variations on internal structure between the extremes, there are no obvious correlations between structure and agency size, age, or budget.

More important in our analysis are the substantive factors of the organization's work, environment, and values. The first two factors—work and environment—are relevant to structure in all organizations, but have different meanings for the structure of social change organizations, as explained below. Values (or ideology) are generally seen as highly relevant to nonprofits (and less so to structure in other organizations), but here we find a somewhat more complex relationship than is often described.

Social Change Work and Structure

A substantial literature suggests that organizations should be structured in ways that support the work they are trying to perform. It is argued that technical aspects of the work itself—including the interdependencies and complexities of tasks—should inform structural choices relating to the grouping of activities and the centralization of authority.[7] What we find in SCOs is that it is more the *aim* than the technique of work that matters, and the aspect of structure that varies in conjunction with work is the level of constituent participation, not the manner of grouping activities nor, for that matter, the internal decision-making structure.

In particular, we find a relationship between the organization's approach to the work of social change and the structure of constituent influence. As shown in figure 4-6, all of the organizations with the strongest form of constituent participation (Faith in Change, Residents Making Change, Community Voice, and Respect) operate with the same approach to social change, one that links individual transformation to collective action; furthermore, they represent three quarters of the SCOs that take this approach (one-quarter have weaker forms of constituent participation).[8] In addition, Community Choices, which is shifting to this social change approach, is adopting the strongest form of constituent participation.

Among organizations that work to support activists or activist groups (Urban Watch, Advocates for the People, Center for Critical Information, and Community Choices), all but Community Choices use the least powerful form of constituent participation, a choice that is consistent with their relative distance from individual client-constituents. These organizations also tend to have the most concentrated internal authority. Similarly, Rights for All—the sole representative of a legal advocacy approach that focuses on dismantling barriers to individual empowerment—also operates with limited constituent participation and is structured internally as a decentralized hierarchy.[9]

Organizations adopting a social change approach that emphasizes individual transformation and empowerment are the most diverse in terms of constituent participation. Three of the five (Teaching Tools, Sheltering Our Own, and Neighborhood Reach) operate relatively independently of constituent influence,[10] and the other two (Dare to Dream and Growing Roots) are more participatory. These SCOs also vary somewhat in internal structure, although none are completely democratic.

Given what our SCOs are aiming to accomplish, the variation in constituent participation—rather than internal decision-making structure—makes sense. Where a theory of change entails individual transformation coupled with collective action (primarily among the organizing groups), constituent capacity building requires participation in agenda-setting and social action; staff members must be responsive and accountable to constituent decisions but need not necessarily make their own operational decisions in a fully democratic manner.

In contrast, where a theory of change involves no individual transformation, either because the organization supports collective action through groups or its primary work is to dismantle formal barriers (the various types of advocacy groups), a very different kind of constituent involvement may be required. In these cases, regular contact with constituents and a sensitivity to their changing needs and circumstances is needed to inform agency programs, but it is not clear that anything would be gained through stronger participation by constituents in the organization itself.

Finally, where a theory of change does entail individual transformation but with the aim of personal self-determination more than collective action (primarily in the service agencies), the level of constituent participation may need to vary by the type of capacity the organization aims to build. Teaching Tools, for example, aims to change youth culture by building the capacity of individual young people to be peace-makers. Although TT must be open to understanding young people and how the training works for them, the type of skills TT seeks to build do not necessarily require significant client input. By contrast, Growing Roots and Dare To Dream are both engaged in developing self-advocacy, systemic consciousness and political awareness in their clients, along with concrete skills; this type of capacity building arguably requires deeper client engagement in program design (as exemplified in the adult learning program begun at DTD through client action).

Some of these organizations might be more effective with a different form of participation, but there is nonetheless a definite logic to the relationship between structure and work, and it does not argue for the same type of participatory structure in all social change organizations.

Environment and Legitimacy

The literature on organizations also suggests that environmental conditions—particularly complexity and stability—have important implications for organizational structure. Rule-driven, multi-layered bureaucracies can be quite effective in simple and stable environments, but complexity or rapidly changing circumstances call for different systems of coordination and decision-making. Following Mintzberg's theory,[11] dynamic environments require rapid decision-making, which means that authority is either highly centralized or "selectively decentralized" (flowing to the organizational position with appropriate expertise for a particular problem). Highly centralized structures with limited layers of authority (what Mintzberg calls "simple structures") work well in dynamic but simple environments, whereas more organic structures with distributed authority (what Mintzberg calls "adhocracies") are effective in dynamic and complex environments.

We do see some patterns that are consistent with these expectations. For example, our most bureaucratically structured organizations are those in arguably the most stable environments (they have established relationships with funders, and their services are tailored to a relatively unchanging niche). And our flat hierarchies (simple structures, with centralized authority but minimal layers) seem to face more dynamic environments. At first glance, our most democratically structured organizations seem to resemble what Mintzberg calls an "adhocracy," but he envisions this form as one in which authority is distributed by *technical expertise*. The democratic structures seen in our organizations differ in at least two important respects: they include *group* decision-making processes—as opposed to the "selective decentralization" of the adhocracy—and they are driven not so much by an organic responsiveness to environmental complexity as by the demands of mission and legitimacy—both external and internal.

Community Voice, for example, has a mission of promoting economic equality and participatory democracy by increasing constituents' self-determination through collective action. Fidelity to the mission requires that CV's decision-making structure be both democratic and faithful to the organization's principles of working for justice and opportunity. As Stephen Jencks explained, "I think that people should control all of the significant decision-making power and there should be total accountability." His own role should entail working with the board and members to create accountability mechanisms, "and also to make as few decisions as possible, to the extent that the organization is about people exercising their own decision making power." Staff member Alex Montoya echoed some of these arguments, saying, "The reason we became membership–led was because we felt that working collectively with the community . . . not only *for* the community but *with* the community, would bring more social change." He went on to assert that the development of the full-staff collective was a response to pressure from within the organization:

> Before they had a little collective group who would make decisions, like five people would just be on that group. But the other staff had a problem with that, because the majority of people who were on that group was white. . . . I had a problem with it, and other staff had a problem. Like why are you guys making decisions for us when we could make decisions, and don't we have one person of color [who could do this]? I know they're not making decisions that would mess us up, or hurt us in any way, but we still want our say in it. And they abolished that group and they made it a staff collective.

Alex's comment highlights the importance of legitimacy—in contrast to technical competence—in SCO decision-making: the objection to the previous structure was not with the quality of the decisions but with the lack of voice felt by those who were not involved. CV has moved to a collective, community-based decision-making structure, but as noted earlier, this effort sometimes comes up against the reality of unequally distributed special skills or technical expertise.

SCO structures must be responsive to the demands of their task environments (as noted by Mintzberg) as well as the legitimacy concerns of their institutional environments (as discussed by institutional theorists such DiMaggio and Powell).[12] Complicating the picture for SCOs is the possibility that different stakeholders will have varying expectations of appropriate organizational structure. Among constituents—including, sometimes, staff members—collective structure and community decision-making provide a certain kind of legitimacy. But a hierarchical structure with clear authority and accountability assigned to a single leader may be needed to legitimize an organization in the eyes of some funders and other important institutional actors.[13]

Adhering to Values

Closely related but not identical to the issue of legitimacy is the role of values or ideology in shaping organizational structure. Although ideology is not often identified in the general literature on organizational structure, it is highlighted in the literature on nonprofit structure, in which some argue that commitment to a particular set of values may motivate the choice of decision-making system, apart from considerations of effectiveness.[14] We find values to be relevant not only to the choice of a democratic structure but to refinements of that form. As Community Voice's Steven Jencks explained, membership decisions should be accountable to the organization's principles. Having just noted that CV existed to help residents exercise their own power, he went on to say:

> But I think that also, we have a political vision and it's important . . . to be clear about what the mission is, so that it's not just [that] you become a member of the organization and then you rule the organization. It's similar I guess to some sort of constitutional democracy where actually there are a set of values or precepts people accept by becoming members. . . . [For instance] if people are homophobic then they should probably not join, or they should know that the organization is not homophobic and doesn't support homophobia and is going to work against its manifestations.

Community Choices was another organization in which leaders spoke of the need to ensure consistency between decisions and principles. Its new membership-driven structure includes the expectation that members will provide a "signature of agreement" with the organization's mission and a commitment to action in one or more CC campaigns. The board/membership committee structure will reflect existing major activity areas that operationalize CC's mission. And although a majority of the board will be elected by the membership, there will also be appointed board positions for those who bring either technical expertise (and other forms of support), or who represent critical allies in CC's regional network. An arrangement in which voting members commit explicitly to the organization's mission is analogous to a "constitutional democracy." Structural features such as additional types of board representation and committees that parallel existing programs may also provide ballast against the possibility of a membership moving too far from core values.

Structuring Organizations for the Work of
Social Change

Research on structure in activist organizations often frames the problem as a choice of democratic versus hierarchical decision-making systems in which groups must trade off ideological purity (in democratic structure) against efficiency and effectiveness (in hierarchy). Polletta (2002) argues against this dichotomization, maintaining that participatory decision-making in the context of social movement groups can have *strategic value*, including "solidary, innovatory, and developmental benefits."[15] We also find a relationship between participation and the requirements of work involving social change, but we note that organizations adopt different theories of change—thus requiring different structures—and we distinguish between systems for constituent participation and the structure of internal decision-making. When the theory of change entails individual transformation linked to political action, a high degree of constituent participation is not only appropriate but necessary for success. But a staff can be directed by constituents without necessarily being structured democratically for internal or operational decision-making. Given the appropriate level of constituent involvement,[16] SCOs can be effective with internal democracy, hierarchy, or some mix, so long as those who staff the organization are attuned to the demands, strengths, and weaknesses of their form. Similarly, the model of board composition and involvement can and should vary according to the work of the organization. As discussed in the following sections, each form has its own challenges that must be recognized and managed if SCOs are to perform effectively.

Working with Democratic Staff Structures

Among our four SCOs with the strongest constituent involvement,[17] only two have staff collectives. A strong form of democratic organization may be important in the circumstances exemplified by these SCOs: when the staff members are from the constituency (as at Respect) and/or when one aspect of the organization's social change mission is to serve as a model of alternative approaches to work and organization (as in both Respect and Community Voice).[18] Linda Jefferson described how Respect's structure was central to mission:

> I mean some of us get more and more education as we're in it and we become *professionalized*. But none of us are really professionals, and we don't want to have that label or that stance. . . . This is about a mass movement; it's about coming from the heart and the core of the ordinary person. . . . And I think having it a collaborative helps to keep it that way so that somebody doesn't become so professional that they're talking about the people in the third person. See, we want to write in the first person: our families, our communities, our issues, our problems, our elected officials. . . . And I think that's what our readership really appreciates, feeling that it's really the voice of the people who are being spoken about in the paper.

She went on to acknowledge that the collective form could be difficult to sustain, as people "come with their different views of how an organization should be." Members disagreed about the need for organizational infrastructure: for some, "it's very difficult that we don't have an office" but others worried about being "co-opted . . . get[ting] so into building the organization that we forget to do the organizing we need to do." Building and maintaining an organization, particularly in poor people's movements, can drain resources, and in groups like Respect there is recognized value in the process of struggling to do things as a collective.

An alternative view is that a certain level of organizational infrastructure can free up resources for mission-related work, and that informal, consensus-based decision-making can itself be very costly. Steven Jencks of Community Voice inclined more toward this view, worrying that as their staff grew, "having a collective governance structure is also more challenging." He had heard from other leaders that he would probably want to grow, despite his current hesitation: "They've definitely said, 'Oh yeah, you say you don't want to grow and then you get to the position where you could do something really exciting and positive and excellent and then you end up wanting to do it."

Participants in democratic organizations must figure out ways to avoid drowning in arguments over minor issues, but even more importantly, must be able to work through serious internal divisions (which occur but are muted in hierarchies). A third challenge is to avoid hidden exercises of unequal power that can result in formally democratic groups being unintentionally subject to informal sources of authority. These threats to legitimacy and effectiveness can be mitigated through a combination of principles-based decision-making, a high level of awareness on the part of all participants, and attention to capacity building for all staff members. When the process of internal democracy works well, it is transformative for those who participate, demonstrating the kind of the change that SCOs seek in the society at large.

Working with Hierarchical Staff Structures

Among our SCOs with more hierarchical internal structures (i.e., all but the two collectives) we find varying forms of constituent participation. Here, for purposes of assessing the particular challenges of internal hierarchies, we assume the organization has adopted an appropriate level of constituent involvement for its social change work; if this is not the case, the challenges to effectiveness are of course greater than those associated with internal hierarchy alone.

The potential efficiencies of hierarchical organization and the legitimacy of this form in the eyes of some stakeholders are significant advantages for accomplishing certain kinds of tasks. But for SCOs especially, there can be major threats to effectiveness in hierarchy, primarily deriving from the loss of staff ideas, information, enthusiasm, and commitment when participation is severely limited or uneven. The result is problematic for any organization, but most subversive in SCOs, given that staff members are supposed to work for the development and empowerment of others. Furthermore, the failure to distribute responsibility inhibits the development of new leaders and can take a toll on those currently in positions of authority. All of the directors of the SCOs we studied take seriously the need to involve other staff members in decision-making, but reports from other staff members suggest that not all are as effective at this task as they could be. And there are several organizations in which so much power resides with the director that it is not at all clear how the agency would continue if he or she left.

A central challenge for hierarchical structures in SCOs is maintaining transparency and consistency. Among the groups we studied, lack of staff participation was less problematic than uneven participation—situations in which it wasn't clear when staff input would be consequential, or which staff members would be involved in any given decision. Also difficult were cases in which directors believed they were more open than their staffs perceived them to be. Clarity and consistency, along with an appreciative view of staff input, are essential in hierarchically structured SCOs. In addition, principles-based decision-making is a powerful counter-weight to the potential disadvantages of hierarchy, just as it is to the excesses of democracy. As one director explained, although he held final authority for decisions, he sought to avoid arbitrariness by listening to everyone and then making decisions that held the agency accountable to shared, articulated principles that were derived from the organization's mission.

Varying Roles for Boards

Finally, just as SCOs can function effectively with either democratic or hierarchical staff structures, so they may successfully involve their boards to different degrees and in different ways.[19] As in the case of nonprofits generally, some SCOs make very little use of their boards and do not necessarily suffer as a result (though it is hard to know if they would be *more* effective with more active boards); in others, the board plays a significant role and makes an important contribution to the organization. We note that the role and contribution of boards vary by the type of SCO and its social change work. In some of our service organizations, boards partner with top staff members in strategic planning and fund-raising, and provide a sounding board for the director; boards in these agencies tend to be made up primarily of individuals with professional expertise and high-level community positions. By contrast, in some organizing groups boards set the action agenda, and staff members support and facilitate what the board wants to do; in these cases, boards are made up primarily of constituents. In most cases, boards include a mix of member types ("professional" boards include some constituent representation, and constituent boards include some substantive experts or network contacts), but the balance varies depending on the role of the board and the orientation of the SCO.

Within our sample of organizations, the greatest weakness associated with board practices is the possibility that SCOs with very passive boards are missing an important source of information and guidance. For example, one organizing group has a long-term leader with a passive board; a project director in this agency observed,

> I also think organizations like this quite often have boards of directors that are completely inactive. "Oh, it's a not–for–profit, let's just name so–and–so to the board . . . he's a good friend of mine." . . . We need an active board that's out there in the community, that have their finger on the pulse of what's going on, to lead us and guide us and give us suggestions about what should be done and give us some vision. . . . Because sometimes when . . . we're all in an organization and the goal is the same, we kind of get tunnel vision. Sometimes, we need someone from the outside looking in . . . to provide us some vision and guidance.

It may not be surprising that this is an organization in which staff members also complain about ineffective internal management. In some ways, the problem of a director making inadequate use of the board parallels the problem of a director making insufficient room for staff participation. The desire to avoid interference from an ill-informed board or incompetent staff members is understandable but prompts the question of why the board or staff could not and should not be improved.

No structural form—whether it involves board, staff, or constituents—will ensure effectiveness in a social change organization, but structures do matter for SCOs. Choices about structure and the ongoing management of different arrangements should reflect the fit between mission and form, as well as an awareness of the trade-offs inherent in different configurations.

CHAPTER FIVE

RESOURCES

Spinning Straw into Bricks

You should never have the illusion that the Ford Foundation is giving you a grant because they really believe in real social change. . . . [Make that assumption] and you're going to be really surprised . . . because the minute you start really making some real changes, you're not going to have that money. In fact, you might even have that institution going against you. So you should never have that illusion that Philip Morris is giving you money, that they really want to, you know, change the politics. . . . Bullshit. They're giving you money because you could help them maybe with their legislative agenda, to keep filling people with smoke, with cigarettes, and those are the [real reasons]. But you think you'll take that money and hopefully do something good with it, understanding there's like real limits to it. So it's like a tricky business.

ANTONIO MENA
Advocates for the People

All organizations confront the problem of ensuring adequate resources to accomplish their goals. Profit-making enterprises do so primarily by providing products or services directly to paying customers. Many nonprofits do this as well, but they must also rely on donor support or third-party payments in order to provide "public goods" for which there is no market, or services for which clients are unable to pay the full cost. Rather than engaging in a direct exchange with consumers, nonprofits must appeal successfully to the charitable motives of private donors—including foundations and corporations, or to government for the support of publicly mandated activities through grants or contracts. Donor support may come in the form of cash grants, in-kind contributions of goods or services, or volunteer labor.

Among nonprofits generally, revenue strategies have been shifting. Although private contributions from individuals, corporations, and foundations have grown over time in absolute terms, the nonprofit sector has also grown, and with this growth has come increased competition for funding. The difficulty of obtaining adequate donations, along with the instability of this funding source and the constraints attached to it—including the fact that it is rarely available for capacity building and ongoing programs— have prompted many nonprofits to turn to other sources. The major alternative for most is "commercial activity," usually fees for services, charged either directly to the consumer or to a third party payer such as government.[1] In 1998, among all reporting "public charities" (those tax-deductible nonprofits filing informational tax returns) other than hospitals and higher education, fully *half* of all revenues were derived from fees, 22 percent from private contributions, and 14 percent from government grants. If funding (as opposed to "operating") organizations are excluded, the proportion derived from fees is even higher.[2]

For social change organizations, the challenge of obtaining adequate funding from contributions is particularly pronounced. As suggested by Antonio Mena and a number of other respondents, SCOs are not only dependent on private altruism but may be in the position of soliciting support for activity that is threatening to the interests of funders. Indeed, although precise figures on social change funding are hard to obtain, studies suggest that a relatively minuscule proportion of the dollars available for charitable purposes is given for this type of activity.[3] Among the reasons are the reluctance of funders to be "too political," pressure on funders to make up for reductions in government-funded service programs, a growing concern for demonstrable effectiveness and/or pressure for measurable results that are difficult or impossible to see in social change activities, and the under-representation of disadvantaged populations in foundation decision-making positions.[4]

With their particularly constrained access to donations, SCOs might be expected to turn along with other nonprofits to program-service revenues, but this is an option available only to some of them. The possibility of generating significant revenue from program-related fees is limited to those agencies that provide services that can be charged either to government or to users. Furthermore, even if revenues can be generated from services, there are significant associated costs, leaving a slim margin, if any, for social change work that requires additional effort. Non-programmatic forms of commercial activity, including establishing for-profit subsidiaries or entering into partnerships—such as cause-related marketing—with for-profit organizations, are theoretical options but unlikely to be strong sources of support for SCOs.[5]

Most SCOs, then, have limited options for financial support and must leverage other resources to accomplish their missions. In the following analysis we consider resources in the broadest sense, not limiting the discussion to funding or even to the other standard categories of in-kind donations and volunteer labor, but identifying any important asset or capacity (internal or external) that can be leveraged for desired outcomes.[6] We find that the particular ways in which our SCOs meet their resource challenge vary according to their social change orientations: each orientation is characterized by a set of constraints and opportunities that shapes the SCOs' resource strategies. The strategies differ in the primary types of resources used, the relationship between those sources of support and the impacts sought, and their strengths and vulnerabilities.

Table 5–1 summarizes primary funding sources, total revenues, fund balances, revenue-to-expense ratios, and critical non-monetary resources, by social change orientation, using our framework from chapter 1. Groups are divided first according to whether they aim at collective action or individual empowerment, and then within each of these divisions, according to the centrality of individual transformation in the approach to social change. As the table indicates, all SCOs rely to some degree on grants and contributions, but the mix of funding sources, along with other critical resources, varies by social change approach. In the following discussion we take up each of these approaches and describe the resource strategy associated with it, beginning first with the two collective action approaches.

Supporting Collective Action

A glance at table 5–1 reveals two important features of resource strategies of SCOs emphasizing collective action: on average they have much lower revenues, and with one exception, they receive far less government support than those emphasizing individual empowerment. Government funding is not only unavailable for much of the organizing and advocacy work of these groups, it is seen as potentially corrupting. For Steven Jencks of Community Voice, "there's . . . the fear that getting government money might limit our capacity to hold the government accountable," and Mark Lightner of Uniting Youth for Change hypothesized that "if we were bound by government, we wouldn't even be able to make the assumption that there might be a connection between the policy of the state and a rise in vi-

Table 5-1 Funding and other critical resources, by social change orientation

	Social Change Orientation			
	Collective Action		Individual Empowerment	
Organizations	Individual transformation	No individual transformation	Individual transformation	No individual transformation
	Providing space/skills for individuals to come together in collective action	Providing groups with information, analysis, and networks to motivate/inform action	Meeting basic needs and skill-building for individual empowerment	Dismantling formal barriers that prevent individuals from accessing needed services
Organizations	Rt, FC, RMC, CV, UYC, COP	CC, AP,[a] UW, CCI	DTD, SOO, TT, NR	RFA
Median fund balance[b]	$407,881	$461,284	$852,408	$1,583,587
Median annual revenues[b]	$657,167	$760,405	$1,443,894	$2,420,885
Median annual ratio of revenues to expenses[b]	1.02	1.17	1.08	1.15
Median percentage support from non-governmental grants/contributions[b]	90.5%	84.8%	57.5%	51.8%
Median percentage support from government grants[b]	0%	0%	25.8%	47.3%
Median percentage support from government service fees[b]	NB: Two agencies, RMA and COP, reported some, but only COP consistently reported substantial figures (an average of 63.6%)	NB: Only one agency, CC reported any, an average of less than 3%	0%	0%

Table 5-1—cont.

| | Social Change Orientation | | | |
| | Collective Action | | Individual Empowerment | |
	Individual transformation	*No individual transformation*	*Individual transformation*	*No individual transformation*
Other important sources of revenue	• membership dues	• non-governmental program service revenues		
Other critical resources	• constituents • publicly owned real property • public agency participation	• other activists/coalitions • board expertise and links to networks (not FR boards) • potential service revenues	• political and funding ties • collaborations • cross-class contact • volunteer labor	• pro-bono counsel from private firms • public-interest partners • skilled interns/fellows • community groups

[a]Figures for AP are not included because it has become part of a larger organization and data on its resources as a single unit are unavailable.
[b]Figures are taken from Form 990 for the period 1997–2002 where available (some returns are missing for some years).

olence in the schools; we couldn't even push people to think in [that] way."
The exception is a group whose organizing and collective action is embedded within a service model: Community Ownership Program brings together low-income residents to take ownership of abandoned or foreclosed
properties. Although the local government does not necessarily subscribe
to all of COP's aims, they do want a solution to the problem posed by these
properties, and COP can help with that, "so there's this coincidence of
goals." At the same time, the director realizes that they are far from secure
in this relationship: "One misstep and a vindictive commissioner and we
could be out of business tomorrow."

Within the group of SCOs oriented toward collective action, there are
different resource strategies according to whether the model of social
change emphasizes individual transformation (as an integral part of collective action) or focuses on providing support to activist groups or leaders
(with no emphasis on individual transformation). We take each of these up
in turn.

Strategy One: Leveraging the Power of the Community

For the six organizations that bring individuals together in collective action, some monetary support in addition to foundation grants and contributions is provided by community institutions such as churches and individual members themselves. One agency (COP) relies on government
contracts for its services, but as noted, this is an unusual model for organizing groups. Three other resources are central for these SCOs: constituents for all organizations; publicly owned land and buildings for some;
and for one organization, the assistance of those working in the public
agencies that are targeted for change. Each type of resource constitutes an
important element in the social change strategy of the organizations that
rely upon it.

Most indispensable for all SCOs that bring people together for collective action are the constituents themselves, because in this approach it is
they who do much of the work of social change.[7] As members of structurally disadvantaged communities, they represent their concerns before
the public, the media, and elected officials; they stand up to employers and
social service agencies that fail to live up to their obligations; they apply
political pressure in various forms, including large-scale demonstrations;
and they recruit, educate, and support other constituents. Consequently, the
first order of business for most of these SCOs is finding people in the com-

munity who are capable and committed, developing relationships with them and then bringing them into relationship with one another. "And then you have the critical mass of talent that's able to do all these things," explained director Pete Veratek of Faith in Change. "On a normal day we'll be in five different places but the organizer will only be in one of them. But the world doesn't understand. . . . They think everybody's paid." He chuckled as he added, "So we have a series of meetings with the mayor with twelve people. I'm the only paid person there."

Central to this model of social change work is the SCO's ability to leverage large numbers of constituents with small numbers of paid staff members who can support the constituents and help to coordinate their efforts. Limited victories can be won with even relatively small membership groups—especially when backed up with the threat of more aggressive action or litigation—but more systemic changes require larger numbers of active constituents. When asked about resource needs, directors at these SCOs often noted how much more they could accomplish with one or two more full-time organizers. Right now, Community Voice's impact is often limited. As Steven Jencks noted:

> I mean, a group of twenty-five workers went to a boss the other day and said, "You owe these four workers two thousand dollars." The boss became scared and paid them all. So that's an example of really direct power that's very limited direct power. If you wanted to change the minimum wage in the city or state, there would be no way to do it with the kind of numbers of people we have and the particular people that we're organizing.

Jencks would like to double CV's core membership—those with whom the organization works most intensively to develop their political and leadership skills. This group would then be "well positioned to bring other people into the organization and also into the larger movement for social justice." But it would take another staff position to do this.

> So we have lots of really incredible, experienced members. . . . [B]ut I think that in order to get that kind of really well–trained core, it would need to be at least one person's full–time job. And then [we would] . . . double our membership of people who have some of those skills, and definitely are engaged and care about the organization and the work. And then also widen our network of people who we could contact for events. And I think that that would give us a critical mass to be able to really create leverage, some kind of larger scale political changes in the city, which then I think because of its centrality in the United States would be really helpful in creating model legislation that could be used in other municipalities.

Three social change goals can be achieved directly out of the mobilization of constituents: an increasing sense of the community's own political power, a redistribution of resources in its favor, and changes in the behavior of public institutions to accommodate its needs. Although some of these SCOs use constituent power almost exclusively, others rely on one or two other types of non-monetary resources to bring about redistribution and institutional change. These resources are publicly owned property (or rights to acquire privately held property) and public agencies themselves.

Four of our SCOs have engaged in housing and community development efforts in which they have leveraged publicly owned property or rights to property in depressed areas in order to address the needs of local residents. In all cases, the mobilization of constituents is central to the process, whether the aim is the rehabilitation and acquisition of abandoned buildings for cooperative ownership, or the redevelopment of vacant land in accord with the social and economic priorities of the community. Whereas redevelopment generally benefits private developers and individuals, in these cases the active engagement of constituents—sometimes in sweat-equity efforts, sometimes in political advocacy with public officials—produces a different kind of outcome in which the benefits accrue to the community.[8]

Finally, public agencies themselves can become resources in the effort to achieve institutional reform, when used in combination with the ideas, energy, and legitimacy supplied by constituents. Uniting Youth for Change often locates its organizing efforts in public schools where it works not only with students but with others in the school setting to analyze problems and act on them. When it works in communities, it brings together actors from a variety of public and sometimes nonprofit institutions to work on problems together, such as improving relationships between police and local youth.

Pressure on the Poor   The particular challenges of the resource strategy described here have to do primarily with its reliance on constituents—who themselves have been disadvantaged—and the need to sustain the active participation of large numbers of people.[9] In addition, unless the SCO is exceptionally successful with foundations, its funding base will be quite limited and unstable. These problems are felt most acutely in Respect, where even the "staff" work is done by constituents, who are predominantly low-income women. Their work is at the mercy of other demands on them, and under new welfare-to-work requirements, they have found that members have less time available for volunteer advocacy. At the same time, training and development needs are constant. A similar problem was noted by one of the constituent leaders at Faith in Change, when he observed that local churches that supported FC would find themselves in a bind as the economy went into recession. "There's more pressure being put on [us] . . . because people are out of work, welfare is at an end where people are going to be going to the church for food. They're knocking on the church's doors with all these problems. So the church has to be careful not to fall into the trap of just doing the work that the government used to do."

Strategy Two: Working through Other Groups

A different resource strategy is employed by SCOs that facilitate collective action by providing information, analysis, and other support to activist individuals and groups. Whereas SCOs that organize individuals look to those constituents for support—including deriving supplemental income from memberships—those that work through other activist groups use their partnerships as an important asset. Activist "clients" may provide supplemental income in the form of program revenues if they pay for information and analysis or other services, they may collaborate with the SCO to produce social change tools, or they may do the direct work of advocacy, using information supplied by the SCO. In any case, the ultimate social change goals of resource redistribution or institutional reform are accomplished indirectly.

Urban Watch, for example, accomplishes its social change mission by providing critical information to activists and non-profit social service providers—a group of people that is, according to Rachel Beck, "largely under-resourced . . . completely strapped, [and] that . . . needs to be using its time as efficiently as possible." With limited research capacity, an activist group might require several days to track down an important piece of political or policy information, but through UW's website, the data can be obtained with "maybe a couple of computer clicks . . . in five, ten minutes." The impact can be "enormous," Rachel said. "Now, the people on the ground are designing their own information." UW derives some financial support from its users in the form of paid subscriptions for its newsletter, but it is also able to draw on revenues for employment advertising in the local nonprofit sector; program service revenues provide as much as 36 percent of its financial support, an unusual and enviable position for an SCO.

Relying to this degree on program service revenues is uncommon, but depending on other activists to get the work done is not. When Antonio Mena was asked about the kinds of resources his organization needed, he responded that "an important resource is just the constituency. . . . [They serve] as the recipients of the kind of information we generate and also as a kind of resource in providing us with information and feedback. . . . I could pile up hundreds of reports, very nicely done with very nice recommendations that nobody's listened to. . . . But unless you can develop a constituency and a kind of political base that'll make these policy-makers listen, it's all for nothing."[10] On an issue like voting rights, Advocates for the People would seek out possible partners, bring them together into an issue network, and then provide them with the technical assistance needed to accomplish the work.

Similarly, Ellen Mayhew of the Center for Critical Information said her organization works toward social change by providing support "for the activists who are working on the front lines. . . . We supply them with the information and analysis that they need to do their work." CCI relies heavily on collaborations in its work, exchanging expertise for the knowledge and organizing effort of its partners. In a joint project with a local resource center serving women of color, CCI will provide data-gathering and analysis on the issue of marriage-promotion among welfare recipients. In return, the women's center will help CCI produce popular education materials. "They would be in some ways teaching us how to do something that we're committed to learning how to do, and we would be providing them with the materials that come out of it for them to use in their work."

As already noted, Community Choices is shifting in its social change orientation, and its resource strategy is changing as well from one that has relied heavily on organizational partnerships and to some degree on program service revenues, to one in which it will leverage a large resident membership in organizing campaigns—though it hopes to retain its ties to other groups and to continue collaborative work on behalf of common constituencies.

For the partnership-based resource strategy to be successful, SCOs must have both networks that connect them to other groups, and the specialized knowledge and expertise that make them attractive partners. They acquire these assets by hiring appropriate staff members, but also through board composition. In contrast to the fund-raising boards of service agencies, these boards tend to reflect substantive expertise and linkages to potential partners.

A Narrow Niche　　In theory, this group of SCOs should be able to generate program service revenues from the services provided to activist clients, but in practice their ability to do this is limited. The most successful is Urban Watch, which survives in part by selling subscriptions and employment advertising to larger, more mainstream nonprofit customers. Other SCOs do some of this—and perhaps could do more—but they are constrained by the limited resources of the groups they serve. The result is that these particular SCOs tend to be heavily reliant on a limited pool of foundations and individual contributors willing to support political work and not necessarily expecting a direct connection to disadvantaged constituencies. Sufficient support for capacity building on top of immediate program activities is difficult to come by, and yet the work requires highly skilled and knowledgeable staff members such as researchers, journalists, and lawyers. Overall, this resource strategy may be the most constrained, and these groups have among the smallest budgets of all our SCOs (see table 5-1).

Supporting Individual Empowerment

In contrast to the SCOs that emphasize collective action, those working for change through individual empowerment rely significantly on government support, along with private grants and contributions, and these SCOs tend to have much larger budgets. Although they intend to have some systemic impact, their emphasis on individual empowerment rather than collective political action positions them to draw on government support in a way other SCOs may not be able—or wish—to do. The problem, of course, is that such support is provided explicitly for *services*; unless the social change work is embedded within the service itself, it must be conducted as an additional effort by the organization.

The specific ways in which these SCOs access government support, and the other critical resources on which they draw, vary according to whether the organization's social change approach emphasizes individual transformation (through service provision and capacity building) or the dismantling of legal barriers (with no emphasis on individual transformation), as we explain below.

Strategy Three: Selling Service, Providing Empowerment

SCOs in this group rely heavily on financial resources, combining government grants for the provision of essential services—such as shelter to victims of domestic violence or homelessness—with foundation or individual support for work that promises to go beyond strict service provision—for example, skill building to help families not only move out of poverty, but become advocates for themselves and their community. Social change work is often accomplished on top of the funded services, through political capacity building with clients in the course of service provision or through the direct advocacy work of SCO leaders and staff members. Two non-monetary resources are especially critical in this strategy: linkages to funders and policy-makers, and collaborative relationships with other agencies. In addition, although all SCOs make use of volunteers or interns, unpaid or subsidized labor is particularly prominent in agencies providing direct services.[11] Finally, there is at least the potential for cross-class contact and subsidization in most of these groups, and some organizations make use of this as part of their strategy for change.

Varying types of networks are a relevant resource for all SCOs, but for this group, political and fund-raising connections are essential assets. Boards of directors often include very prominent and sometimes wealthy individuals, and executive directors tend to have strong personal networks; indeed, it is striking to hear these leaders describe the extent to which their organizations depend on personal ties. In explaining her work at Dare to Dream, director Dorothy Morrison noted, "I've been here a long time so I know a lot of people and I know a lot of resources, so I can make connections and make things happen." When others would compliment her on what she'd been able to do, she would say, "look at the people that I'm surrounded by." Her ties extend not only to funders but to policy-makers: when a group of advocates for the homeless sought a meeting with a state legislator to lobby for eligibility-requirement changes, she was able to arrange it—and they succeeded in having the law changed. Similarly, the director of Teaching Tools has developed relationships with elected officials as well as high-profile entertainers who support TT's work in a variety of ways. His board also includes a number of individuals with strong networks in relevant areas.

These SCOs also rely heavily on institutional partnerships to accomplish their work, drawing on others to provide specialized services needed by their constituents or community, joining forces with similar agencies to increase the effectiveness of their political advocacy, or locating their services within other institutions to leverage resources or even to change the larger institution itself. The director of Sheltering Our Own described a number of projects in which her staff recognized "we cannot do it alone" and reached out to bring in partners with complementary capacities, such as a conference on domestic violence that required a partnership with a local medical school. Similarly, Dare to Dream works constantly in collaboration with other agencies to meet the needs of its constituents and in coalition with similar providers for advocacy purposes (as in the effort to increase housing assistance).

Teaching Tools and Growing Roots both partner with public schools to bring their programs to young people, and in the course of the process hope to have an impact on the schools themselves. But TT has taken collaboration even farther, developing a growth model that relies on partnerships with other agencies. Rather than opening a separate program office in another city, they provide their training through an existing agency that has good resources, that is already running programs in the local schools, and that is interested in TT's curriculum. Speaking of this partnership, director Jay Stanley said, "We cannot succeed without them."

A third critical resource, common to almost all our SCOs but especially prominent here, is the labor of volunteers or interns, including those from national service programs such as VISTA or AmeriCorps. Neighborhood Reach, for example, uses over two hundred volunteer tutors in its adult literacy program. For Teaching Tools, volunteers allow it to deliver its program on a much larger scale than it could do with only paid staff members. Volunteers provide a variety of services for Dare to Dream, including serving as tutors and mentors to clients in adult education and transition to work programs. Sheltering Our Own would not be able to provide the services it does to multiple linguistic and ethnic groups without volunteer translators, hotline operators, and numerous other unpaid workers.

Growing Roots depends on volunteers to provide a variety of support services to its young clients, but also to strengthen the organization's own ties to its community. For organizations like Growing Roots and Neighborhood Reach that serve particular geographic communities, the pattern of former clients returning as volunteers—or even enacting both roles simultaneously—is especially meaningful. Neighborhood Reach at one point decided to move away from the term "clients" to the idea of "participants" in recognition of the fact that people's roles could be multiple and changing. The former director gave an example of an older woman who had learned computer skills at NR, then become a teacher for others. "She really became expert and today she's a volunteer. She runs one of the open access classes. So there she is; she comes for her hot lunch; she participates in the activities for the seniors; but she has this other role where . . . we rely on her to do some other things."

Finally, the nature of the work done by these groups means that sometimes they are in a position to facilitate cross-class contact that can promote social change, or to use the resources of better-off constituents to support service to those less advantaged. This strategy is not well developed in any of these agencies, but is probably more prominent in Neighborhood Reach than most, in part because NR's early history included substantial volunteer work and support by wealthier citizens. In reflecting on this history, the former director noted that the move toward more government funding and professionalized services in the 1960s and 1970s, although positive in some ways, had reduced cross-class contact and as a result had eliminated an opportunity for political education of the wealthy. Today there is an effort at the agency to revive some of that contact in ways that can promote greater understanding as well as extending services. Providing programs on a sliding fee scale is one way, but more complex efforts are also possible. In one new initiative, NR is working with a local parent group to support the improvement of a neighborhood school that currently serves mostly lower-income families of color, but where middle-class residents would send their children if the school could be made stronger. If successful, the effort could produce long-term benefits for the community as a whole.

Staying the Course for Change　The direct service work of these SCOs requires substantial resources, and even with support from volunteers and partners, these organizations rely heavily on government and foundation funding. As noted earlier, this support is primarily available for services rather than social change work, so that SCOs in this category are faced with a difficult balancing act. They must continue to provide the services that are attractive to funders—and needed by clients—but simultaneously attend to the larger goal of systemic change. The risk is that funders' preferences or requirements will constrain program activities so much that social change work is inhibited or crowded out. Government funding is especially subject to conditions that can inhibit the work or limit the kinds of constituents served. Furthermore, when funding is plentiful only for a particular type of service, organizations may be encouraged to stray from the focus of their missions, to duplicate services and even to engage in destructive competition with other groups. Some SCO leaders in this category expressed great frustration over the challenges of sustaining support by "sell[ing] your work to people who don't get it," and they yearn for more financial independence, but there are no obvious solutions to the problem.[12]

Strategy Four: Aikido—Using the State against Itself

Only one of our SCOs represents the fourth approach to social change, which entails attacking the barriers that prevent marginalized groups from exercising their legal rights, including accessing mandated services and support. Rights for All is home to a variety of legal advocacy projects that rely on foundation and government funding, but the mix of private and public support varies among projects, which are financially independent of one another. The independence of programs allows for different funding strategies within the same organization: less politically sensitive projects are able to access government grants, while more radical projects seek support from the most progressive foundations and individuals. Furthermore, this structural arrangement spreads the agency's financial risk; if external funding priorities change, projects may end (or in some cases, where funding increases greatly, they may spin off), but the agency as a whole remains. RFA's work also draws on several significant non-monetary resources, including pro bono counsel from local law firms, partnerships with other legal advocacy groups, interns from law school clinics, relationships with community organizations where outreach is conducted, and of course the law itself. Finally, as with other SCOs that require significant financial support, RFA has strong networks through its board members.

In its effort to use the law as an instrument of social change, RFA targets precedent-setting and class-action cases on behalf of significantly disadvantaged groups such as homeless people, immigrant workers, and mentally ill prisoners. In this work it regularly depends on the services of pro bono counsel from private firms, and also on collaborations with other legal advocacy groups. RFA employs its own staff attorneys, but they could not undertake the number and kind of cases they do without the support of private firms, some of which have committed to providing substantial amounts of pro bono services, out of a mix of altruism and concern for community relations.[13] In addition, RFA attorneys partner in some cases with attorneys from other public-interest advocacy groups, effectively spreading the cost of the work.

A related resource available to an agency like RFA is relatively skilled volunteer labor. Because of the cutting-edge nature of its work, RFA regularly attracts large numbers of interns and fellows from a variety of service programs. Volunteers are costly to manage but their value increases with the length of their stay, and some of RFA's fellows are with the organization as long as two years—enough time for them to constitute an important asset.

Finally, RFA's particular approach to legal advocacy depends on knowledge provided by potential clients about the kinds of oppressive practices they confront or the service failures they experience. To target its efforts most effectively, RFA gathers information from clients in the places they frequent, rather than waiting for individuals to come to the agency. Outreach is conducted in a variety of community service locations, including soup kitchens, drug treatment centers, and programs serving at-risk youth; as a result, collaborative relationships with these kinds of agencies constitute another essential resource in RFA's strategy. These linkages also bolster support in the political and funding communities, as they distinguish RFA's approach from other legal services, and testify both to RFA's commitment to constituents and its community support. And as noted above, the strong networks forged by the agency's board, director, and project leaders are an additional critical asset when it seeks external support.

Strengths and Vulnerabilities   Like the service agencies discussed above, RFA's strategy requires significant levels of financial support, even as it manages to leverage pro bono resources and partnerships with other groups. In the rights-based approach to social change, however, the service delivery itself can have immediate structural impact—when the legal work is precedent-setting or involves a class rather than an individual. For SCOs in this category, then, there is less tension between providing funded services and meeting a social change mission.[14] Nevertheless, an organization like RFA is vulnerable to shifts in external funders' priorities, as well as to changes in the availability of pro bono services. The sustainability of the organization is ensured to some degree by the existence of financially autonomous projects, a structure that diversifies financial risk and provides flexibility. The downside is that a project that provides important work but loses its funding will not be maintained by the agency, and in the extreme the agency would have its activities driven entirely by the preferences of outside funders.

The Challenges of Scaling and Sustaining
Efforts for Change

These SCOs have all managed to devise resource strategies that allow them to continue engaging in social change work. At the same time, all strategies have their limitations in terms of the breadth and depth of change that can be supported.

Groups that work through collective action, whether by bringing individuals together or by supporting other groups/activists, have very limited access to funds and must rely heavily on the mobilization of constituents in the first case or the work of other groups in the second case in order to achieve their goals. Relying on constituents for a major share of the work—and in some cases, for funding as well—is consistent with the philosophical orientation of the organizing groups, and with their goal of building power among those who have been excluded from decision-making systems. But limited access to and instability of funding may prohibit these groups from achieving the size needed for significant impact. Steven Jencks of Community Voice felt this constraint keenly, and observed that it was common in groups that work through constituent mobilization. "I think it's not an accident," he said, "that . . . organizations . . . get to the 'We can mobilize five hundred people' level [and] don't get much bigger, because the funding [of] groups like ours is completely not strategic." Funders provide support for three years and then stop, he explained, presumably with the idea of distributing funds to more groups. He saw this as a self-defeating approach. "We're not trying to let every flower bloom," he argued. "We're trying to win stuff and we're really on the defensive, and we're getting our asses kicked. So I would think that [strategy] doesn't make sense. Organizing folks is not going to be self-sustaining; unless you put in a huge front-end investment, you get like forty organizers, you create . . . a lot of organizational infrastructure, and then you could maybe make it self-sustaining."

He maintained that funders will provide support to an organization until its budget reaches five hundred thousand or a million dollars; then they stop. In effect, this means "we [the funders] let you cross the threshold of barely relevant and then we stop funding you." At that point the group either stops growing or becomes a service organization in order to attract more support. In either case, those who want to work on social change through constituent mobilization become frustrated and leave the field.

On the issue of scale, it should be noted that there is a range of organizational size and impact among the SCOs in this group, with Community Voice in the middle. One agency that is somewhat more successful in mobilizing larger numbers of constituents—albeit still falling short of the impact Stephen Jencks envisions—is Faith in Change. Two characteristics of FC are relevant to its somewhat greater success: it relies in significant measure on community institutions such as churches for funding and also for the identification of resident leaders. And it has access to the networks of a national organizing group. At the same time, though, there are community members not reached by FC's approach, who may be picked up by an organizing model more like that of Community Voice.

The other group of SCOs that works through collective action, those that support the activism of others, also has a problem of limited access to funds. Their work appeals to a narrow niche in the funding community, those willing to support progressive, politically oriented projects that do not directly serve disadvantaged communities. These SCOs must solicit funds to support the analytic and research products they provide to other activist groups, who are themselves unable to purchase such products at their full cost. The potential for impact among these SCOs is greatest when their reporting and analysis motivate others and inform their actions for change, necessitating strong linkages to client-activists and a high level of responsiveness to their needs in terms of both substance and timeliness. But funding is granted primarily for research and dissemination, not linkages and responsiveness; these must come on top of the basic production effort. Furthermore, the long funding cycles of many foundations makes it especially difficult for these organizations to address rapidly changing political conditions and information needs. As much as any of our SCOs, this group requires significant infrastructure and operating support if it is to have maximum impact, but such support is virtually impossible to come by.

Organizations that work toward individual empowerment through blending service provision with political capacity building would seem to be in an enviable position in terms of access to resources, as those with the largest total revenues and access to the widest assortment of funding sources. However, the services they must provide are generally quite costly, and these groups tend to operate with relatively slim margins. In fact, their average ratio of yearly revenues to expenses for the six-year period we examined (1997–2002) is lower than the figure for organizations providing information and analysis to other groups (see table 5-1). In terms of social change impact, the challenge for those working through individual-level service is to ensure that service provision does not eclipse social change work. When the social change work is separate from service, for example when a director works with other organizations to lobby for a new state policy, this work must somehow be supported on top of work that is directed at service provision. An alternative is to embed political capacity building and individual empowerment work within the service model; most of our SCOs try to do this, but with varying levels of effectiveness. In either case, the challenge is to ensure that the social change work for which the organization is not being funded directly nevertheless gets done. This challenge is especially difficult to meet in a fiscal environment in which program funding is under constant downward pressure, as has been the case of late. Both government and foundation budgets have been constrained at the same time as service needs have risen, creating strong pressure for service providers to reduce costs and to pare down service activities to the most streamlined level.

The relatively larger size of these organizations may be an advantage, however, for it makes possible the building up of infrastructure that can be used to support unfunded activities. We note that the median fund balance of the organizations in this category is higher than that associated with either of the two preceding groups, but this reflects primarily the financial status of the largest and by far the oldest service agency, Neighborhood Reach.

In the fourth, rights-based, social change approach we have only one organization, and so the observations we make about the resource strategy in this approach must be particularly tentative. RFA is undoubtedly similar in many ways to other groups that might be placed in the same social change category—particularly other legal advocacy groups—but it has some important differences that are especially relevant to resource strategy. Of all the organizations in this study, RFA is the one with the strongest financial resources, reflected both in its relatively high revenue-to-expense ratios and sizable fund balances over time. On the issue of resources, RFA's project-based strategy is particularly important and may not be representative of other SCOs that would fall into this general category. Its projects are all independently funded and therefore able to appeal to organizations that may have widely different agendas, including some that favor individual service and others that are interested in larger change. More importantly, although the organization may help some project directors to locate funding and prepare proposals, RFA will not take on projects that are unable to support themselves (and a portion of the general expenses). This is an essentially market-based strategy, weeding out projects on the basis of the capacity of their directors to bring in support. In terms of social change impact, the risk of course is that potentially useful work that cannot be supported externally will not be undertaken. Furthermore, if a project becomes large enough, it may spin off into a separate organization; in such cases, the project's revenues and specific assets go with it. Finally, we should note an important limitation of this approach to social change that is not peculiar to RFA, but shared by all legal advocacy SCOs, which is that it is circumscribed by the law. Changes beyond the reach of legal action cannot be effectively addressed through a rights-based approach.

Implications

In summary, the resource strategies associated with particular social change approaches have complementary strengths and weaknesses. Those oriented toward collective action tend to have very limited budgets and small sizes, but the funds they are able to solicit directly support their social change work. By contrast, funding for the agencies that are focused on individual empowerment is linked to service activities. In the case of a legal advocacy group, the service itself—legal representation—can be employed as a social change tactic when the cases are precedent-setting and/or class-action lawsuits. In some ways, the service groups that work on change through individual transformation and empowerment are in the most challenging position in terms of the relationship between their sources of support and their social change work.

These agencies can engage in some social change work as a separate activity—and most do—but their greatest potential in terms of leveraging resources for change lies in developing service models in which social change work is embedded. Examples are Dare to Dream's inclusion of leadership and advocacy training in a skill-development course serving poor women, or Growing Roots's emphasis on awareness and activism in its youth development program. This kind of work requires a special commitment and creativity; funders may resist it, and service-oriented nonprofits may fear a loss of favorable tax status if they engage in arguably "political" activities.[15] Change-oriented services also depend on the active engagement of constituents. For some clients, participation will be an opportunity to give voice to their own analysis and for others, it will be an opportunity to build awareness, but in either case, their engagement will be critical in the integration of transformative social change work into service provision. Finally, funders must recognize the need to support capacity for work that goes beyond meeting urgent needs or remediating individual disadvantage—whether that means funding SCOs that do direct social change work through collective action or supporting the larger social change efforts of those working through service provision.

At this stage, although all of these SCOs accomplish a great deal with what they have, even the most resource-rich groups are not in a position to effect change on the scale and depth they envision. To significantly in-

crease their impact, they must accomplish one or more of the following efforts: obtain large infusions of resources to support the growth of their individual organizations; draw even more energy and support from constituents; and/or link together with other SCOs in a more intentional way.
Given current fiscal realities and increasing strain on the public and nonprofit infrastructure, the first option is an unlikely solution for most SCOs.
The second option may be feasible up to a point—for some organizations
and particular constituent groups—but many constituencies are themselves
increasingly resource-constrained. The third option, then, merits closer
consideration. In the following chapter we assess our SCOs' actual experience with collaboration, and in the conclusion we consider the possibilities
for something more.

CHAPTER SIX

COLLABORATION

Mission Driven Partnerships

Well, collaboration for us is a natural . . . even more so [now] with our explicit . . . systemic change focus. Right? Because to build power at the scale necessary, you can't do it alone. And we would never . . . aspire to be an organization that could organize directly over a whole region. It's just not doable. So we know we need allies . . . and I think that we've been pretty successful at collaborating and coalition building . . . in part because we—in the beginning anyway—were not seen as an organization with our own turf.

MYUNG KIM
Community Choices

All organizations must work in partnerships when they want to accomplish something they cannot do alone, and SCOs are no different. Indeed, with their limited resources and large missions, they are particularly likely to require partners, and the stronger their capacity for collaborative work, the greater the potential for systemic impact. Ultimately, significant social change requires movement building—an issue we take up in the final chapter; however, an intermediate step is collaborative effort. In exploring the particular forms, benefits, and challenges of collaboration in the experience of our SCOs, we hope to develop insights relevant to the task of building a movement.

In keeping with the general literature on inter-organizational collaboration, we use the term to refer to the process by which two or more groups work together to accomplish something that cannot be done—or not done as effectively—by a single group.[1] Some definitions also specify that the activity is not governed by either contract or hierarchical authority,[2] but we do not exclude circumstances in which organizations are involved with others in formal relationships. Most writers also note that different kinds of partnerships entail different levels of complexity and commitment, but there is no consensus on terminology. Some place "collaboration" on the more advanced end of a scale that includes "cooperation" and "coordination," but others use the terms interchangeably; additionally, some distinguish collaboration from "coalition." We discuss different forms of collaboration but do not adopt a strict typology.

Collaboration is a popular idea among funders and academics—those that do not necessarily have to practice what they preach—but among practitioners the term often evokes discomfort, sometimes even scorn. One popular simile holds that "collaboration is like teenage sex: everyone talks about it, everyone thinks everybody else is doing it, and the few that *are* doing it, aren't doing it very well." Another oft-quoted phrase defines collaboration as "an unnatural act between non-consenting adults."[3] More sanguine comparisons emphasize the benefits but do not deny the challenges: collaboration is like marriage, jazz, or a journey without a map.[4]

Collaboration is hard in the way human relationships can be hard, and often what makes it work are factors not unlike those that support interpersonal cooperation. The literature identifies a long list of factors that influence the success of collaboration, including shared purpose and potential for mutual gain, resources, commitment, communication, clarity, trust, respect, leadership, equity among partners, shared conceptual frames, and compatibility of organizational cultures. We find that many of these influences are relevant to collaborative practices among our SCOs without regard to their particular social change orientation, but for certain factors—the potential for mutual gain, resources, shared frames, and cultural compatibility—there is variation by orientation, and as a result collaborative practices differ. Social change tactics and resource strategies are particularly relevant: SCOs must work with other groups to gain the power or resources needed for mission attainment, but power and resources are also a source of inter-organizational tension in a competitive environment.

In general, where the social change orientation inclines toward collective action, linked with constituent transformation and mobilization, the dominant form of collaboration is participation in *political coalitions*. An orientation toward collective action through other activists (with no emphasis on individual transformation) is associated with *complementary alliances and match-making*. Where the change model is individual empowerment, linked to individual transformation, collaboration tends to involve *service partnerships and issue-area networks.* Finally, where the aim is individual empowerment through dismantling legal barriers (with no element of transformation), collaboration consists predominantly of *joint production*—in this case, of lawsuits. These general categories are discussed below, along with the relevant forces shaping collaboration in each case, and exceptions to the overall patterns.

Political Coalitions

Political coalitions tend to be short-lived, motivated by a specific issue, and focused on bringing about a particular action by public authorities. Among our SCOs, we find this form of collaboration most often among those working toward collective action through constituents (predominantly organizing groups). Sometimes an SCO will be asked to join a coalition started by another group, in which case the SCO will consult its constituents as to the desirability of participating. More often, however, the coalition will be an outgrowth of an issue that has been identified as critical by the SCO's own constituents but is not something the organization can accomplish on its own. As Community Voice leader Stephen Jencks explained, "work[ing] in coalition . . . is basically the only way that we're going to be able to achieve broader social change with the amount of power that we have."

CV has engaged in a number of efforts in which it had to "piece together a campaign, a coalition with enough strength to balance out the power of the [vested interests]." In one campaign for a city ordinance that would benefit immigrant workers, CV recognized the need for a critical mass of support to prompt a powerful city council member into action. They established a group of coordinating committees and solicited "sign-on" support from a long list of other groups, but it wasn't enough to move this particular council member. Recognizing that what was needed was active support from organized labor (an important constituency of the councilman), CV pitched the issue to the unions. The more progressive ones joined the campaign readily, but special effort was needed with one. "Luckily we found a good person there to push it through the bureaucracy, [and] I think they were a really important, quiet ally on the campaign." Ultimately, a critical mass of support was established, a political tipping point reached, "and then we kind of had the winning equation" when a powerful council member signed on and eventually the mayor was forced to do so.

Community Ownership Program and Respect both join forces with other groups to address political issues relevant to their particular missions and constituencies. In COP's case this joint effort usually focuses on support for low-income housing efforts and involves state and local housing nonprofits, organizing groups, and legal aid organizations. Respect is closely affiliated with other low-income women's groups but also makes common cause with organized labor, health care advocates, and legal services. Respect members contribute their bodies, voices, and sometimes cash to collaborative efforts to increase awareness of issues relating to poverty, hunger, and homelessness. "Whatever somebody tries to do, we try to be supportive of them in any way we can," said Linda Jefferson. "I think [most] groups really want us to participate, and they think we have something to add, and it strengthens them by having us there."

Although political coalition work is most strongly associated with SCOs working toward collective action through individual transformation, not every group with this orientation relies heavily on this form of collaboration (nor are they the only SCOs that engage in it). One moderating influence has to do with the target of change: for example, the campaigns of Uniting Youth for Change aim to affect institutional environments (primarily in schools) rather than influence political decisions, and so UYC relies less than other organizing groups on political coalitions. In addition, when the work of organizing groups emphasizes service development in their communities—as is particularly true for Residents Making Change, collaborative strategies include service partnerships as well as political coalition building.[5]

Conflicts over Resources and Ideology

The extent of collaboration among collective-action, constituency-based groups is constrained by conflicts over resources (including turf) and ideology. As explained in the previous chapter, these SCOs must build large membership bases both to survive and to accomplish their social change objectives. They rely on constituents for action and in some cases for financial support—directly through dues from individuals and their community organizations such as religious institutions, and indirectly from foundations who look to the size of an SCO's active membership to assess its effectiveness. Other research has found that generalist organizing groups, particularly those affiliated with national federations, are especially likely to compete over both turf and organizing ideology.[6] Such groups may find they have adequate support from within their federation to be able to accomplish goals without building local coalitions. By contrast, more specialized and independent groups are somewhat less likely to be in direct competition with each other and more likely to need coalition support.

Among our SCOs, the reported experience of collaboration is generally consistent with these patterns, but even those that engage regularly in joint actions find the effort challenging. When the partnership involves organizations with complementary roles—for example, a membership-based group linking with a policy advocacy organization—direct competition is not a concern, but lack of respect for the differing contributions of the partners may be. On the other hand, partnerships between organizing groups may be inhibited by competition for membership or funding, unless the bases are distinctly different. According to Steven Jencks of Community Voice, competition makes it hard for groups like his to learn from each other. Funder-sponsored arenas in particular may not feel like safe places for honest communication, given the enormous pressure that SCOs feel to demonstrate performance.

> I think [it] creates this weird culture where people are constantly self-promoting and talking up stuff and exaggerating stuff, and it makes it hard to have reasonable conversations even when there's no foundation person in the room because people are thinking, "Oh my, that person might talk to this person or that person, and I can't tell them that there were only twelve people at that meeting because they're going to think we're shitty organizers," and I think it's a real obstruction to critical thinking and analysis of the work.

Either type of collaboration—between complementary or similar organizations—can also be inhibited by disagreements over process and politics, given the centrality of ideology in SCO work. Although "open conversations and criticism and self–criticism are really useful," as Jencks noted, "dialogue about legitimate political disagreements [is] challenging, because . . . people are so invested and identified with whatever political position they have."

Complementary Alliances and Match-Making

Two other forms of collaboration, what we call "complementary alliances" and "match-making" (where an SCO joins allies to each other), are most common among the SCOs that emphasize collective action primarily through other groups. Because the social change work of these particular SCOs consists of supplying information, analysis, and linkages to activist groups, their relationships tend to be complementary ones. The Center for Critical Information, for example, works with client groups in order to develop products for their use. In some cases they engage another organization in joint production of those materials that neither could produce alone, for reasons of limited expertise. In its campus activism project, for instance, the Center has created an advisory committee of people from interested organizations who have helped to design its research, reviewed drafts of the reports, participated in a conference on the project, and who plan to use the final report when it is completed.

Advocates for the People and Urban Watch provide information and analysis to others, but their collaborative activity also includes bringing third parties together—actively in the case of AP, and more passively (but still consciously) in the case of UW. Advocates for the People spends considerable effort *developing* potential partners—that is, identifying groups or leaders in the community that can act on its policy research and analysis—and then linking them to each other. Director Antonio Mena notes that staff members working on particular issues will play the role of "facilitator"—locating activists that have an interest in the issue, putting them in touch with each other, and helping to establish a "functioning group."

The idea of providing a location in which third parties can learn about each other and begin to make connections is something Urban Watch director Rachel Beck calls "non-collaboration collaboration." As journalists, said Rachel, they are "lone wolves" who "don't play well with others." But they feel they play a central role in building or sustaining a network of progressive interests in their city. She described a time when the local conservatives had united behind a particular candidate but the Left was splintered among "social work types," "peace advocate types," "transit types," and others, who lacked a coherent message and tended to fight amongst themselves.

> So when we started we [said] . . . the first thing is that we're not going to go there. We're going to work with everyone but we are not going to work *for* anyone. So that we had this stark independence, [for] which I think [it] was helpful being journalists, because journalists can do that. . . . I don't know, for some reason we had trust, and so we would go around to all these different camps in whatever field that we're working on and talk to them . . . and . . . our view of this, at least, was that we would create collaboration within the pages of our reports. Because we heard what one guy was saying here, and we heard what another guy was saying here, and these two guys might actually have some really angry words to say to each other because they're very com-

petitive in terms of their ideas but we're like, you know what? Two–thirds of what these guys are saying overlaps completely.

UW would do its own analysis and act independently, but at the same time would support a larger, shared effort. It sought to identify common themes as well as areas of contention, creating "a sense of who the players were and where the divisions were and why. And so that's the way we'd be collaborative."

Differentiation Supports Cooperation

By definition, collaboration is part of the work of SCOs oriented toward collective change through other activist groups. For groups with this orientation, relationships tend to be built primarily with complementary organizations, and in particular with those the SCO intends to support in its own work. Collaboration is not without frustrations; as for other SCO types, partnerships can founder on disagreements over style and substance, insufficient clarity or uneven commitment. But direct competition for resources (including legitimacy) may be less of an issue when partners can appeal to different sources of support, or if approaching the same source can differentiate their appeals. By the same token, funding for these groups is so limited that there are times when they must target the same source with a similar appeal—a factor that undoubtedly works against collaboration.

Moving from Complementary Alliances to Coalitions

Some exceptions to the general types of collaboration in this group can be found in the activities of Advocates for the People and Community Choice, both of which engage in political coalitions on top of complementary alliances or match-making. For both AP and CC, there is a greater connection between the SCO and a community constituency than for other groups in this category. In AP's case, the organization does not work with individual constituents but does represent the interests of a particular racial/ethnic community in its analysis and advocacy, and as a result, it does act in coalition with other groups on issues of direct relevance to communities of color.

CC's situation is somewhat different and instructive about the relationship between social change orientation and collaborative processes. As CC moves toward a different orientation—shifting from working in support of other groups to developing its own membership base—its collaborative interactions are changing from complementary alliances (in which it provided technical expertise and support) to more political coalitions focused on constituent issues. In contrast to the traditional organizing groups, however, CC has a history of supporting other agencies, a history that shapes its more enduring and deeply collaborative relationships with others. Its approach is evident in Myung Kim's description of an effort to convene a series of dialogues among groups interested in healthy and affordable housing. It was a situation, he said,

> where we wanted to do some pretty deep sharing and recogniz[ed] that we didn't want to just say, "Let's pick something and work on it." Because we wanted there to be a deeper connection between the organizations and the movement, recognizing that everybody was already working 200 percent on the stuff they [had] already defined, but how do you actually do this in a way that starts to change people's approach and framework so that as we continue to do our work we start growing together. . . . You know, there were a lot of meetings to try and define the kind of the terrain that we were talking about. . . . We started to take a look at it from the perspective of our constituency, because we all were serving the same constituency, and we said, "Well, let's create a couple of case studies of people that we work with and how their experience of these issues cuts across everything that we're doing."

In this particular case, CC ultimately deferred to another agency to take the lead in trying to move the agenda, but offered to provide support. In another campaign, however, CC's role was more central and ongoing. In consultation with its constituency, the organization had begun to work on the problem of air pollution in the neighborhood and sought to bring in other groups that were concerned about the same issue. The original plan was to campaign for cleaner fuel in city buses.

> And what that coalition did, initially, was, even though we defined some goals . . . we actually didn't do what was done in some other more traditional advocacy campaigns, where you stay very narrowly focused on specific demands and you just stick to those and you build whatever coalition is necessary to get those demands through. What we did was, we said, we've got to make sure, one, that people actually agree with us that this is a problem. We had a pretty good assurance because of all these different groups and our youth who were already involved in defining the issues, but we said we've got to enlarge that set of folks, and we held a series of three forums and about 400 people came out to these three different forums.

To their surprise, the coalition partners learned that their constituents placed a high priority on a different set of transit issues than the ones highlighted by the coalition. As a result of listening to their common constituents, the coalition members defined "transit justice" as their broader framework of concern and within that framework identified a set of equity issues relating to transportation funding and access. This set of issues eventually defined the principles guiding the immediate campaign and the organized group that grew out of it. According to CC director Myung Kim, "What we knew within the coalition then was that, given our approach, we couldn't just stay narrowly focused. We actually had to define our issues in this broader transit justice framework."

Community Choices's collaborative alliances have a depth and endurance that goes beyond the typical political coalition of traditional organizing groups, and it seems likely that CC's past work and history with its partners supports this deeper collaboration. In this context, it is noteworthy that CC has worked to reassure allies that in connecting more directly with individual constituents, it is not competing for members—the plan is for membership costs to be low and multiple memberships to be common among the constituents—and it has retained a program that continues to provide critical services to its partners.

Service Partnerships and Issue-Area Networks

Among SCOs aiming at individual empowerment through transformative work with clients, two general types of collaboration predominate. In *service partnerships*, SCOs coordinate with different types of service providers to create programs that meet client needs. For example, Dare to Dream has extended its programming for homeless women into the areas of workforce development, adult education, professional childcare training, and leadership development by partnering with a variety of local agencies ranging from community colleges to women's advocacy groups that have capacity in complementary areas. Neighborhood Reach has engaged in a similar type of partnership but with the roles reversed: it provides a host of services including adult literacy, pre- and after-school programs, and senior support, to the low-income tenants of a local nonprofit housing agency. Growing Roots works with public school administrators to reach its target constituency, and Teaching Tools' basic program model is collaborative, relying on the schools in which it provides training to support its work and ultimately sustain the curriculum after TT moves on. The anti-domestic violence work of Sheltering Our Own requires interaction with other community-based groups that serve its constituency, as well as relationships with local criminal justice agencies.

A second form of collaboration common among these SCOs is participation in *issue-area networks*, in which agencies join forces with similar
groups to share information, exchange technical assistance and referrals,
and engage in issue-related advocacy. As an agency that serves women in a
particular ethnic group, SOO links with other shelters to ensure referrals of
women to the agency best able to serve them. Neighborhood Reach's
childcare program participates in a network of over a hundred providers
that trade advice on training, staff development, and accessing resources. A
local consortium of youth workers, to which NR also belongs, allows staff
members engaged in this highly demanding work to share ideas and emotional support, and to coordinate activities addressing common problems
such as gang violence. Provider collaboratives may even be supported in
some way by the state, as is the case with the consortia of child care
providers and adult literacy trainers to which NR belongs.

These SCOs also work with others on issue advocacy through both
grassroots networks and the participation by directors in statewide or national campaigns and commissions. Government-sponsored campaigns
and commissions do bring groups together for joint effort but are often
time-limited and politically constrained. Potentially more powerful are locally generated networks of similar agencies, such as the association of
shelter providers in which Dare to Dream participates. Members not only
provide mutual assistance but also maintain a statewide political network
in which individual shelters establish relationships with their own political
representatives. With this type of network, the group can advocate effectively for policies to benefit their constituents, including higher Section 8
funding and more affordable housing programs.

These kinds of efforts generally rely on collaborations among similar
agencies, but they can also extend to very different types of organizations
that happen to share a concern for social justice. Among our service-
oriented SCOs, Dare to Dream seems to engage with the widest variety of
partners; in a recent initiative to raise awareness and advocate for solutions
to the problem of homelessness, it has worked with women's groups, religious organizations, and legal aid programs.

When and Why It Works

SCOs working for social change through services that transform and empower their clients are in some ways well positioned for long-term collaboration with a variety of other groups that either serve the same constituency
or work on the same issue. Complementary service activities—such as
DTD's partnerships with educational providers—enhance programming in

line with the missions of participating agencies, do not involve direct competition, and may appeal to funders in a way that increases total resources available. Joining forces with similar groups may be more problematic insofar as competition is an issue, but this kind of collaboration can also produce mutual gains—in the form of additional public funding, more favorable legislation, or other support for the constituent population or type of service provided. In both kinds of partnership, there are potential benefits not only in terms of service to the constituency (mission attainment) but for organizational sustenance as well.

The major challenges to collaborative efforts among these SCOs are not unique to this group; they include lack of clear agreements, differences in service philosophy, and the time and effort it takes to sustain joint activities when additional resources are not available to support the work.

Joint Production

The fourth social change orientation—which emphasizes individual empowerment but through dismantling external barriers rather than through transformative capacity building—is represented in our sample of SCOs by Rights for All. RFA's primary mode of collaboration has been the joint production of work, in this case public-interest lawsuits, in which it partners with other legal advocacy groups or private law firms. RFA also interacts with other organizations to identify clients and potential issues and locates outreach activities in a variety of settings that include service agencies—a kind of co-location of services that constitutes a limited form of collaboration. Recently RFA has taken on a project providing representation for other community groups rather than individual clients, and this work will entail a different type of collaboration in keeping with the greater emphasis on collective action in this project. If this type of work assumes greater prominence in RFA's portfolio of activities, the organization's collaborative efforts may come to resemble the complementary alliances of those oriented toward collective action through activist groups. But at present, the community action project is more the exception than the rule at RFA, and joint production of lawsuits remains its dominant mode of collaboration.

RFA's director argues that collaboration is easiest and most productive when the partners bring different capacities and resources—as when his group partners with a private law firm seeking to fulfill its *pro bono* obligations. In such a situation, the two groups bring something different and gain something different from the collaboration, and there is little competition over politics or resources. More difficult are the collaborations with other legal services agencies, where differing ideologies along with competition for funding and clients can make partnerships much more difficult. As RFA attorney Tony Capra explained,

> The city is a big place and . . . unlike a lot of smaller cities in the rural communities, there are a lot of lawyers . . . for the poor—nowhere near the need, but there are a lot. There are a number of organizations, and they're vying for the headlines and the spotlight and the funding, and my ego sometimes gets caught up in what our role on the food chain is. Size, notoriety, our name in the paper. And I would have to let go of some of that ego and just realize we play a role, we do good work, and if we're not getting all the headlines all the time then fine.

The resource strategy associated with legal-advocacy SCOs relies on a combination of public and private funding in which competition for support can be intense and collaboration aimed at increasing resources seems rare. In this context, differentiation by service and funding niche may help otherwise similar groups work together.

Cross-Cutting Influences on Collaboration

Collaborative practices vary across social change orientations, but in almost all cases, a dominant influence in favor of collaboration is the desire to achieve broader impact and better serve constituent groups. *Political coalitions* create the power base needed to influence public decision-making in favor of constituents; *complementary alliances* extend the reach of SCOs across locations and areas of expertise; *service partnerships and issue networks* support more comprehensive programs for client capacity building; and *joint production* of legal advocacy increases the likelihood of successfully representing the most marginalized populations. Partnerships may involve similar organizations—serving or representing different groups but concerned with the same issue, or complementary ones—serving or representing the same neighborhood or constituency but focused on different issues; but in both situations the "mutual gain" sought usually reflects the agencies' social missions.[7] In short, it is larger commitments that push SCOs into collaborative ventures.

Working against collaboration are organizational needs. SCOs tend to have very limited resources and competition over these—including competition over membership, recognition, and funding—can make groups reluctant to cooperate in circumstances where the pool of resources cannot be enlarged. Furthermore, collaboration itself is costly, drawing resources away from other work. Even when organizations are willing to work together, they may be unable to sustain collaborative efforts without additional support.

Political differences also inhibit collaboration. These can arise when organizations or their leaders are strongly—perhaps overly—identified with particular practices; in such cases, political differences may reflect organizational rather than social commitments. But there can also be disagreement on the matter of the goals of social change—especially when constituencies have conflicting interests, or groups differ strongly on tactics; in these cases, political differences reflect something beyond organizational concerns.

As we have seen, the factors that support or inhibit collaboration vary with social change orientation, shaping the degree and type of collaboration in which different kinds of SCOs are likely to engage. SCOs engaged in collective action with individual transformation generally compete for membership, and they may also have strong political differences that work against long-term collaborations. At the same time, their focus on political change and need for critical mass draw them into coalitions. Those focused on collective action without transformation by contrast work toward change primarily if not entirely through other activists, and these SCOs tend to develop strong collaborative relationships as a matter of routine,[8] often creating links between other groups as well. SCOs coupling individual empowerment and individual transformation draw on third-party resources, such as public funding that can sometimes be enlarged through joint effort with similar organizations, and the goal of increasing service effectiveness motivates complementary partnerships. These SCOs also tend to establish longer-term collaborations of various types. Finally, for SCOs working toward individual empowerment without transformation (of which we have a single example), the most straightforward collaborations are those in which partners bring different resources and seek different benefits. Perhaps because this orientation is associated with legal advocacy, collaborative activity is highly focused and limited to certain kinds of relationships.

Variation within Social Change Orientation

Differing strategies and circumstances shape collaborative patterns across social change orientations, but we also find also that the depth and consistency of cooperative efforts vary *within* these orientations. Among SCOs oriented toward collective action and individual transformation, Residents Making Changes stands out as exceptionally collaborative, engaging with a variety of different kinds of organizations in long-term partnerships as well as short-term coalitions. Among SCOs oriented toward individual empowerment and individual transformation, Dare to Dream is exceptional—routinely partnering with a variety of different kinds of organizations in both service activities and political coalitions.

In some cases, particular historical or environmental influences may make collaboration less costly, more beneficial, or simply more expected than is generally the case. Residents Making Change, for example, was established in part through the efforts of individuals associated with other community groups, and RMC still allocates board positions to representatives of such groups. These structural connections support ongoing partnerships and ensure the accountability of RMC not only to individual constituents but also to other community groups in its neighborhood.

Perhaps more importantly, however, we see variation linked to differences in leadership attitudes and capacity. SCO directors vary significantly in their attitudes and practices relating to collaboration. On one end of a spectrum are those for whom the desirability of collaboration is "overblown," hindered by widespread "turf" and "ego" issues. For these directors, as one put it bluntly, "the concept of collaboration . . . for social change organizations is largely crap." He acknowledged that collaboration could be a means to a positive end, but often seemed to be inappropriately valued as a "good thing in and of itself." In the experience of these respondents, collaboration works best when the self-interest of both parties is clearly served.

By contrast, Dorothy Morrison of Dare to Dream—a routinely collaborative SCO—noted that a "critical" aspect of the agency's effectiveness was that "we have a ton of collaborations. We work with everybody under the sun, but [always] with those people who are really focused on the same direction." Partnerships worked, she said, when the participants agreed that the effort should be "focused not so much on the great growth and preservation of their own organization, but . . . on the purpose for which the organization exists." She noted that most of her own learning, in fact, had "come from doing and it has come from collaborating with others. . . . I learn from the women that I interact with, I learn from trying to kind of move around and effect change, and I learn from colleagues and people who have other kinds of skills and resources that collaborate and work with me." Seeing collaboration as a way to enhance her organization's work, she was inclined to share with others. Of her support of new groups in the field, she said, "you create something, [and] if it's really good you share it with everybody. You don't put a price tag on it. You say we've learned this. How can we help you? How can you help us? How together can we help the families?"

Antonio Mena, another unusually collaborative director, observed that working with others constituted an essential part of the work of Advocates for the People—"not even something we think about, we just do it." He recounted how, at a funder-organized meeting on coalition building, after everyone spoke and after he had described his group's efforts, "people would come up to me and say, 'Oh, my God, you're doing all this fantastic work.' And I'm saying to myself, how could you do your work without working with other people?" Although external factors undoubtedly make collaboration easier or more difficult, these kinds of comments suggest that some directors strongly favor collaboration and are more likely to do what is necessary to make it happen regardless of other factors.

Going to the Next Level

In chapter 3 we noted the struggles of SCO leaders to balance not only the trade-off between mission and margin common to many nonprofits, but the additional tension between dedication to a single organization's mission and commitment to the larger cause of social justice. In the context of collaboration we find a parallel set of concerns. At one level, SCOs must balance the operational costs against the mission-related benefits associated with collaboration. When these benefits are great enough, SCOs will engage in the kinds of collaborative activities described here, which focus on achieving particular political or social outcomes that reflect organizational missions and constituent needs. But there is another—in a sense higher—level of collaboration alluded to by some of our respondents that occurs very infrequently. At this level, collaborators would provide a space for communal agenda-setting, acknowledge a common good that is more than the sum of separate interests and respond to collective agenda-setting by changing and growing.

Communal agenda-setting. Josh Klinger, the newest director of Neighborhood Reach, envisions this level of collaboration even if he has not yet managed to accomplish it. He noted that a particular challenge in successful collaboration is taking responsibility for sustaining joint effort without dictating the agenda. "And so that's one of the things that we're kind of struggling with when it relates to collaboration, is how do you provide the platform without actually designing the platform?" In his community, there are many organized groups—"assets," in the language of social capital—but "none of them are at one table at any given time forming a shared agenda. So my notion is that without saying we're forming something new that's mind–boggling to people, just say 'We want one place in the community.' We can call it a council, we can call it a forum." With representation from all the neighborhood's different constituencies, it would be "almost like a neighborhood legislative body in some way" whose agenda would be to explore what it is that "as a whole, as a community of the West Side . . . we need to do."

Acknowledging the common good. In the view of an RMC board member, the most critical work of collaboration is "fighting for the common good and helping our community to hold itself accountable to a common good." Recognizing that action starts with self-interest, he said it cannot stop there. He defined a set of concentric circles with organizational or individual self-interest at the center, surrounded by a sort of "shared interest" beyond which would be "the community good, the common good, something that really is bigger than any shared interest." In the absence of a clear sense of this common good, the community risks being torn apart by internal tensions. And even at this level, larger systems need to be taken into account for sustainability. In the long term, we must attend to all levels, and there must be "some entity in a community" that helps us do this and holds us accountable to the task.

Changing and growing in collaboration. As explained above, Community Choices and its partners have sought a "deeper connection" in which organizations actually change their approaches and frameworks in a way that allows them to grow together in their work. In the example described by CC director Myung Kim, several community-based organizations came together in coalition with the aim of improving resident health by decreasing air pollution. Their initial plan was to campaign for the adoption of cleaner fuel in city buses, but after engaging community residents in an agenda-setting process, they realized the need to attend to broader transit issues. The collaborative framed the problem in terms of a larger "transit justice framework" that highlighted disinvestment in mass transit infrastructure and the inequitable distribution of transportation resources. Within this frame, the coalition was able to organize transit users into a group that campaigned for greater equity in transit policies and won real concessions from the state government. Furthermore, the transit users' group has continued to organize and campaign for its agenda.

Arguably, the promise of change is greatest in collaboration that makes space for communal agenda-setting, seeks out a vision of the common

good, and supports learning and change by participants. These features—
and the experience reported by Community Choices, in particular—reflect
an approach similar to what Himmelman (2001) calls "collaborative empowerment" as opposed to "collaborative betterment." In the latter approach, collaboration among community-based organizations is initiated
by powerful outside institutions, including private funders or fiscal inter-
mediaries, government agencies, and universities. Himmelman argues that
in this context, power remains primarily outside the collaborative, which is
funded only for the short-term and develops no capacity to demand increased resources for the community. By contrast, in collaborative empowerment, the process is driven by community-based organizations and their
constituencies. Integral to this effort is the enhancement of local capacity
in terms of both means (leadership and organizing) and ends (greater participation in public decision-making).[9]

The aims of this kind of collaboration go beyond the winning of a single
campaign or the provision of a particular service to the strengthening of
democracy. The effort requires SCOs to develop a shared analytic understanding, a commitment to larger goals, and an openness to mutual influence—qualities also relevant to the task of movement building, a concern
we take up in the next chapter.

CHAPTER SEVEN

ORGANIZATIONS, MOVEMENT, AND THE FUTURE OF SOCIAL CHANGE

So everybody needs housing, everybody needs healthcare, everybody needs
to have a job that treats them with dignity, everybody needs child care if
they want it . . . those are the things that everybody needs, and that's how I
think we build those coalitions because people can see, ha, I'm no different
from you, I need that stuff too.

LINDA JEFFERSON
Respect

We undertook this study with the aim of better understanding a class of
nonprofit organizations that has received little attention from social movement researchers but which constitutes an important element of progressive social change work in the United States. Our exploratory investigation
of sixteen social change organizations has begun to define some of the
characteristics of these kinds of organizations—the commonalities and
differences in their theories of change; the requirements, rewards, and difficulties of their work; special leadership challenges; options for and implications of decision-making structures; alternative resource strategies associated with particular approaches to change; and varying forms of
collaborative effort.

Among the lessons of this exploration, we have noted that SCOs share a
common commitment to constituent engagement and participatory efforts
but vary in the mode of empowerment they emphasize and the centrality of
individual transformation in their approaches to systemic change. These
dimensions of SCO theories of change link different types of agencies in
unanticipated ways: for example, organizing and service groups share a
commitment to transformative work, while service groups share with legal

advocacy agencies an orientation toward individual empowerment rather than collective action.

In terms of staffing requirements, we find that critical to all SCOs is a systemic political analysis that SCO workers come by in different ways. Other qualities—staff skills, knowledge, and motivations—vary with the type of work for change in which an organization engages, but all groups struggle with low compensation, high expectations for commitment to the work, and competing demands for personal needs (such as time with families). SCO leaders face the same sorts of demands as other nonprofit managers but in addition must be able to set direction in a participatory way; must support staff engagement, growth, and transformation; and must balance the demands of organizational maintenance with larger efforts for change. Most leaders have limited formal preparation, and almost none are trained in the special tasks of SCO leadership. On-the-job development of new leaders is in many ways preferable to formal education, but places heavy demands on under-resourced organizations and existing managers.

In examining decision-making structures, we find there to be two distinct dimensions—the internal decision-making practice of staffs and directors and the external avenues of influence available to constituents—and that the two do not necessarily co-vary in predictable ways. An SCO can have relatively centralized internal authority and yet be highly responsive to its constituency; similarly, a democratic internal structure does not necessarily imply great openness to client influence. A number of factors affect structure, but we find the SCO's approach to change, its guiding values, and the demands of its environment to be especially relevant.

Resource strategies—including the use of non-financial resources—also vary with social change orientations. Perhaps not surprisingly, those oriented toward collective action have the most limited budgets and rely the least on government support. Change-oriented service agencies and legal advocates may have much greater budgets, but they also have significant commitments to service activity that must be provided with these funds. If they are to engage in social change activity, it must be embedded within the service model or supported with resources squeezed out of whatever margin exists.

Finally, the shape of SCO collaborative activity relates to social change orientation as well. For some, political coalitions are a predominant form of collaboration; others work with large institutions to promote change from within, create service partnerships to support clients, establish issue networks to fight for common goals, or engage in co-production of services. Across all types of SCOs, the primary motivator for collaboration is a commitment to change and desire to serve constituents. Inhibiting collaboration are organizational concerns—limited resources, competition for members and funds, and conflicting visions or strategies for change.

Ideas and Insights on Movement Building

We turn now to the question of whether these kinds of organizations can be aggregated into a larger movement for change, what their potential is, and how that potential can best be tapped. We begin by revisiting the social movement literature. Although it has little to say about organizations of the type we have studied, it does offer some observations about the relationship between organizations and movements, observations that may be helpful as we try to envision the role of SCOs in larger change efforts.

A second source of insight is the debate among progressives over how best to build a movement. Here we find on one side an argument for a centralized approach to messaging, mobilization, and policy definition that raises important concerns about the drawbacks of SCOs. This view is countered, however, by an analysis that identifies critical functions in movement building that can best be fulfilled by grassroots groups in touch with constituents.

Drawing on these writings and taking into account what we have learned of SCOs through our study, we identify the primary contributions SCOs can make to the building of a progressive movement and then the challenges to these groups taking up this expanded role.

Movements and Organizations

Social movement theorists differ in their views of the roles of organizations in movements. In both the political process model (e.g., McAdam 1999 [1982]) and resource mobilization theory (e.g., McCarthy and Zald 1973) organizations are seen as providing essential movement infrastructure.[1] But more radical theorists such as Piven and Cloward (1977) argue that organizations are detrimental to movements: they redirect resources from protest to organizational maintenance and shift power from those fighting oppression to elite sponsors.

McAdam's later work tries to bridge the gap between these different approaches by highlighting three problems that organizations must guard against: *oligarchization*, whereby "a certain class of individuals . . . come[s] to value the maintenance of the organization over the realization of movement goals" (McAdam 1999 [1982], 55); *co-optation*, whereby external support "threatens to tame the movement by encouraging insurgents to pursue only goals acceptable to external sponsors" (55); and *dissolution of indigenous support*, which occurs as "insurgents increasingly seek to cultivate ties to outside groups" thereby weakening their own indigenous links (55–56). These are concerns we should keep in mind as we think about the possible role of SCOs in a larger progressive movement.

In terms of how grassroots organizations might *build* a movement, however, the literature offers little guidance. Many social movement theorists tend to treat organizations as secondary to the movements of which they are a part rather than independent sources of mobilization. An important exception is Aldon Morris (1984), whose work on the civil rights movement elaborates the roles of various types of pre-existing organizations in growing and sustaining the movement (and developing new movement-identified organizations). In Morris's analysis, the civil rights movement was aided by three types of organizations: indigenous institutions (such as black churches and colleges) that provided infrastructure, continuity, indigenous control and cultural legitimacy; local movement centers (community-based activist groups such as the Montgomery Improvement Association or the Southern Christian Leadership Conference) that organized protest activities, informed tactics, and unified efforts; and movement half-way houses (non-indigenous groups that are dedicated to change, such as the Highlander Folk School and American Friends Service Committee) that contributed additional resources, such as popular education, activist training, and publicity. Morris clarifies how existing organizations can support and promote a nascent movement, and some of his conclusions are relevant to the roles that could be played by SCOs in a progressive movement today.

In short, the social movement literature identifies many ways in which SCOs could contribute to a larger movement *if* one were to appear. What this literature—even Morris's analysis—does not supply is a sense of how these diverse, independent grassroots groups could work together to *generate* a movement. A critical missing piece is the sense of shared identity or consciousness that would motivate large-scale coordinated effort and develop a *collection* of efforts into a *collective* endeavor. Are SCOs a blessing or a curse in the task of developing shared consciousness and commitment to change?

The Debate among Progressives

A number of prominent progressives have argued that SCOs do not constitute the best infrastructure for an effective movement. Critics such as

Michael Shuman (1998) and Todd Gitlin (1995) suggest that support of these kinds of organizations actually detracts from movement building by encouraging the proliferation of small groups, based on social identity characteristics or specific programmatic goals that undermine a more centralized strategy. In their view, a persuasive analysis and unifying national vision, linked to a coherent policy framework, is the way to move a progressive agenda forward. In this paradigm, small, independent SCOs are seen as ineffective at best and divisive at worst. Funding that could be used to support national policy groups is effectively squandered on local programs and identity-based work (related to race/ethnicity, gender and sexual orientation) that inhibits the development of a broader class-based movement, especially one that would appeal to white middle- and working-class families. Those holding this view believe that the strongest engines for progressive change are either research institutes (think-tanks) that can develop appealing policy ideas and frame appropriate messages or national groups with local affiliates that can mobilize people to support issue campaigns.[2] Those who favor a more centralized approach to movement point to lessons learned from the political Right, which they believe has succeeded through media investment, the development of sophisticated political tactics through large institutions, and centrally guided voter mobilization.

But this view is not embraced by all progressives. Hardisty and Bhargava (2005), drawing on past research on the Right, claim that the argument for a top-down approach both misreads the strategies of the Right and ignores the underlying issues that face a political progressive movement today. In explaining the gains of the Right, they identify several key elements that can be instructive for progressive movement building. These include the importance of allowing ideological diversity while aligning to a common purpose reflected in a set of beliefs and principles; listening to the constituent base to understand what people are thinking and feeling; recruiting a broad group of supporters through base building not only for mobilizing voters but to continually stay close to constituents; and using insider and outsider politics to project "a clear, principled and uncompromising voice of progressive values and policies" (Hardisty and Bhargava 2005, 23). The authors argue that "mass organizing must be informed by visionary principles as well as nuts-and-bolts techniques," that can "grow out of the everyday work that activists in sub-movements do on various issues" (26). Progressives need the "overarching principles" that Hardisty and Bhargava believe are developed in a "step-by-step process of slowly creating broad consensus" using the kind of active listening employed so successfully by the Right (26).

Hardisty and Bhargava's analysis strongly suggests that SCOs could play an essential role in movement building, and we outline below what we see as the most important potential contributions of these organizations. At the same time, we acknowledge the legitimacy of concerns raised by social movement theorists and progressives who argue for a more centralized effort. We do not adopt these critiques in full, but rely on them to inform our analysis, as they call our attention to the tensions among organizations and between organizations and movements. For example, of McAdam's three dangers, we find the problem of tension between maintaining organizations and supporting movement to be the most significant for SCOs, and we elaborate on this in our discussion of conflicting demands on leaders below. But in the case of SCOs, the result is not so much the problem of oligarchization that McAdam identifies, in which a small number of organizations would come to dominate a movement, but a matter of individual organizational imperatives standing in the way of aggregation of effort. The problem of co-optation is a challenge we noted in our earlier discussion of resources, but it is not one of the primary threats to SCO participation in movement building that we identify here, because we find that SCOs work hard—and relatively successfully—to balance competing claims. Similarly, we see the threat to indigenous support posed by cultivation of ties to outside groups as a greater issue for larger groups than for grassroots SCOs. We do, however, take up issues relating to resources and the relationships between organizations in our section on obstacles to movement building.

We turn now to the contributions SCOs can make, and subsequently take up the challenges. It is an open question whether unification or fragmentation ultimately will dominate, but we conclude the chapter with some hopeful observations.

The Movement Building Potential of SCOS

Echoing the argument of Hardisty and Bhargava, we see four important ways in which SCOs could contribute to building as well as sustaining a progressive movement: they can serve as entry points for mobilization of diverse constituencies, develop indigenous movement leadership, help to build shared consciousness based on a common analysis, and contribute to a process that would identify and advance unifying principles. The first two items speak primarily to the functions of infrastructure fulfilled by organizations on behalf of nascent or developing movements; the second two address the difficult challenge identified above, of promoting a shared consciousness of the need for change.

Entry Points for the Mobilization of
Diverse Constituencies

At Community Voice, immigrant residents learn their rights, develop political skills, and organize collective action to bring resources into their neighborhood and ensure better access to public services. Working with Uniting Youth for Change, students in inner-city schools investigate the problems in their institutions and use their knowledge to work with other stakeholders for change. Supported by Community Choice, bus riders from low-income neighborhoods identify resource gaps and unequal services, then map political power structures and act collectively to improve transit equity.

SCOs promote civic and political engagement by the traditionally disenfranchised groups who represent a progressive movement's natural constituencies. Given the problem that disadvantaged groups are often politically ill-informed and may be discouraged from participation,[3] this SCO work is a critical first-step in the process of large-scale mobilization. Can SCOs and their members take the next step and link their efforts, to form larger initiatives? We do see evidence of such efforts in a number of localities. Among the groups we studied, the regional partnerships of Community Choice, the cross-class mobilization of Respect, and the statewide networks being developed by Dare to Dream all involve inter-organizational action that reaches beyond single neighborhoods and individual issues or identity groups.

These are promising albeit limited starts, but other research suggests that deep, long-term progressive alliances may be growing more common. In Los Angeles, for example, a long-term collaboration among organizations from different sectors has produced some notable gains on a progressive agenda (Nicholls 2003; Mann 2005; Milkman 2000; Pastor 2001). An analysis of the Los Angeles case suggests that the formation of an "organizational infrastructure" linking labor, community-based organizations, and a local university, has allowed a diverse set of actors to develop trust and a thick network of relationships that support action and learning over time (Nicholls, 2003). Most recently this coalition was active in the election of a progressive candidate for mayor; SCO participation included educating constituencies about the differences between candidates and encouraging activism in constituents and staffs.[4]

Other examples may be found in the Progressive Leadership Alliance of Nevada (PLAN); the Western States Center of Portland, Oregon; and the development of NGO New Mexico.[5] This last case illustrates the process of how aggregation of effort can begin. NGO New Mexico is a newly formed statewide nonprofit association whose board includes representatives from mainstream groups and progressives interested in deeper social change. One of the most progressive members, the executive director of the SouthWest Organizing Project, recommended that the board postpone developing a policy agenda until it had talked with its member organizations about the values that would guide their advocacy and capacity-building work. NGO New Mexico then held four meetings in different parts of the state to discuss these issues and to build relationships among groups that otherwise might never cross paths. Now NGO New Mexico's first executive director is using the results of these meetings to formulate a set of values that will drive the association's advocacy and policy work.

It is the SCOs' focus on constituents that not only positions them as entry points but supports the possibility of broader mobilization. The commitment to constituents motivates organizations to work together, and the participation of constituents means that relationships are built not only among organizational leaders but among constituents themselves.

Developing Indigenous Leadership

Movements require large numbers of people but also credible leadership. National figures are important but there is no substitute for strong local leaders who show others like themselves that it is possible to stand up against oppressive systems. Writing about civil rights organizing, Payne (1995) has challenged the assumption that the most important motivator for mobilization was visible national leadership (as embodied in Martin Luther King, Jr.). Rather, he argues that it was a combination of local political and economic conditions along with community-level leadership that led to action. In fact, it was the risk-taking activities of those at this level that provided crucial information for building the national agenda for change.[6]

Several of the SCOs in our study have explicit leadership development programs, where the goal, as explained by an RMC board member, is to make not individual leaders, but "community leaders, [who] . . . see that power rests with the community and in the community. They serve the community." Organizing groups in particular are likely to have invested time, energy, and thought into leadership training of local residents who become not only the source of agendas but the voice of campaigns. Clients and community members learn how to speak up in public settings, to represent their groups to decision-makers, and to mobilize neighbors and coworkers. They inspire each other as they lead by example and demonstrate the possibilities of change on both personal and political levels. As a new leader in Faith in Change's community told an older leader from the same neighborhood, "Roy, I used to watch you. I used to look at you talk, I used to admire the way you talked, and I really like the things you say and the things you do. I want to do . . . the same stuff."

Building Shared Consciousness Based on a Common Analysis

Perhaps *the* central challenge to the building of a progressive movement in the U.S. is the need to develop a broadly shared social understanding and commitment to change. The critics of SCO-based initiatives are concerned that focusing on specific identity group concerns or particular issues will detract from broader coalitions. We argue that commitment grows out of particular experiences of oppression (sometimes vicarious), but that there must be a link that connects those particular experiences, and that the most powerful link is an analysis that locates the causes of deep inequality within social structures rather than individual failings. A common understanding of systems of power can help to build a sense of unity.[7]

One of the important roles that SCOs can play is to provide information and analysis that helps people see how often invisible systems have an impact on their lives. For some SCOs—primarily change-oriented service agencies, and those involved in organizing—constituent empowerment comes through a process of individual transformation in which constituents (and sometimes staffers as well) begin to understand their circumstances in the context of larger structural factors rather than entirely through a framework of individual responsibility. Many advocacy groups also contribute to this effort, not through transformative work with individual clients but by informing people in the society at large. Through this type of consciousness-raising, individuals come to understand their own experiences and options in a new and powerful way.

A systematic approach to the transformation process is most evident in the field of organizing, where resource manuals are common: such books as *Organizing for Social Change* (Bobo et al. 2001) and, more recently, *Power Tools* (Castellanos and Pateriya 2003), a workbook by Strategic Concepts in Organizing and Policy Education (SCOPE), detail the process. The National Organizers Alliance has also developed a curriculum based on varying approaches that can be used by organizers to "create new strategies to unify people into long-term alliances across constituencies, issues, and organizations."[8]

These resources identify various techniques that can serve as building blocks for larger movement, but they are aimed primarily at organizing groups, ignoring the potential of other types of SCOs that also do transformative work—in particular, change-oriented service agencies.[9] Mass mobilization would be furthered by modifying and promoting these techniques and analyses to these other types of social change organizations. Service providers committed to social change often include education on systemic issues in their work, but there are fewer texts and tools available to these groups than to organizers. An exchange of ideas between those working in different types of SCOs, and the production of materials drawing on their similarities and differences, would help to build a larger base of constituents. However, there has been a long-standing antipathy toward service provision by organizing groups who see service providers as only putting band-aids on problems rather than working to solve them.

There is no reason that this divide cannot be closed. The on-the-ground work of transformation based on political and critical analysis operates by drawing on the experiences of constituents and staff, and works to challenge the assumption that individuals are the only ones responsible for their own situation—whether it be their financial well-being, their health status, or the education of their children. Political education highlights how systems work to reinforce certain privileges for some but not all, and helps people think about how those systems can be changed. Bridging the divide between different SCOs that are all interested in a larger movement for change means we must address the larger question of what are we all working toward?

Establishing a Process for Identifying Unifying Principles

Hardisty and Bhargava argue that a progressive movement does not require ideological uniformity as long as a set of overarching principles underlies its diversity. Unifying principles are not something that can be created in the offices of think tanks but require an exchange of ideas and experiences among many groups, including diverse constituencies, policy professionals, academics, politicians, funders, and others. In particular, the process requires that those in dominant positions seek out and actively listen to those with less power.

SCOs offer one public space in which this conversation could take place (in a few cases, *is* taking place). Located within severely disadvantaged neighborhoods and serving marginalized groups, they provide a venue in which relatively voiceless people can express themselves. Two elements of process are critical here. First, new ideas often come from the margins and SCOs are a place in which such ideas can be aired. Second, understanding nonmaterial motives is particularly critical for movement building, yet tends to be ignored (Dobbin 2001; Goodwin, Jasper, and Polletta 2001). SCOs offer a venue in which participants can express both material and spiritual aspirations. Focus groups may provide information, but they do not engage people in a holistic developmental process as full participants.

Although the SCOs in our study were working in separate issue areas and with different approaches, they all had the desire to see a different type of society where people who had been disadvantaged by social and economic systems had more power over their lives. To move forward, SCOs will need to reach out to groups beyond their immediate clients and beyond even other SCOs and their constituencies, to promote a conversation that includes all who can be linked by common needs and visions—in a word, "everybody" that Linda Jefferson's comment (at the opening of this chapter) encompasses.

Challenges to SCOs in Building Movement

We have outlined some ways in which SCOs can be important contributors in building a movement for social change, but their successful involvement in this effort is by no means assured. In this section we discuss what we see as the three main factors that work against SCOs in the role of movement builders. These include the competition for resources; the difficulty of bridging the gap between national and local groups; and the conflicting demands on and motivations of SCO leaders. Although some would see these problems as a reflection of the narrow interests and/or incompetence of SCO leaders and staff, we are more inclined to interpret these difficulties in terms of the conditions in which SCOs operate—even as we acknowledge that SCO workers have their failings.

Competition for Resources

Proponents of a centralized approach to change worry that the resources invested in SCOs divert funds that should be invested in organizations that are better positioned for impact—reflecting concerns about both the scale of SCOs and the challenge of producing something useful in the absence of a larger, coherent progressive agenda. Our analysis is different. We believe that the problem is not simply a matter of limited resources but that certain features of the funding process tend to undermine movement building by aggravating competition and inhibiting political action.

As noted in chapter 5, SCOs struggle constantly with the need to identify reliable sources of support. Responding to funder preferences for "new ideas" and to constantly shifting priorities, directors devote considerable time and energy trying to sustain funder interest and thinking about how to package their activities to maintain their appeal. The result is a culture of distrust among potential allies whereby groups are likely to stress their differences from other SCOs, rather than their common vision and goals. To the extent that SCO leaders are heavily invested in their own organizations, competition for support aggravates this problem.

Even though many funders promote collaboration (and will make funds available for, or even tied to, collaborative effort), their procedures may still undermine such efforts. If resources are allocated only for the collaborative effort (and often insufficient resources, at that), the participating organizations—in need of ongoing support—have strong financial incentives to limit their participation to the minimum required. In addition, organizations are ever wary of the need to keep up appearances with funders, and this need can make it especially difficult to have honest exchanges with potential collaborators at events that are sponsored by funders. Competition for funds can result in SCOs exaggerating their successes or claiming that theirs is the only or most important group in their field.[10]

All nonprofits are subject to these conditions, but there are additional constraints on philanthropic resources for SCOs. The growing concern for performance measurement and accountability (by itself reasonable and some would say overdue) may, if it leads to inflexible definitions and narrow expectations, limit support for activities with long-term, uncertain or hard-to-define outcomes. At particular risk are time-consuming efforts at building relationships that cross issues and geography. A second factor limiting resources for this work is the possibility that funders are uncomfortable with political work or ambivalent about supporting movement building as such.

Recent research into foundation funding of think tanks suggests that conservative foundations are more willing to support overtly political activities than are mainstream or liberal foundations. Rich (2005) analyzed spending by conservative, mainstream, and progressive foundations and found that contrary to common belief, it was not the case that more money was available for policy research from conservative foundations, but that the groups they funded were more committed to explicitly ideological work than were the research institutes supported by mainstream or liberal foundations. Rich quotes the research director of a progressive think tank: " 'If you're on the left, you have to go to the foundations and say you're neutral, unbiased—not politicized. You're certainly not liberal. If you're ideological, they don't want to support you. It's frustrating—because, by contrast, if you're on the right, the foundations will only fund you if you toe the ideological line, if you want to do battle for the conservative cause.' "[11]

There may never be enough money to support all worthwhile progressive activities, and consequently there will always be some competition. But some of the obstacles to movement building may relate more to funding procedures and priorities than to scarcity per se. Rather than approaching allocation as a zero-sum game, progressives should be developing strategies that link local base-building with state and national policy and political work.

The National-Local Divide

A second significant barrier to SCOs building a larger movement for change is the local scope of their work, including, for many, the lack of connection to a larger political picture. The problem is not simply that a larger vision is missing, but that the development of such a vision is impeded by the tensions between local groups and national organizations.

SCOs often express frustration at the funding of national groups that they perceive as lacking accountability to a constituent base, but the complaint is more than an issue of resources; it also reflects competition for recognition, ideas, and respect. Although some national organizations with local chapters do engage in a kind of vertical collaboration, and some grassroots groups do make connections to national interest networks, alliances tend to be limited to single issues (sometimes even single organizations), and the relationships are often marred by mutual suspicions.

National groups often find local organizations overly parochial and competitive with each other, and complain that it can be difficult to establish productive local connections. However, local SCOs experience national organizations as controlling and disrespectful; they feel that nationals ignore what local groups have to contribute or that the nationals expect them to carry out policy agendas in which they have had little involvement. As Community Voice's Stephen Jencks argues, the disconnect is neither consistent with progressive values nor politically viable:

[The problem is] particularly fresh in my mind because of the election. . . . [T]he idea that we're going to be able to win stuff through a flurry of advertising during a five-month lead up to an election is crazy. It's just outrageous. And the thing that I would say this election tells us is that the . . . base-building, hearts-and-minds kind of thinking [and] work that has gone into the Republican ascendancy is what we need to be doing. So all these folks who were giving fifty million dollars to the DNC will be much better served by giving forty of it to community organizations and then giving ten million at the tail end to mobilize the folks, so that you don't have kids from New York knocking on doors in Miami, you have a strong organization in Miami with lots of members, good databases, relationships with people. . . . [A]nd then they also can be an active force, not just in the election, but in general when you're trying to win things at the state, city or national level.

The bottom line is that while local groups lack the skills and resources needed for large-scale campaigns (and are sometimes divided), national organizations are missing the kind of local understanding that comes with long-term community-based work. SCOs are potentially strong partners for progressive national think tanks and advocacy groups: with their strong connections to communities, SCOs can help more distant organizations develop ideas and policies that will resonate with the people who must be mobilized for action and in turn provide essential political education on the ground.[12] Conversely, the information and analysis that national groups develop can be used by those working locally to strengthen their own efforts.

A successful movement will require both a venue and a process for building relationships that is supportive of groups at national, state, and local levels. But joint production takes time, commitment, and a willingness to set aside one's own agenda and assumptions to learn from others. Even if national groups were to develop a greater openness to local organizations, would SCO leadership be up to the challenge?

Conflicting Demands on Leadership:
Individual Interests or Shared Movement

A major obstacle to movement building at all levels, but particularly for SCOs, is the commitment of leaders to their own organizations. It takes unusual drive and dedication to establish and maintain a social change organization and the leaders in our study have these qualities in abundance. But it is precisely the skills that are needed to push individual organizations forward that can deter people from moving together into a larger force for change.

We often felt in our interviews, especially with directors, that the sheer strength of will required to create and sustain these organizations left little time or interest for developing a more generalized vision for change. When asked what made their organizations social change groups, few leaders mentioned working with others toward change (and those that did were often frustrated by the lack of coordination or interest). Indeed, as reported in chapter 3, at least one director saw his own organization as a kind of movement in itself, especially as it continued to develop and expand. Understandable though this organizational identification is, it is a highly problematic stance in movement building.

Even if leaders are inclined to contribute to broader efforts and can find the resources for this work, they may be ill prepared for the task. Most of the directors in our study had little training for their roles, and although they had worked hard to learn how to run a single organization, the management skills they had developed were not necessarily those needed for contributing to a larger movement.

Beyond exhorting individual leaders to take a more generous, broader view, the best ways to address this problem are to try to change some of the conditions that promote commitment to organizations over a movement. These include more strategic funding arrangements and generous support for relationship building and broader social change work. It is also possible that some of the leadership and turf battles could be eased by communities and supporters recognizing long-term leaders for their contributions. Those who have spent a lifetime serving in social change organizations often feel neglected by those interested in larger movement building. It is important that we acknowledge their work, including the financial sacrifice many have made, and learn from their experience. At the same time, the field must be open to newer generations of leaders that are not carrying the same history, and must help them figure out how to build and sustain organizations in the context of a larger movement.

Looking Forward

Grassroots social change organizations are a critical resource for progressive movement building in the United States. They provide political education and sites for constituent engagement, and they are beginning to create networks across issues and/or communities; they promote home-grown leadership among marginalized groups; they contribute to a shared understanding of the problems of inequality and injustice; and they offer a public space for the dialogue needed to identify common principles.

At the same time, there are serious obstacles to their effectiveness in movement building, including resource competition, lack of cooperation between grassroots and national groups, and the conflicting commitments of SCO leaders. These problems do not have to be completely debilitating, but overcoming them will require even greater levels of openness, cooperation, and generosity than we have seen to date from all sides. Funders must be willing to provide more consistent support for social change work, including long-term, cross-issue and cross-constituency relationship building. National and state-level actors and groups will have to develop strategies that are more respectful and inclusive of local groups. And SCO leaders must be genuinely interested in setting differences aside to work on common goals, and in spending the time to work out consensus on values and principles.

On the last point, we are hopeful. One of the distinguishing qualities of our SCOs is the enormous dedication of staffers and constituents to their vision of social change. At a time when concern is often voiced about moral commitment in American life, those working in SCOs demonstrate the importance of passion and strong beliefs as a motivation for sustained action and for building larger efforts. In addition, we found that many social change groups have a large reach in spite of their small size. Linda Jefferson, a long-time member of the Respect collective, has edited a book about poverty and the struggles of low-income women, and she speaks frequently at national conferences as well as in local classrooms. Jay Stanley and his staff at Teaching Tools advise schools around the country on how to adapt TT's anti-violence training to fit their own needs. And Myung Kim is part of a national network of small, locally based environmental justice groups that meet regularly to share tools and strategies, and to discuss ways to have broader impact.

SCOs have built a valuable infrastructure of organizations that although sometimes fragile have managed to survive and even grow throughout different political regimes. Spread throughout the country, these organizations have human, financial, and physical resources that can serve as part of the foundation for larger change. Their often long-term presence in local communities has attuned them to the political issues, assets, opportunities, and constraints of those communities. And the infrastructure supplied by SCOs extends beyond their engagement with particular constituencies. In many cases, these groups hold a kind of public space that can be an important counterweight to the current trend toward privatization in American society. It is in this space where the engagement of constituents and their transformation into informed citizens can happen, and indeed is happening as people make changes for themselves, their families, their communities and beyond.

APPENDIX

Study Methods

In keeping with the exploratory aims of this research project, the study relied on qualitative methods of data-collection and analysis. Organizations
and individual respondents were selected based on theoretically relevant
characteristics rather than for statistical generalizability, and data were
gathered primarily through in-depth, semi-structured interviews. Interview
material was supplemented by data from informational tax returns (IRS
Form 990), agency documents, websites, published media or research accounts, and informational forms completed by agency respondents. Interview transcripts were analyzed for content relating to research concerns
and for prominent themes in the respondents' accounts of their experience.
The analysis was conducted using QSR N-Vivo, a computer program designed for analysis of qualitative data.

Sample Selection: Organizations

The aim of the research was to increase understanding of small nonprofits
that engage in social change work—whether or not such work is their *only*
purpose—without necessarily trying to assess the extent of their impact.
Our basic definition of a social change organization, then, was one whose
mission included reference to systemic change, and whose work promoted
the increased power of disadvantaged groups, communities, or interests—
with the understanding that this effort might be conducted in conjunction
with other activities such as direct service. We chose to use a somewhat

broad definition for two reasons: first, we wanted to learn more about how practitioners themselves thought of social change work, and second, we wanted to understand more about the connection between social service and social change in the hope of developing insights that could strengthen this connection.

Using our basic definition, we solicited names of social change organizations that might be good candidates for the study from academics and practitioners familiar with nonprofits in two urban areas of the northeastern United States. We were constrained to this region for practical reasons: we planned to visit the agencies and conduct multiple in-person interviews, and we also felt it would be important to have some familiarity with the surrounding communities. Conducting the research in two urban areas did provide some contextual variation, but the fact that the study organizations come from a single region does limit the study's generalizability to the extent that our conclusions depend on local demographics, economic conditions, funding opportunities, and political structures.

From the suggestions received, we compiled a list of over one hundred organizations that we thought worthy of initial investigation, and we developed very brief profiles of most of these agencies (a few we were unable to learn more about, and some we decided were inappropriate before we gathered data on them). Working with this list, we screened for organizations that met the following criteria:

- a mission statement that referred to changing conditions or systems, not simply ameliorating individual suffering or disadvantage;
- relatively small size, ideally with staffs of at least five people and no more than forty, and annual budgets between $300,000 and $2,000,000; and
- independent, locally based organizations rather than chapters of national groups.

The next step was to winnow the list of eligible groups to a sample of realistic size that would reflect balanced variation along certain critical dimensions. Given the particular kinds of questions we wanted to explore, and what we had learned from reviewing the nonprofit literature and interviewing practitioners, we determined that the most important dimensions of variation would be the following:

- issue area (e.g., youth development, health care, environmental justice, domestic violence);

- organizational structure (e.g., bureaucratic, collective, membership-based);
- primary funding source;
- age;
- size;
- community/constituency served;
- founder-led versus having a history of leadership transition;
- location (half in one urban area and half in the other); and
- basic type of nonprofit (from the literature: service, advocacy, organizing).

Finally, because one of our motivating issues had to do with social change leadership and generational transition, we sought variation in the characteristics of organizational leaders (executive directors) in terms of age, race/ethnicity, and sex. For the most part, our screening assessments were based on secondary data about the organizations from a variety of sources, rather than interviews with people in the organizations.

Ultimately we identified eighteen agencies that we hoped to include in the study, of which all but two agreed to participate. The final sample of sixteen organizations deviated from the initial design in certain respects— for example, several organizations had budgets higher than the original limit (and one was smaller), some had slightly larger staffs, one was affiliated with (but not dependent on) a national group, and one had merged into another somewhat larger local organization.[1] See table A-1 for characteristics of the final group of organizations in which respondents were located; note that data are incomplete in a few cases. Because this was an exploratory study, the sample was constructed to capture theoretically relevant diversity and not to reflect the composition of social change organizations as a whole.[2] The data gathered in this study shed light on the work and challenges of social change nonprofits and raise interesting questions for broader studies, but were not intended to be the basis for statistical generalizations about all social change nonprofit organizations.

As planned, the agencies ranged in size from small (staff size five or less; smallest annual budget $76,000) to medium-sized (the largest had a staff of fifty-four people with a budget of $3.3 million); the median number of staff members was approximately nineteen and the median budget roughly $1.3 million.[3] Though the oldest agency had been in existence for over a hundred years, the median organizational age was about 17 years, with five agencies in existence less than a decade. By design, about half of the agencies with an individual director were headed by older leaders (ages

Table A-1 Characteristics of study organizations

Category	Pseudonym	Age	Annual year 2000 budget [a]	Number of employees [a]	Basic activities and goals
Advocacy	Advocates for the People (AP)	30[b]	$2,201,301[b]	22[b]	Political action, research, and networking to achieve full participation for the Latino community
Advocacy	Center for Critical Information (CCI)	20	$576,895	6	Opposition research and analysis, in support of the work of progressive groups and individuals
Advocacy	Rights for All (RFA)	17	$2,294,529	39	Legal representation and organizing of socio-economically marginalized groups
Advocacy	Urban Watch (UW)	26	$878,496	5	Local-issue research and analysis to serve social justice activists and policymakers
Advocacy/ organizing	Community Choices (CC)	9	$584,266	13	Citizen education, training, networking, and litigation to address environmental inequalities and sustainability
Advocacy/ organizing	Community Voice (CV)	8	$457,660	16	Community organizing and legal representation of eco- nomically marginalized neighborhoods
Organizing	Community Ownership Program (COP)	29	$1,821,177	23	Development of cooperatively owned and managed hous- ing for low-income people
Organizing	Faith in Change (FC)	22	$514,614	24[c]	Organizing and education of local residents for more ef- fective political participation and advocacy
Organizing	Respect (Rt)	13	$76,027	n/a[d]	Self-organizing and education for the empowerment of low-income persons
Organizing	Residents Making Change (RMC)	18	$1,292,541	18	Supporting community decision-making and control of development in diverse, low-income neighborhood
Organizing	Uniting Youth for Change (UYC)	10	$1,243,172	19	Organizing and training inner-city youth to develop stronger schools and communities
Service	Dare to Dream (DTD)	20	$2,144,471	40	Providing services and support to homeless and other low- income families in a way that promotes their move- ment out of poverty; advocating for policy change

Table A-1—cont.

Category	Pseudonym	Age	Annual year 2000 budget [a]	Number of employees [a]	Basic activities and goals
Service	Growing Roots (GR)	8	$651,326	7	Providing services to support the development of Black and Latino youth in poor neighborhoods
Service	Neighborhood Reach (NR)	111	$3,287,756	54	Supporting stabilization of at-risk individuals and groups, nurturing community, bringing together economically diverse segments of the population
Service	Sheltering Our Own (SOO)	7	$1,373,501	10	Serving particular racial/ethnic group to support women's freedom from domestic violence; advocacy and education for changing attitudes
Service	Teaching Tools (TT)	5	$1,406,309	36	Anti-violence training for youth, in service of safer, more democratic schools/culture

[a] Budget figures are total annual expenses as reported on Form 990 for the year 2000. Numbers of employees are also taken from that document, except in cases where the Form was incomplete; in these cases we obtained figures from the respondents directly. Note that the Form 990 staff-size figure is the "total numbers of employees" as of a given date. Full-time-equivalent (FTE) "staff size" may be higher or lower: if many employees are part-time, the number on the Form 990 will be high, but if many workers are independent contractors rather than employees, the total reported may be low compared to "staff size."

[b] AP was an independent agency that merged into a larger organization; the figures for budget, age, and staff size are for the larger organization.

[c] We understand FC's regular FTE to be much lower than this number; we assume the figure reported on the Year 2000 Form 990 included many part-time and/or temporary workers related to a special project undertaken during this period. The number of employees reported on the 2002 Form 990 was 6.

[d] Respect is staffed by members of a predominantly unpaid collective.

forty-five and above) and about half by younger leaders (ages forty-one and below).

The organizations were diverse in many respects. Most had predominantly female staffs (the median percent male was only 30 percent), though three were just over half male. People of color were also heavily represented among agency staffs: the median figure for the proportion of the staff that was white was only 27 percent, and only four agencies had staffs that were predominantly white (53–92 percent white). Agency directors were somewhat more likely to be white: of organizations headed by a single director, over half had a white leader. Compared to staff members, directors were disproportionately male—about 64 percent of agencies with a single director had a male leader. As noted in chapter 1, organizational activities were highly varied, and included legal assistance to marginalized communities, community-based social and economic development, organizing poor women for self-advocacy, educating and organizing youth, advocating for environmental justice, and working against domestic violence.

For those curious about how organizational context varied with leader characteristics, we note that agencies headed by younger leaders were different, on average, from those headed by older leaders.[4] Older leaders tended to head larger, older agencies. The median age of these agencies was twenty-one years (none was younger than ten years old); median budget $1,980,000 (the smallest was $515,000), and median staff size twenty-four (smallest six). By contrast, organizations headed by younger leaders had a median age of eight years (two-thirds were less than ten years old), a median annual budget of $1,086,000, and a median staff size of fifteen. The staff demographics between the two groups of agencies were similar for gender (median about 30 percent male) but slightly different for race: the median percent white was 26 percent in agencies with younger leaders, versus a median figure of 31 percent white among older leaders' agencies.

The agencies headed by our respondents of color were, on average, of similar size to those headed by white respondents. Notably, however, agencies headed by people of color had staffs that were considerably less white (21 percent median versus 45 percent median among agencies headed by whites) and slightly less male (29 percent median versus 33 percent median). Agencies headed by women were roughly the same age and size on average as those headed by men. Median staff demographic figures were similar across these two sets of agencies (about 30 percent male and roughly 30 percent white for each group).

Table A-2 Initial interview respondents categories and characteristics

Respondent Categories	Number	Age range	People of color	Women
Directors[a]				
older[b]	9	45–69	3 (33%)	4 (44%)
younger[b,c]	8	27–41	5 (63%)	3 (38%)
Members of collectives[a]				
older	1	54	1 (100%)	1 (100%)
younger	1	32	0 (0%)	1 (100%)
Staff members				
older	3	50–62	1 (33%)	2 (67%)
younger[d]	16	21–42	11 (69%)	10 (63%)
Board members				
older	1	60	0 (0%)	0 (0%)
Total respondents	39	21–69	21 (54%)	21 (54%)
Leaders/collective members	19	27–69	9 (47%)	9 (47%)
Staff members	19	21–62	12 (63%)	12 (63%)
Board members	1	60	0 (0%)	0 (0%)

[a]Respondents in the "Directors" category include two who were entitled "co-director," and one of these was from an organization that later transformed into a collective. Respondents in the "Collective Members" category had no titles and no history of formal organizational leadership.

[b]Included among the older directors are two women of color from the same organization, one of whom was just retiring and the other of whom was just starting, at the time of our interviews. Among the older directors, five (56%) were founders of their organizations.

[c]The younger directors included four (50%) who had started or re-created organizations they were now heading (one of which was led by a team of two leaders).

[d]Five of the younger staff members were over 35 years old.

Individual Respondents: Leaders

We approached organizations by contacting the formal leaders, requesting their participation, and then conducting our first full interviews with these individuals. Second and sometimes third interviews were conducted with other staff members, as explained below. Table A-2 gives some basic demographic characteristics of the initial group of respondents by organizational position and age group.[5] Thirteen leader-respondents were individual directors of established organizations (i.e., organizations that had been in existence over ten years, or in one case, an organization that was younger but not founded by the current leader).[6] Of this group, nine respondents were older and four were younger. Two of our interviewees were members of a self-described collective and therefore not categorized as single leaders; one of these was older and one younger. Finally, we interviewed four young "entrepreneurs"—founders (or co-founders) of relatively new organizations—one of whom (at forty-one) was slightly older than the other young leaders. It is also noteworthy that several of our older leaders were founders of their organizations, which gave them a particularly strong connection to the organization and undoubtedly shaped their views on the questions we asked. Of the nine older, single leaders, five were founders and one had been with the organization for most of its life (over twenty years, far longer than anyone else in the organization).

The 19 leaders we interviewed were distributed relatively evenly across the four race/gender categories: five were women of color, four were men of color, four were white women, and six were white men. The ten older leaders were evenly divided by gender but more of them were whites (six) than people of color (four). More of the older leaders of color were female, and more of the older whites were male. Among younger leaders, five of the nine were people of color and five were men. Here the whites included two men and two women, and the people of color included three men and two women. Finally, it should be noted that three of the four co-leaders/collective members were women, and three of the four were people of color, so among single leaders the proportions of men and whites were higher than among all leaders.

Staff Respondents

Once a leader had been interviewed, he or she was asked to identify a younger staff member with some responsibility who could represent a different view of the organization. We followed up on these referrals and arranged interviews with the designated staff members. In order to explore generational leadership transition issues, we had intended to interview staff respondents who were under the age of thirty-five, but on conducting the second set of interviews we learned that several of the staff respondents were older.[7] In most cases, the staff members in question were only slightly older (still members of Generation X), but in a few cases were old enough to be members of the Baby Boom generation. To learn as much as possible about the organizations, we went ahead with all these interviews, and in addition, in some organizations we conducted a third interview to ensure adequate representation of the youngest staff members in our sample.[8] As shown on table A-2, of the nineteen staff members we interviewed, eleven were ages 21–34, five were slightly older members of the younger generation (36–42), and three were old enough to be considered part of the Baby Boom generation (50–62). All of the staff respondents aged thirty-five and over had significant responsibility within the organization. Among the youngest respondents there was more variation on this dimension, but most did have some autonomy and/or responsibility in their work.

The inclusion of a range of ages among staff members turned out to be revealing in several ways. Interviews with the oldest staff members allowed us to investigate the phenomenon of a leader preparing to leave an organization by bringing in a second-in-command who was much closer in age to herself than to younger staff members. Interviews with the older members of Generation X provided a perspective on the organizations that was quite different from the views of either the leaders or the youngest staff members.

Finally, in terms of the demographic characteristics of the staff respondents, almost two-thirds were people of color and the same proportion were women. These proportions did not vary significantly across the age groups within the staff respondents, except for the lower proportion of people of color among the oldest staff members (two of the three were white).

Strengths and Limitations of the Respondent Sample

The inclusion of respondents at different levels of the organization allowed us to develop a more complete understanding of the organizations, particularly in areas where different types of respondents were likely to report different perspectives (as in discussions of organizational decision-making). In addition, the considerable demographic diversity in our respondent group ensured important variation in experience that might have been missed with a more homogeneous sample. A limitation of the sample is that it did not include clients or constituents (except when a staff member was also a constituent), a reflection primarily of resource constraints but also of confidentiality concerns. We did make an effort to obtain additional, external perspectives on the organizations by consulting popular and academic accounts of their work. For example, in one case where we had questions about whether the organization was as open to constituent participation as the staff suggested, we were able to locate a dissertation written about one of the organization's programs, that provided extensive material based on participant observation and interviews with clients.

Data-Collection Procedures

The initial round of interviews—of a formal leader and at least one staff member—was conducted in late 2001 and early 2002. Interviews took place at the respondent's organization, and ran from 50 to 180 minutes in length, sometimes over multiple sessions. They were conducted by project staff members (all women, about half of whom are women of color) using semi-structured topic guides that had been developed for the different categories of respondents. Primarily open-ended questions were posed, and respondents were encouraged to describe their experiences and concerns in their own terms.[9] Topics included the following areas:

- the mission and work of the organization; whether and how it contributed to "social change";
- the organization's structure and decision-making processes;
- the respondent's path to the work, personal motives, beliefs and experiences;
- organizational leadership needs and opportunities for leadership development, as well as the respondent's own training in this area; and
- the effects of race and gender on leadership and decision-making.

In addition, we obtained demographic data on the respondents and their organizations, and we supplemented interview data with information from a variety of secondary sources, as noted above.

In 2004, we again contacted the study organizations to request a follow-up interview with the director, to explore topics on which we felt additional information would be valuable, and to learn of any major changes that had taken place in the study organizations. We were able to complete follow-up interviews in thirteen of the sixteen organizations (in three organizations, directors were unavailable for a follow-up interview), and in all but two of these groups, the leader we originally interviewed was still at the organization. The exceptions were Neighborhood Reach and Urban Watch. At NR, we had initially interviewed both an outgoing director and her replacement, but by the time of our follow-up the replacement had also left, and so we interviewed her successor. At UW, the director (our original interviewee) was in the process of leaving but a replacement had not been hired, so we re-interviewed the departing director. Follow-up interviews were generally briefer than the initial interviews, running from about forty to sixty minutes. Topics covered included the following:

- agenda-setting and program-design processes in the organization;
- critical components of the work itself;
- experiences and attitudes toward collaboration; and
- clarification of decision-making structure and board role.

We attempted to tape-record all interviews in both rounds, but two tapes failed and for the analysis of these interviews we relied on interviewer notes. All tape recordings were transcribed for analysis.

Analysis

Our analysis entailed iterative coding of interview texts, in a process based partly on the grounded-theory approach of Glaser and Strauss (1967) and similar to the techniques described by Emerson, Fretz, and Shaw (1995) and Charmaz (1983). At the outset, all transcripts (or notes) were reviewed and coded for themes relating to the general question of what constitutes social change, with some codes reflecting concepts identified in advance and some reflecting concepts used by respondents. In subsequent steps, themes were added or aggregated, and transcripts re-coded. The first product of the analytic process was the framework we present in chapter 1 wherein we identify key dimensions of similarity and difference among SCOs.

In later analysis, we repeated this process but focused on different questions (having to do with leadership, staffing, structure, resources, collaboration, and movement building). At this stage, coded segments of text were reviewed not only across the whole set of transcripts, but also within categories based on organizational and respondent characteristics. For example, after developing our framework on social change approaches, we used this categorization in subsequent analyses, exploring if and how responses to particular questions varied according to the organization's placement in this framework. We also conducted some analysis by respondent characteristics, noting how leaders' responses varied according to age group, sex, or race, and how responses varied by the respondent's position (director versus staff member).

In some cases we summarized qualitative data into numerical counts for basic frequencies, and we also conducted some quantitative analysis with data from the informational tax returns, again looking for patterns of similarity and difference by organizational characteristics.

NOTES

Introduction: Grassroots Organizations and Social Change

1. The original three-day meeting, sponsored by the Ford Foundation, was held at the Hauser Center for Nonprofit Organizations at Harvard University. The Ford Foundation is also a primary funder of the Building Movement project, which is directed by Frances Kunreuther along with a steering committee of social change leaders. More information on the Building Movement project can be obtained at http://www.buildingmovement.org/index .html.

2. There are some exceptions. See, for example, Berry and Arons (2003); Berry, Portnoy, and Thomson (1993); and the articles in Hula and Jackson-Elmoore (2000).

3. It is not possible to estimate the number of these types of organizations, but evidence such as the explosive growth of nonprofits (particularly smaller ones) supports the notion that SCOs are growing in number (Weitzman et al. 2002).

4. The term "social movement" has been defined in various ways by different writers. Variations on the basic concept of a collective effort to bring about change include the following: the collectivity may be defined to include individuals, groups, and/or formal organizations; the target may be political change, cultural change, or both; and affiliation may or may not be based on a shared identity. Diani (1992, 1) suggests a definition of social movement based on common themes in different theoretical approaches: "networks of informal interactions between a plurality of individuals, groups and/or organizations, engaged in political or cultural conflicts, on the basis of shared collective identities."

5. For an excellent summary, see Robert Bothwell's "The Decline of Progressive Policy and the New Philanthropy" (http://comm-org.utoledo.edu/papers.htm, accessed 6/7/2004); among those cited by Bothwell are Callahan (1999); Hart (2001); Himmelstein (1990); and Ricci (1993). Conservatives have been successful by coordinating a national strategy that has resonance at a grassroots level; whether this actually represents a social movement might be debated.

6. Historical summaries of social movement theories tend to begin with late nineteenth- to mid-twentieth-century writings in which there were several different schools of thought on collective activity, including the "collective behavior" approach deriving from Park and Burgess (1921); the "mass society" perspective (e.g, Arendt 1951); the "relative deprivation" school (e.g., Aberle 1966); and the "institutional school" following Michels (1959)—the

only one to emphasize organizations. However, some have argued that the work of Marx and Engels constitutes a much earlier and in some ways, more important contribution to the field than sociological theories of mass behavior, and that the writings of other Marxists, including Lenin and Gramsci, also require recognition. See Flacks (2004); Tarrow (1998); Bevington and Dixon (2005).

7. See Laraña, Johnston, and Gusfield (1994); Melucci (1989).

8. By definition, the early collective-behavior tradition was concerned with large-group activity outside organizational or institutional structures.

9. This argument was also made by Morris (1984); his typology of organizational roles in the civil rights movement is summarized in our final chapter.

10. The term "social movement organization" originated with McCarthy and Zald (1973, 1977) but has been used by many other social movement researchers. The term "social change organization"—common among practitioners—is largely absent from academic literature. Browsing the index of almost any academic anthology or searching in an academic literature database is unlikely to produce any reference to "social change organizations." For example, a search in EBSCO's Academic Search Premier Database produced a mere seven citations, only one of which (from a popular journal) discussed social change organizations as a topic. Though a search on "social change" returned thousands of citations—in part because *social change* is a subject heading—a relatively small proportion of these related to intentional social change, and of those that did, only a fraction also focused on organizations.

11. For example, see Skocpol (1999) on Washington-oriented, professionalized organizations without members; Meyer and Tarrow (1998) on the institutionalization of social movements. Grassroots SCOs also contrast with another model of organizational impact found in the nonprofit literature—that of "social entrepreneurship" in which a small organization makes an impact by "going to scale" in the manner of a for-profit business; see Letts, Ryan, and Grossman (1999).

12. In one such search, the first 80 links were closely reviewed for content. These 80 links produced 53 relevant sites (after elimination of duplicates and inaccessible sites), of which 30 (56 percent) referred to a single, named organization as a "social change organization," and 23 (44 percent) used the term either as a general concept or to describe a group of unnamed organizations (as in, "we serve social change organizations"). Many sites referred to social change organizations or activists as "progressive," and the specific causes identified by these sites tended to signal a liberal or radical orientation. Only one (2 percent) of the 53 sites examined defined SCOs as including conservative groups (this site was a class assignment requiring students to study an SCO), and two others (one a funding agency and the other a college course syllabus) included moderate or apolitical organizations in their implied definitions. None of the 30 sites that identified a single, named organization as an SCO either stated or implied that "social change" is anything other than politically progressive. Investigation of more sites might turn up some in which conservative groups refer to themselves as SCOs, but the great preponderance appears to be progressive.

13. The relevance of social change terminology to people engaged in the work is also illustrated in an episode recounted by ethnographer Marla Frederick, who studied African American spirituality and religion. She describes an incident in which the members of a politically active community group were debating the symbol to be used on their T-shirts: should it be a Bible (reflecting the spiritual source of their strength) or a hand (the unifying logo of their community organization)? An eighty-year-old member of the group voiced his objection to using the Bible by asking rhetorically, " 'Are we a church or a social change organization?' " Frederick (2000, 150). For the people in this community group, the term captured something significant and positive about their work.

14. The distinction between strictly service agencies and change-oriented groups can be illustrated with the following two mission statements, both from homeless shelters. The first agency—a service-only group—states, "Our mission is to provide a safe and nurturing envi-

ronment to help poor guests maintain their dignity, seek opportunity, and find security in their lives." The second agency—a change-oriented service group—states, "[We are] dedicated to ending family homelessness. Toward this end, we create structures which support families, build communities of interdependence, and challenge systems that threaten basic human rights." For purposes of this book, we would define the second but not the first as a social change organization.

15. A more detailed description of study methods, including respondent characteristics and a discussion of sample strengths and limitations, may be found in the appendix.

16. In one case, the organization was "staffed" by unpaid members of the collective.

17. See for example Minkoff (1994, 2002). The earlier work also includes the category of "protest organizations," but the later article considers only service, advocacy, and hybrid groups.

18. These are not necessarily mutually exclusive categories. Minkoff (2002), for example, discusses the rise of "hybrid" service-advocacy organizational forms among identity-based groups, but most of the agencies in this book were primarily identified with one category.

19. A report on generational issues is available at the project website listed in note 1 above.

20. The age categories were as follows: older leaders were 45 to 69, younger leaders 27 to 41, with all but one under 40.

1. Approaches to Social Change

1. Names of both organizations and individual respondents are pseudonyms, and certain other identifying details have been changed. Transcript conventions include the following: ellipses indicate omitted text; comments in brackets are not the speaker's words but are inserted to make sense of a passage.

2. Our use of the term "grassroots" is consistent with the two definitions given by *The American Heritage Dictionary of the English Language, Fourth Edition*. The first of these is "People or society at a local level rather than at the center of major political activity" and the second is "The groundwork or source of something."

3. See Martin (1990) for a similar treatment of the problem of defining feminist organizations.

4. Examples include the Environmental Defense Fund and the Children's Defense Fund. Some scholars argue that these types of "professionally dominated" organizations are increasingly prevalent in civil society (Skocpol 1999).

5. We also note that there is variation in the degree to which the other SCOs engage participants, and patterns may change over time. For example, in its long history, Neighborhood Reach had transitioned from a highly constituent-involved, advocacy-oriented group to one more focused on traditional service provision, but seems now to be moving back toward a higher level of participation.

6. It can also be argued that under conditions of gross inequality, service provision in itself can be a form of social activism and change. In describing feminist organizations, Martin argues that "feminist goals" include serving women as well as changing society, and she notes that "numerous scholars claim that feminist organizations do things in unique ways. . . . For example, services are delivered in a way that empowers recipients within a social relations context that communicates caring and support. How services are delivered is emphasized as much as the services themselves" (1990, 196). Minkoff (2002, 378) discusses service provision as the primary social change strategy of many identity-based organizations prior to the 1960s, after which time both advocacy and service-advocacy "hybrid" organizations became more common. See also Hyde (1992) on the social change implications of service delivery for feminist organizations.

7. See, for example, *Pedagogy of the Oppressed* (1970), one of Freire's best-known works. In *We Make the Road by Walking* (Horton and Freire 1990), Freire discusses the principles of his work with Myles Horton of the Highlander School, another practitioner of popular education. Other relevant work can be found in the writings of Henry Giroux.

8. The basic approach of agitation for action is detailed in Saul Alinsky's books on community organizing. See *Rules for Radicals* (1989).

9. Or at least, it has not been the primary aim to this point; it does appear that RFA may be moving with some of its projects into more organizing work (resembling Community Choices), and in this case would migrate up in figure 1–1. At this stage, however, RFA illustrates the theory of change that emphasizes individual empowerment without necessarily including individual transformation.

10. See Letts, Ryan, and Grossman (1999); Light (1998); Drucker (1990); Oster (1995); and Wolf (1999). In other work (e.g., Salamon [1999, 2002]), nonprofit organizations are disaggregated along such lines as "subsector" (general activity category), size, public versus member-serving, funding versus operating, and service versus action (based on a legal distinction, where the latter category refers to lobbying groups). Although some of these distinctions are relevant to social change organizations, they are less meaningful than distinctions based on differing social change orientations.

2. Doing the Work

1. See Oster (1995) and Watson and Abzug (2005) for discussions of human resource management in nonprofits and the importance of "fit." Note that in almost all cases we are writing here about paid staff members, even though not all are full-time employees. The one exception is the "staffer" at Faith in Change who was a constituent leader and had received extensive training through the organization both locally and nationally.

2. Dissatisfaction with inequality and belief in principles of fairness appear to be common among Americans, but a critical perspective—an appreciation for systemic causes of inequality and a commitment to structural change—is much less widespread. See Draut (2002); Washington Post/Kaiser/Harvard Survey Project, American Values (1998).

3. For an alternative introduction to community organizing, see Sen (2003).

4. Although issues of gender and class were raised in the interviews, the topic of race seemed to elicit more responses, perhaps in part because all the groups in our study either worked primarily with people of color or served groups that worked with people of color.

5. See Draut and Silva (2003).

6. See Oster (1995).

7. Three organizations that have developed formal political education projects are the SouthWest Organizing Project (SWOP), which offers a youth membership course, a power mapping exercise, and workshops on the city budget (see www.swop.net for information about the agency); People Organized to Win Employment Rights (POWER), which runs a nine-week training called "POWER University," structured one-on-one meetings with members, and regular discussion groups that examine political issues in the context of larger social and economic forces (see www.fairwork.org); and Community Coalition for Substance Abuse Prevention and Treatment, which sponsors a "Political Academy" for youth, study groups for local service providers through its Prevention Network, and ongoing staff training and reflection on structures of domination (see http://www.ccsapt.org/).

8. See Ballard (2005) on the problem of educational debt among nonprofit workers.

9. Recently, Third Sector New-England opened a multi-tenant center that advertises the provision of "affordable, quality workspace that also builds on and enhances cross-organizational collaboration and community." See http://www.nonprofitcenterboston.org/section/569.html, accessed 4/26/05.

10. For example, many nonprofits oppose living wage campaigns because of the impact such a policy would have on their budgets.

11. See Copeland (2005).

12. The Annie E. Casey Foundation has supported the formation of many of these programs including those at Transition Guides, CompassPoint, and the Maryland Association of Nonprofits.

3. Leadership

1. The literature on nonprofit management includes long lists of responsibilities and functions of leaders. For examples, see Young (1987), Herman and Heimovics (1994), Drucker (1990), Wolf (1999).

Note that we focus on formal leaders—in most cases, the executive directors of organizations—but recognize that the exercise of "leadership" is something that can happen at any level of an organization and may at times even be stronger at lower levels. It should be noted that boards of directors also have formal authority for oversight and policy decisions in nonprofit organizations, but highly active boards are not the rule in this group of organizations and we generally do not discuss them.

2. See Moore (1995, 2000) for articulations of his framework on strategy in public and nonprofit organizations.

3. We explained in chapter 1 that our organizations are not for the most part "social movement organizations," but there are similarities between our groups and some (especially local) social movement organizations. For those interested in this comparison, we note that the SCO leadership challenges of participatory decision-making and balancing organizational maintenance against movement building apply also to those who lead social movement organizations; see Polletta (2002). And, as in our SCOs, the leader's need to support transformation and growth of workers may more be relevant for some social movement organizations than others.

4. See Bradford and Cohen (1998), Lipman-Blumen (1996), and Plas (1996).

5. Important internal functions of leadership are identified in Letts, Ryan, and Grossman (1999), Wolf (1999), and Oster (1995). All of these can pose special challenges in SCOs, given the nature of their work. Fund-raising and government contracting options are limited for groups that seriously challenge the status quo, and programs sustained by client fees are constrained by the limited resources of the constituent base. Performance measurement is feasible when a visible product such as low-income housing is being produced, but much less straightforward when the goal is individual transformation or community empowerment.

6. See Fletcher (1999) for definitions and discussion of relational practice at work.

7. Plas (1996) discusses this idea at length.

8. See Chetkovich and Frumkin (2003) for an analysis of the problem of balancing margin and mission.

9. Dorothy Day was co-founder of the Catholic Worker Movement.

10. On the last point, see Daloz (2000) on transformative learning and the development of leaders who serve the common good.

11. See Karp et al. (1999) on Generation X and teamwork.

12. An exception was a group that was part of a national organizing initiative that provided regular, formal training to organizers and constituents.

13. A notable exception was Community Choices, where the leader did not relate significant movement inspiration, but had a deeply collaborative style (see chapter 6 for more detail).

14. "Developing Community Leadership," in *Black Women in White America: A Documentary History*, ed. Gerda Lerner (New York: Pantheon Books. 1972), 352.

15. See Lave and Wenger's analysis (1991) of how vocational training is accomplished through increasingly central participation in a community of practice.

16. It is in the situation of individual responsibility for a project or program that the critical feedback process is most direct: an individual can see the impact of her own work as opposed to the result of shared decisions or implementation.

17. By "transforming" we mean something like taking an organization that existed in very limited form, perhaps was not even incorporated, and building it into something much more active, perhaps even very different in substance.

18. For discussions of nonprofit leadership transition issues, see Hinden and Hull (2002); on the need to develop young leadership, see Development Guild/DDI (2001).

4. Organizational Structure

1. See Martin (1990); Lofland (1996); Baker (1982); Ferguson (1984); Rothschild-Whitt (1979); Alter (1998); and Bordt (1997).

2. At the time of our initial interviews, CC was in the process of clarifying those key principles and shared assumptions, a process that would lead to a shift in its social change orientation and structure with respect to constituent participation, as noted at the opening of the chapter and discussed fully below.

3. The projects are responsible for all of their own fund-raising; the executive director sees this arrangement as a test of the project directors' capabilities and basically lets them make decisions about their own activities without his involvement.

4. Very small stipends and reimbursements for child care, transportation, and other expenses are provided to some members, usually in accord with their level of need.

5. In some cases nonprofits may designate officers or executive directors in response to real or perceived requirements of incorporation and/or funders; the "co-directors" at Community Voice retain this title for these reasons.

6. See Smith and Lipsky (1993); Mintzberg (1981); Gross et al. (1998); DiMaggio and Powell (1983); Milofsky (1987); Bordt (1997); Alexander (1998); and Alter (1998). Gross et al. (1998) describe organizational life cycles in which structural forms in successive phases address the problems arising in preceding phases. The initial phase is informal, energetic, and fluid; the second is more structured; the third is characterized by decentralization (a reaction to over-centralized authority), and this phase is in turn succeeded by a period of consolidation in which ways must be found to integrate the decentralized units. Interestingly, many nonprofit managerial guides have little or nothing to say about structure.

7. See Mintzberg (1981, 1983); Burns and Stalker (1961); Perrow (1967); and Thompson (1967).

8. Only one of these, COP, is at the lowest end of the participation spectrum. COP has a larger professional service element in its programs than is the case in the other organizations in this group, and its model seems be moving from one based heavily on organizing and collective action toward one of individual empowerment through meeting needs and building skills.

9. Although RFA clients are not significantly engaged in the workings of the organization, it does routinely reach out and actively listen to constituent groups, and its mode of representation is one that honors client self-determination.

10. We should note here that even though SOO primarily employs the weakest form of client participation, the clients do have input into site-specific shelter decisions.

11. See Mintzberg (1981, 1983).

12. See DiMaggio and Powell (1983).

13. Ospina et al. (2002) point out that although a traditional conceptualization of accountability relates to appropriate financial management and regulatory compliance, accountability can be defined more broadly to include qualities of performance such as re-

sponsiveness to client communities. Conflicting accountability demands from "above" and "below" can require elaborate negotiation by nonprofit leaders.

14. The argument is sometimes made in literature concerning feminist organizations. See Alter (1998) and Iannello (1992).

15. Polletta (2002, 2), emphasis omitted.

16. An inadequate level of constituent participation will hinder the work of an SCO, whether its internal structure is democratic or hierarchical.

17. The number is five if Community Choices is included.

18. To a lesser degree, Growing Roots is also trying to model an alternative, with its shared leadership and staff participation. In a sense, these groups are engaged in what Breines (1982, 6) called "prefigurative politics."

19. See Axelrod (2005) for a discussion of how board practices should vary with the needs of the organization.

5. Resources

1. See Froehlich (1999); Young (1998); Salamon (1999); and Gronbjerg (1992, 1993) on changing patterns of revenues in the nonprofit sector.

2. The proportion of revenue for *all* public charities (including hospitals and higher education institutions) that is derived from fees is 68 percent; for operating organizations it is 70.5 percent. See Independent Sector (2002).

3. For example, Jenkins (1998) estimates that for the period 1955 to 1977, the "high point" for social movement philanthropy came in 1977, when it amounted to 0.69 percent of total foundation giving. Rabinowitz (1990) estimates that approximately one tenth of one percent of all funds available to nonprofit activities (from all sources) goes to support progressive social change programs.

4. See Hunsaker and Hanzl (2003).

5. Even in the most favorable circumstances and in organizations best-suited to this kind of enterprise, for-profit ventures and partnerships tend to be risky endeavors (Dees 1998). Still, the possibility exists and the idea has been entertained, if not pursued, by one or more of our SCOs. See Shuman and Fuller (2005) for an argument in favor of for-profit ventures as a source of funds.

6. Dees, Emerson, and Economy (2001) recommend that social entrepreneurs think broadly about resources and identify many critical non-monetary assets.

7. We distinguish between strategies that rely on mobilizing constituents and those that use primarily non-constituent volunteers. In the former case, constituents are doing something on their own behalf, and are developing their own skill and power. Volunteers are providing service to others.

8. In some cases, there are legal arrangements that constrain resale or limit the equity gains to new property-owners, to prevent gentrification and to ensure that benefits accrue to the community as a whole rather than individual owners.

9. Mondros and Wilson (1994) describe how much work is involved in recruiting and sustaining an active membership for political action.

10. Advocates for the People works with individuals as well as other groups, but unlike the SCOs that bring individuals together in collective action, those targeted by AP are community or organizational leaders rather than grassroots-level community members.

11. Again, we distinguish volunteer labor from constituent mobilization, for the reasons explained above.

12. Growing Roots's co-leaders expressed an interest in establishing a for-profit enterprise that would both subsidize their other activities and provide a model of economic development for the community, but they had not been able to identify a specific plan that seemed workable.

13. Some firms recognize an obligation to serve, but they are also under public and peer pressure to do so. Some of the firms that assist RFA are signatories to the American Bar Association's "pro bono challenge" in which large firms are asked to commit to providing three to five percent of professional time to pro bono service, at least half of which is supposed to be given to legal work on behalf of the poor.

14. Not all of RFA's cases fall into the system-changing category. As far as those that constitute individual services are concerned, RFA is faced with constraints similar to those of other direct-service SCOs.

15. Berry and Arons (2003) argue that such fears do inhibit nonprofit activism, but that these organizations have more room for political activity than they often realize and that it is crucial that they engage in such activity.

6. Collaboration

1. See Gray (1985, 1989), Himmelman (2001); Mizrahi and Rosenthal (2001); and Mulroy (2003).

2. See Hardy, Lawrence, and Grant (2005).

3. The original authorship of these two quotations is impossible to identify with any certainty.

4. A quick search on the web will produce many references to collaboration using these comparisons.

5. Organizational history is also relevant here: RMC's original membership included representatives of other organizations along with individual community activists.

6. See Hall and Hall (1996).

7. Less frequently SCOs enter partnerships for the immediate benefit of the organization—for example, when they offer mutual support or exchange technical assistance. But these efforts indirectly support mission attainment.

8. The exception in our sample is Urban Watch, which follows a journalistic ethic of independence but still engages others and clearly provides a space for the virtual collaboration of other groups.

9. "In collaborative empowerment coalitions people and communities are not 'targets' of institutional intervention but subjects of their own purposes." Himmelman (2001, 282).

7. Organizations, Movement, and the Future of Social Change

1. For an extended discussion, see Zald and Ash (1966) and McCarthy and Zald (1997).

2. See Lakoff (2004) and Hazen (2005).

3. On the problem of how political knowledge is unevenly distributed, see Delli Carpini and Keeter (1996).

4. On the Villagarosa campaign in Los Angeles, see Cooper (2001).

5. For information on PLAN's activities, see Foege (2000); also Cooper (2003) for a discussion of PLAN's affiliation with a union organizing effort among sex workers. The Western States Center's programs are described in detail on its website, at www.westernstatescenter.org.

6. Payne (1995, 77) notes the importance of three people in particular—Septima Clark, Myles Horton, and Ella Baker—who traveled throughout the south and were instrumental in building local capacity that resulted in action: "Through long experience working with impoverished communities, they had developed a faith in the ability of communities of the poor to provide much of the leadership for their own struggle and concrete ideas about how that ability could be nurtured."

7. Many social movement theorists, particularly those writing in the vein of New Social

Movement theory and other post-structuralist literature, note the importance of a shared interpretive framework to awaken and mobilize previously uninvolved people. See Flacks (2004). We suggest here that the aim is not only mobilization, but the creation of a unifying sense of commitment that can override other differences.

8. Comment found on the National Organizers Alliance (NOA) website, http://noacentral.org/page.php?id=19, describing *The Social Justice Dialogues*. The site also notes that "Organizers can be the catalysts for building a broad-based active social justice movement by engaging others in sharper political analysis connected to strategic action."

9. There are notable exceptions in parts of some fields, such as the early years of the battered women's movement, which included a power analysis of why women were victims of domestic violence. We find, however, that there are few training resources that demonstrate how such analysis can be used to transform the consciousness of clients (and sometimes, staffs) of service agencies.

10. One new funder at a major foundation stated that within a few weeks, four groups had approached her, each claiming to be the only organization working on social change in a certain region. Either they were dismissing the existence of their sister organizations or had failed to realize that others were doing similar work.

11. Unnamed director quoted in Rich (2005, 24). Rich also makes the point that conservative foundations are much more willing to provide ongoing institutional support rather than funding on a project-by-project basis.

12. Many local activists were particularly frustrated by the inattention of national groups (including the Democratic Party) in the 2004 presidential campaign. In one illustrative case, a local organizing group in the southwest offered to assist a national campaign organization with political education among constituents to ensure that voters were informed before being mobilized. The national group refused this help, apparently assuming that no educational outreach was needed, and that get-out-the-vote efforts could be handled by its own out-of-state volunteers. Voting results suggest that this strategy was misguided, as some taken-for-granted constituencies failed to provide anticipated levels of support for the Democratic ticket.

Appendix

1. In the case of the group that had merged, we focused our analysis on the unit that initially interested us (which retained much of the shape it had as an independent organization), and excluded it from the analyses where the only data available referred to the larger agency of which it had become a part (in particular, the financial data reported on its informational tax returns). Since we completed our analysis the two groups have separated and the smaller agency is once again independent.

2. Patton (1987) provides a thoughtful discussion of the difference between "purposeful sampling" for theoretical relevance and random sampling for statistical generalizability.

3. These figures were from the date of the initial sample construction, primarily based on the Year 2000 Form 990 for each organization. Staff and budget sizes have changed somewhat over the course of the study.

4. These observations are based on organizations that had a single director (or in one case, a founder whose group had later transformed into a collective), constituting fourteen of the sixteen organizations in which interviews were conducted. Again, figures are based on the Year 2000 Form 990 returns, with some additional data obtained from respondents at the time of the initial interview.

5. As explained later, one follow-up interview was done with a director not part of the original sample.

6. As noted in table A-2, two of these respondents were associated with the same orga-

nization: one was the recently retired director and the other newly hired. We interviewed both to obtain a deeper understanding of leadership transition issues.

7. When asking for the name of another person to interview, we tried to indicate that we wanted to talk to someone who had some responsibility in the organization, to distinguish potential next-generation leaders from other staff members. It may have been this framing of the request that led some leaders to refer us to somewhat older staff members than we were seeking.

8. We were able to obtain interviews with staff members under age thirty-five in all but three of the organizations, and even in these cases, the youngest staff member interviewed was still a member of Generation X, albeit at the older end (in the 37–42 age range).

9. See Weiss (1994) and Mishler (1986) for discussions of qualitative versus survey interview methods.

REFERENCES

Aberle, David. 1966. *The Peyote Religion among the Navajo.* Chicago: Aldine.

Alexander, Victoria. 1998. "Environmental Constraints and Organizational Strategies: Complexity, Conflict, and Coping in the Nonprofit Sector." In *Private Action and the Public Good,* ed. Walter W. Powell and Elisabeth S. Clemens. New Haven: Yale University Press.

Alinsky, Saul. 1989. *Rules for Radicals: A Practical Primer for Realistic Radicals.* New York: Vintage Books.

Alperovitz, Gar. 2005. *America beyond Capitalism: Reclaiming Our Wealth, Our Liberty, and Our Democracy.* Hoboken, NJ: John Wiley & Sons.

Alter, Catherine. 1998. "Bureaucracy and Democracy in Organizations: Revisiting Feminist Organizations." In *Private Action and the Public Good,* ed. Walter W. Powell and Elisabeth S. Clemens. New Haven: Yale University Press.

The Amercian Heritage Dictionary of the English Language. 4th ed. 2000. New York: Houghton Mifflin.

Arendt, Hannah. 1951. *The Origins of Totalitarianism.* New York: Harcourt, Brace.

Axelrod, Nancy R. 2005. "Board Leadership and Development." In *The Jossey-Bass Handbook of Nonprofit Leadership & Management,* ed. Robert D. Herman & Associates. 2nd ed. San Francisco: Jossey-Bass.

Baker, Andrea J. 1982. "The Problems of Authority in Radical Movement Groups: A Case Study of Lesbian-Feminist Organization." *Journal of Applied Behavioral Science* 18: 323–341.

Baker, Ella. 1972. "Developing Community Leadership." In *Black Women in White America: A Documentary History,* ed. Gerda Lerner. New York: Pantheon Books.

Ballard, Amanda. 2005. "Understanding the Next Generation of Nonprofit Employees: The Impact of Educational Debt." Unpublished master's thesis. http://www.building-movement.org/artman/exec/search.cgi. Accessed on January 3, 2005.

Barber, Benjamin. 1984. *Strong Democracy: Participatory Politics for a New Age.* Berkeley: University of California Press.

Bennis, Warren G., and Richard J. Thomas. 2002. *Geeks and Geezers.* Boston: Harvard Business School Press.

Berry, Jeffrey, and David Arons. 2003. *A Voice for Nonprofits*. Washington, DC: Brookings Institution Press.

Berry, Jeffrey, Kent Portney, and Ken Thomson. 1993. *The Rebirth of Urban Democracy*. Washington, DC: Brookings Institution.

Bevington, Douglas, and Chris Dixon. 2005. "Movement-Relevant Theory: Rethinking Social Movement Scholarship and Activism." *Social Movement Studies* 4 (3): 185–208.

Bobo, Kim, Jackie Kendall, and Steve Max. 2001. *Organizing for Social Change*. Cabin John, MD: Seven Locks Press.

Bordt, Rebecca. 1997. *The Structure of Women's Nonprofit Organizations*. Bloomington: Indiana University Press.

Bradford, David, and Allan Cohen. 1998. *Power Up: Transforming Organizations Through Shared Leadership*. New York: John Wiley and Sons.

Breines, Wini. 1982. *Community and Organization in the New Left, 1962–1968: The Great Refusal*. New York: Praeger.

Brenner, Neil. 1998. "Global Cities, Glocal States: Global City Formation and State Territorial Restructuring in Contemporary Europe." *Review of International Political Economy* 5 (1): 1–37.

Burns, Tom, and George M. Stalker. 1961. *The Management of Innovation*. London: Tavistock.

Callahan, David. 1999. *$1 Billion for Ideas: Conservative Think Tanks in the 1990s*. Washington, DC: National Committee for Responsive Philanthropy.

Castellanos, Patricia, and Deepak Pateriya, eds. 2003. *Power Tools: A Manual for Organizations Fighting for Justice*. Los Angeles: Strategic Concepts in Organizing and Policy Education (SCOPE).

Castree, Noel. 2000. "Geographic Scale and Grass-Roots Internationalism: The Liverpool Dock Dispute: 1995–1998." *Economic Geography* 76 (3): 272–292.

Catalyst. 2001. *The Next Generation: Today's Professionals, Tomorrow's Leaders*. New York: Catalyst.

Charmaz, Kathy. "The Grounded Theory Method: An Explication and Interpretation." In *Contemporary Field Research: A Collection of Readings*, ed. R. M. Emerson. Boston: Little, Brown, 1983.

Chetkovich, Carol, and Peter Frumkin. 2003. "Balancing Margin and Mission: Nonprofit Competition in Charitable versus Fee-Based Programs." *Administration & Society* 35 (5): 564–596.

Clarke, Susan E. 2000. "Governance Tasks and Nonprofit Organizations." In *Nonprofits in Urban America*, ed. R. Hula and C. Jackson-Elmoore. Westport, CT: Quorum Books.

Cooper, Marc. 2003. "The Naked and the Red." *The Nation* 276 (15): 21.

———. 2001. "Villaraigosa's Hot in Los Angeles." *The Nation* 272 (22): 11–15.

Copeland, Craig. 2005. "Employee Tenure: Stable Overall, but Male and Female Trends Differ." *Employee Benefits Research Institute (EBRI) Notes* 26 (3): 2–9.

Daloz, Laurent A. Parks. 2000. "Transformative Learning for the Common Good." In *Learning as Transformation*, ed. J. Mezirow and Associates. San Francisco: Jossey-Bass.

Dees, J. Gregory. 1998. "Enterprising Nonprofits." *Harvard Business Review* 76 (1): 55–65.

Dees, J. Gregory, Jed Emerson, and Peter Economy. 2001. *Enterprising Nonprofits: A Toolkit for Social Entrepreneurs*. New York: John Wiley & Sons.

Delli Carpini, Michael X., and Scott Keeter. 1996. *What Americans Know about Politics and Why It Matters*. New Haven: Yale University Press.

Development Guild/DDI Inc. 2001. "Engaging New Leadership Voices for Catalyzing and Sustaining Community Change." Report to the Kellogg Foundation. Brookline, MA: Development Guild/DDI.

Diani, Mario. 1992. "The Concept of Social Movement." *Sociological Review* 40 (1): 1–25.

DiMaggio, Paul J., and Walter W. Powell. 1983. "The Iron Cage Revisited: Institutional Isomorphism and Collective Rationality in Organizational Fields." *American Sociological Review* 48: 147–160.

Dobbin, Frank. 2001. "The Business of Social Movements." In *Passionate Politics: Emotions and Social Movements*, ed. J. Goodwin, J. Jasper, and F. Polletta. Chicago: University of Chicago Press.

Draut, Tamara. 2002. *New Opportunities? Public Opinion on Poverty, Income Inequality and Public Policy: 1996–2002*. New York: Demos.

Draut, Tamara, and Javier Silva. 2003. *Generation Broke*. New York: Demos.

Dreier, Peter, John Mollenkopf, and Todd Swanstrom. 2001. *Place Matters: Metropolitics for the Twenty-first Century*. Lawrence: Kansas University Press.

Drucker, Peter. 1990. *Managing the Nonprofit Organization*. New York: HarperCollins.

Emerson, Robert M., Rachel I. Fretz, and Linda L. Shaw, 1995. *Writing Ethnographic Fieldnotes*. Chicago: University of Chicago Press.

Ferguson, Kathy. 1984. *The Feminist Case against Bureaucracy*. Philadelphia: Temple University Press.

Flacks, Richard. 2004. "Knowledge for What? Thoughts on the State of Social Movement Studies." In *Rethinking Social Movements: Structure, Culture, and Emotion*, ed. J. Goodwin and J. Jasper. Lanham, MD: Rowman & Littlefield.

Fletcher, Joyce K. 1999. *Disappearing Acts: Gender, Power, and Relational Practice at Work*. Cambridge, MA: MIT Press.

Foege, Alec. 2000. "Silver Ballot." *Brandweek* 41 (36): 14–15. September 18.

Frederick, Marla. 2000. "The Cultural Politics of Religious Experience: African American Women's Spirituality and Activism in the Contemporary U.S. South." Ph.D. diss., Duke University.

Freire, Paulo. 1970. *Pedagogy of the Oppressed*. New York: Herder and Herder.

Froelich, Karen A. 1999. "Diversification of Revenue Strategies: Evolving Resource Dependence in Nonprofit Organizations." *Nonprofit and Voluntary Sector Quarterly* 28 (3): 246–268.

Gitlin, Todd. 1995. *Twilight of Our Common Dreams: Why America Is Wracked by Culture Wars*. New York: Metropolitan Books.

Glaser, Barney, and Anselm Strauss. 1967. *The Discovery of Grounded Theory*. Chicago: Aldine Atherton.

Goodwin, Jeff, James M. Jasper, and Francesca Polletta. 2001. "Introduction: Why Emotions Matter." In *Passionate Politics: Emotions and Social Movements*, ed. J. Goodwin, J. Jasper, and F. Polletta. Chicago: University of Chicago Press.

Gray, Barbara. 1985. "Conditions Facilitating Interorganizational Collaboration." *Human Relations* 38 (10): 911–936.

——. 1989. *Collaborating: Finding Common Ground for Multiparty Problems*. San Francisco: Jossey-Bass.

Gronbjerg, Kirsten. 1992. "Nonprofit Human Service Organizations: Funding Strategies and Patterns of Adaptation." In *Human Services as Complex Organizations*, ed. Y. Hasenfeld. Newbury Park, CA: Sage.

———. 1993. *Understanding Nonprofit Funding*. San Francisco: Jossey-Bass.

Gross, Susan, Mathiasen, Karl, and Franco, Nancy. 1998. "Organizational Life Cycles: Revisited." *MAGNews* (Summer). http://www.managementassistance.org/page4k.html. Accessed on January 22, 2003.

Hall, Leda McIntyre, and Melvin Hall. 1996. "Big Fights: Competition between Poor People's Social Movement Organizations." *Nonprofit and Voluntary Sector Quarterly* 25 (1): 53–72.

Hardisty, Jean. 2000. *Mobilizing Resentment: Conservative Resurgence from the John Birch Society to the Promise Keepers*. Boston: Beacon Press.

Hardisty, Jean, and Deepak Bhargava. 2005. "Wrong about the Right." *The Nation* 281 (15): 22–26.

Hardy, Cynthia, Thomas Lawrence, and David Grant. 2005. "Discourse and Collaboration: The Role of Conversations and Collective Identity." *Academy of Management Review* 30 (1): 58–77.

Hart, Stephen. 2001. *Current Dilemmas of Progressive Politics*. Chicago: University of Chicago Press.

Hazen, Don. 2005. "The Right Wing Express." *AlterNet*. http://www.alternet.org/mediaculture/21192/. Accessed on June 1, 2005.

Herman, Robert, and Dick Heimovics. 1994. "Executive Leadership." In *The Jossey-Bass Handbook of Nonprofit Leadership and Management*, ed. Robert D. Herman and Associates. San Francisco: Jossey-Bass.

Himmelman, Arthur T. 2001. "On Coalitions and the Transformation of Power Relations: Collaborative Betterment and Collaborative Empowerment." *American Journal of Community Psychology* 29 (2): 277–284.

Himmelstein, Jerome L. 1990. *To the Right: The Transformation of American Conservatism*. Berkeley: University of California Press.

Hinden, Denice Rothman, and Paige Hull. 2002. "Executive Leadership Transition: What We Know." *Nonprofit Quarterly* 9 (4): 24–29.

Horton, Myles, and Paulo Freire. 1990. *We Make the Road by Walking: Conversations on Education and Social Change*. Philadelphia: Temple University Press.

Hula, Richard, and Cynthia Jackson-Elmoore, eds. *Nonprofits in Urban America*. Westport, CT: Quorum Books.

Hunsaker, John, and Brenda Hanzl. 2003. "Understanding Social Justice Philanthropy." Washington, DC: National Committee for Responsive Philanthropy.

Hyde, Cheryl. 1992. "The Ideational System of Social Movement Agencies: An Examination of Feminist Health Centers." In *Human Services as Complex Organizations*, ed. Y. Hasenfeld. Newbury Park, CA: Sage.

Iannello, Kathleen. 1992. *Decisions without Hierarchy: Feminist Interventions in Organization Theory and Practice*. New York: Routledge.

Independent Sector. 2002. *The New Nonprofit Almanac and Desk Reference*. San Francisco: Jossey-Bass.

Jenkins, J. Craig. 1998. "Channeling Social Protest: Foundation Patronage of Contemporary Social Movements." In *Private Action and the Public Good*, ed. Walter Powell and Elisabeth Clemens. New Haven: Yale University Press.

Karp, Hank, Danilo Sirias, and Kristin Arnold. 1999. "Teams: Why Generation X Marks the Spot." *Association for Quality and Participation* (July/August): 30–33.

Kipfer, Stefan. 2004. " 'Metropolitics' and the Quest for a New Regionalist Corporatism in the United States: Comparative Notes and Critical Comments." *Antipode* 30 (4): 740–752.

Kirby, Andrew. 2004. "Metropolitics or Retropolitics?" *Antipode* 30 (4): 753–759.

Lakoff, George. 2004. *Don't Think of an Elephant: Know Your Values, Frame the Debate*. White River Junction, VT: Chelsea Green.

Laraña, Enrique, Hank Johnston, and Joseph Gusfield. 1994. "Identities, Grievances, and New Social Movements." In *New Social Movements: From Ideology to Identity*, ed. E. Laraña, H. Johnston, and J. Gusfield. Philadelphia: Temple University Press.

Lave, Jean, and Etienne Wenger. 1991. *Situated Learning: Legitimate Peripheral Participation*. Cambridge: Cambridge University Press.

Letts, Christine, William Ryan, and Allen Grossman. 1999. *High Performance Nonprofit Organizations: Managing Upstream for Greater Impact*. New York: John Wiley & Sons.

Light, Paul. 1998. *Sustaining Innovation: Creating Nonprofit and Government Organizations That Innovate Naturally*. San Francisco: Jossey-Bass.

Lipman-Blumen, Jean. 1996. *Connective Leadership: Managing in a Changing World*. Oxford: Oxford University Press.

Lofland, John. 1996. *Social Movement Organizations: Guide to Research on Insurgent Realities*. New York: Aldine De Gruyter.

Mann, Eric. 2005. "Building the Anti-Racist, Anti-Imperialist United Front: Theory and Practice from the L.A. Strategy Center and Bus Riders Union." www.thestrategycenter.org/polanalysis-ericmann1.html. Accessed on June 6, 2005.

Martin, Patricia Yancey. 1990. "Rethinking Feminist Organizations." *Gender & Society* 4 (2): 182–206.

McAdam, Doug. 1999 [1982]. *Political Process and the Development of Black Insurgency, 1930–1970*. Chicago: University of Chicago Press.

McCarthy, John D., and Mayer Zald. 1973. *The Trend of Social Movements in America: Professionalization and Resource Mobilization*. Morristown, NJ: General Learning Press.

———. 1977. "Resource Mobilization and Social Movements." *American Journal of Sociology* 82: 1212–41.

Melucci, Alberto. 1989. *Nomads of the Present: Social Movements and Individual Needs in Contemporary Society*. Philadelphia: Temple University Press.

Meyer, David S., and Sidney Tarrow. 1998. "A Movement Society: Contentious Politics for a New Century." In *The Social Movement Society: Contentious Politics for a New Century*, ed. David S. Meyer and Sidney Tarrow. Lanham, MD: Rowman and Littlefield.

Mezirow, Jack. 2000. "Learning to Think Like an Adult: Core Concepts of Transformation Theory." In *Learning as Transformation: Critical Perspectives on a Theory in Progress*, ed. Jack Mezirow and Associates. San Francisco: Jossey-Bass.

Michels, Robert. 1959. *Political Parties*. New York: Dover.

Milkman, Ruth. 2000. "Immigrant Organizing and the New Labor Movement in Los Angeles." *Critical Sociology* 26 (1/2): 59–81.

Milofsky, Carl. 1987. "Neighborhood-based Organizations; A Market Analogy." In *The Nonprofit Sector: A Research Handbook*, ed. Walter W. Powell. New Haven: Yale University Press.

Minkoff, Debra C. 1994. "From Service Provision to Advocacy: The Shifting Legitimacy of Organizational Forms." *Social Forces* 72:943–969.

———. 2002. "The Emergence of Hybrid Organizational Forms: Combining Identity-

Based Service Provision and Political Action." *Nonprofit and Voluntary Sector Quarterly* 31 (3): 377–401.

Mintzberg, Henry. 1981. "Organization Design: Fashion or Fit?" *Harvard Business Review* 59 (1): 103–118.

——. 1983. *Structure in Fives: Designing Effective Organizations*. Englewood Cliffs, NJ: Prentice Hall. 1983.

Mishler, Elliot. 1986. *Research Interviewing: Context and Narrative*. Cambridge, MA: Harvard University Press.

Mizrahi, Terry, and Beth Rosenthal. 2001. "Complexities of Coalition Building: Leaders' Successes, Strategies, Struggles, and Solutions." *Social Work* 46 (1): 63–78.

Mondros, Jacqueline, and Scott Wilson. 1994. *Organizing for Power and Empowerment*. New York: Columbia University Press.

Moore, Mark H. 1995. *Creating Public Value: Strategic Management in Government*. Cambridge, MA: Harvard University Press.

——. 2000. "Managing for Value: Organizational Strategy in For-Profit, Nonprofit, and Governmental Organizations." *Nonprofit and Voluntary Sector Quarterly* 29 (1): 183–204.

Morris, Aldon D. 1984. *The Origins of the Civil Rights Movement—Black Communities Organizing for Change*. New York: Free Press.

Mueller, Carol M. 1994. "Conflict Networks and the Origins of Women's Liberation." In *New Social Movements: From Ideology to Identity*, ed. Enrique Laraña, Hank Johnston, and Joseph Gusfield. Philadelphia: Temple University Press.

Mulroy, Elizabeth. 2003. "Community as a Factor in Implementing Interorganizational Partnerships: Issues, Constraints, and Adaptations." *Nonprofit Management & Leadership* 14 (1): 47–66.

Nicholls, Walter Julio. 2003. "Forging a 'New' Organizational Infrastructure for Los Angeles' Progressive Community." *International Journal of Urban and Regional Research* 27 (4): 881–896.

Orfield, Myron. 2002. *American Metropolitics: The New Suburban Reality*. Washington, DC: Brookings Institution Press.

Ospina, Sonia, William Diaz, and James O'Sullivan. 2002. "Negotiating Accountability: Managerial Lessons from Identity-Based Nonprofit Organizations." *Nonprofit and Voluntary Sector Quarterly* 31 (1): 5–31.

Oster, Sharon. 1995. *Strategic Management for Nonprofit Organizations: Theory and Cases*. Oxford: Oxford University Press.

Park, Robert E., and Ernest W. Burgess. 1921. *Introduction to the Science of Society*. Chicago: University of Chicago Press.

Pastor, Manuel. 2001. "Looking for Regionalism in All the Wrong Places: Demography, Geography, and Community in Los Angeles County." *Urban Affairs Review* 36 (6): 747–782.

Pastor, Manuel, Peter Dreier, J. Eugene Grigsby, and Marta Lopez-Garza. 2000. *Regions That Work: How Cities and Suburbs Can Grow Together*. Minneapolis: University of Minnesota Press.

Patton, Michael Quinn. 1987. *How to Use Qualitative Methods in Evaluation*. Newbury Park, CA: Sage.

Payne, Charles. 1995. *I've Got the Light of Freedom*. Berkeley: University of California Press.

Perrow, Charles. 1967. "A Framework for the Comparative Analysis of Organizations." *American Sociological Review* 32: 194–208.

Piven, Frances Fox, and Richard A. Cloward. 1977. *Poor People's Movements: Why They Succeed, How They Fail.* New York: Vintage Books.

——. 1992. "Normalizing Collective Protest." In *Frontiers in Social Movement Theory,* ed. A. D. Morris and C. M. Mueller. New Haven: Yale University Press.

——. 2000. "Power Repertoires and Globalization." *Politics & Society* 28 (3): 413–430.

Plas, Jeanne. 1996. *Person-centered Leadership: An American Approach to Participatory Management.* Thousand Oaks, CA: Sage.

Polletta, Francesca. 2002. *Freedom Is an Endless Meeting: Democracy in American Social Movements.* Chicago: University of Chicago Press.

Purcell, Mark. 2004. "Regionalism and the Liberal-Radical Divide." *Antipode* 30 (4): 760–765.

Rabinowitz, Alan. 1990. *Social Change Philanthropy in America.* New York: Quorum Books.

Radcliffe Public Policy Institute. 2002. *Life's Work: Generational Attitudes toward Work and Life Integration.* Cambridge, MA: Harvard University Press.

Ricci, David M. 1993. *The Transformation of American Politics.* New Haven, CT: Yale University Press.

Rich, Andrew. 2005. "War of Ideas: Why Mainstream and Liberal Foundations and the Think Tanks They Support Are Losing in the War of Ideas in American Politics." *Stanford Social Innovation Review* (Spring): 18–25.

Rothman, Jack. "Countering Fragmentation on the Left." *Social Policy* 30 (4): 42–46.

Rothschild-Whitt, Joyce. 1979. "The Collectivist Organization: An Alternative to Traditional Bureaucratic Models." *American Sociological Review* 44: 509–527.

Salamon, Lester. 1999. *America's Nonprofit Sector: A Primer.* 2nd ed. New York: Foundation Center.

——. 2002. "The Resilient Sector: The State of Nonprofit America." In *The State of Nonprofit America,* ed. L. Salamon. Washington, DC: Brookings Institution Press.

Schumpeter, Joseph A. 1950. *Capitalism, Socialism, and Democracy.* New York: Harper and Brothers.

Sen, Rinku. 2003. *Stir It Up: Lessons in Community Organizing and Advocacy.* San Francisco: Jossey-Bass.

Shuman, Michael H. 1998. "Why Do Progressive Foundations Give Too Little to Too Many?" *The Nation.* January 12–19.

Shuman, Michael H., and Merrian Fuller. 2005. "Profits for Justice." *The Nation,* January 24.

Sites, William. 2004. "Progressive Regionalism: A 'Deliberative' Movement?" *Antipode* 36 (4): 766–778.

Skocpol, Theda. 1999. "Associations without Members." *American Prospect.* 10 (45): 66–73.

Smith, Steven Rathgeb, and Michael Lipsky. 1993. *Nonprofits for Hire: The Welfare State in the Age of Contracting.* Cambridge, MA: Harvard University Press.

Tarrow, Sidney. 1998. *Power in Movement: Social Movements and Contentious Politics.* 2nd ed. Cambridge: Cambridge University Press.

Taylor, Charles. 1994. "The Politics of Recognition." In *Multiculturalism: Examining the Politics of Recognition,* ed. Amy Gutmann. Princeton: Princeton University Press.

Taylor, Verta, and Nancy Whittier. 1992. "Collective Identity in Social Movement Communities: Lesbian Feminist Mobilization." In *Frontiers in Social Movement*

Theory, ed. Aldon D. Morris and Carol McClurg Mueller. New Haven: Yale University Press.

Thompson, James D. 1967. *Organizations in Action*. New York: McGraw-Hill.

Tocqueville, Alexis de. 1960. *Democracy in America*. New York: Vintage Books.

Washington Post/Kaiser/Harvard Survey Project, American Values. 1998. "National Survey of Americans on Values." http://www.kff.org/kaiserpolls/1441-index.cfm. Accessed on December 1, 2005.

Watson, Mary R., and Rikki Abzug. 2005. "Finding the Ones You Want, Keeping the Ones You Find: Recruitment and Retention in Nonprofit Organizations." In *The Jossey-Bass Handbook of Nonprofit Leadership & Management*, ed. Robert J. Herman and Associates. 2nd ed. San Francisco: Jossey-Bass.

Weisbrod, Burton A. 1997. "The Nonprofit Mission and Its Financing." *Journal of Policy Analysis and Management* 16 (4): 541–555.

———. 1998. "The Nonprofit Mission and Its Financing." *Journal of Policy Analysis and Management* 17 (2): 165–175.

Weiss, Robert S. 1994. *Learning from Strangers: The Art and Method of Qualitative Interview Studies*. New York: Free Press/Simon & Schuster.

Weitzman, Murray S., Nadine T. Jaladoni, Linda M. Lampkin, and Thomas H. Pollak. 2002. *The New Nonprofit Almanac 2000*. San Francisco: Jossey-Bass.

Wolf, Thomas. 1999. *Managing a Nonprofit Organization in the Twenty-First Century*. New York: Simon & Schuster.

Young, Dennis. 1987. "Executive Leadership in Nonprofit Organizations." In *The Nonprofit Sector: A Research Handbook*, ed. Walter W. Powell. New Haven: Yale University Press.

———. 1998. "Commercialism in Nonprofit Social Service Associations: Its Character, Significance, and Rationale." *Journal of Policy Analysis and Management* 17 (2): 278–297.

Young, Iris M. 2000. *Inclusion and Democracy*. New York: Oxford University Press.

Zald, Mayer, and Roberta Ash. 1966. "Social Movement Organizations: Growth, Decline, and Change." *Social Forces* 44:327–340.

INDEX

The fictional names of organizations and staff members discussed in the book are indexed here. These entries of pseudonyms have the notation (pseud.) after them.

Third Sector New England, 182 n9
Thomas, Ken, 179 n2
Thomas, Richard J., 45
transformation: of constituents, 36, 56, 130, 157–158, 163; individual, 14–15, 18–22; and SCO staff, 49–50
transformative learning, 29–30, 183 n10

unions. *See* labor, organized
United Way of New York, 51
Uniting Youth for Change (UYC) (pseud.), 8, 28, 30, 33–34; and constituent empowerment/ participation, 17, 94, 155; funding, 113–116; and individual transformation, 21; and leadership/leadership development, 53, 71; organizational structure, 86–87, 93; partnerships/collaboration, 135; resources, 118; staff members, 45
Urban Watch (UW) (pseud.), 8, 15, 22, 38–39, 64, 176; funding, 114–115, 119, 121; and leadership/leadership development, 69–70; organizational structure, 93, 102; partnerships/collaboration, 119,

137, 186 n8; and social change orientation, 24–25

values. *See* ideology
volunteers, 113, 118, 123, 125–126, 185 n7; pro bono, 125, 142–143
Veratek, Pete (pseud.), 16, 23–24, 29, 30, 62, 79, 117. *See also* Faith in Change
Volunteers in Service to America (VISTA), 123
voter mobilization, 153

welfare recipients, 14, 67, 118, 119, 120. *See also* Respect
Wenger, Etienne, 184 n15
Western States Center, 155
women. *See* gender
women's movement, 31, 65–66

youth: work with, 13, 155. *See also* Community Voices; Growing Roots; Teaching Tools; Uniting Youth for Change

Zald, Mayer, 3, 151, 180 n10

Printed in the United States
105219LV00009B/4-9/A